To Kathie
and Dean

Many great meals
together!

Love
Teri

05-14-88

American
Seafood
Cooking

American Seafood Cooking

The Best of Regional Recipes

George Kerhulas

Exeter Books

NEW YORK

Dedicated to my mother, Emily H. Kerhulas;
my father, Alex T. Kerhulas; my brothers,
Chris and Ike Kerhulas; their wives,
Cathy and Nicki; my grandmother, Veneta
Harakas; and the memory of my grandfather,
George Nicholas Harakas.

COPYRIGHT © 1985 BY FOOTNOTE PRODUCTIONS LTD.
First published in USA 1985
by Exeter Books
Distributed by Bookthrift
Exeter is a trademark of Simon & Schuster, Inc.
Bookthrift is a registered trademark of Simon & Schuster, Inc.
New York, New York

ISBN 0-671-07609
Typeset by CST, Eastbourne, East Sussex, U.K.
Food photography by Judd Pilossof
Food styling by Susan Culver
Book design by Mixed Media
Color origination by Hong Kong Scannercraft Company Ltd.
Printed by Lee Fung-Asco Printers Ltd.
Printed in Hong Kong
This book was designed and produced by
Footnote Productions Ltd.
6 Blundell Street
London N7 9BH

CONTENTS

Introduction   6

Appetizers and Sauces   8

Soups   38

Stews and Casseroles   48

Salads   64

Fish   92

Molluscs   184

Crustaceans   198

Index   220

THE BEST OF REGIONAL RECIPES

The seas, bays and rivers define our boundaries, but they also open up a whole new world of culinary exploration. Too often we eat the same seafoods again and again: shrimp, sole, cod, a celebratory lobster. Many other creatures move under the water's surface, however, and hundreds are good to eat. The recipes in this book are designed to help you take full advantage of the sea's bounty.

From the days when fresh fish and shellfish were the sole prerogative of coastal dwellers to the present, when air transport has made it possible for everyone to savor the gifts of the sea, seafood cookery has been one of the least understood aspects of the culinary arts. Seafood is delicate. It demands care in preparation, precision in cooking, artistry in presentation . . . a light touch.

And seafood demands the utmost care in shopping. Fish must smell fresh, be firm to the touch, have clear eyes and clean gills. Molluscs—clams, mussels, oysters, scallops—must be sweet-smelling and tightly closed. Crustaceans—crabs, lobsters, shrimps— should be lively, springy and waft forth an odor of the sea. When buying whole fish or shellfish, there will obviously be a certain amount of waste, but one must estimate the appetites of the potential

consumers. I know of some people who can eat three pounds of shrimp at one sitting, but that would normally be enough for six as a main course. Fillets of any fish can be allowed at the rate of 6 to 8 ounces per person, depending upon the accompaniments and sauces. A richly sauced dish will demand less in the way of fish to fill one, whereas a simple grilled trout will be much less satiating. Similarly, the simpler the preparation— and really good fish demand the simplest preparation possible—the more important it is that the fish be absolutely fresh.

Do not indiscriminately throw every fish into the frying pan! With rare exceptions, this will cause untold damage to the fish and disappointment to your palate. Frying, like most direct high-heat methods of cooking, will cauterize the poor creature, usually resulting in overcooked, dry and tasteless (except for the overwhelming taste of fat) food. Fish is one of the most delicate of protein foods. Cook it gently. And if you do fry it, do so in either good butter or first-class olive oil. Almost everything else will taste rancid or make for a greasy slab on your plate.

Molluscs are at their best raw or lightly steamed. Overcooking will toughen them to the point of near inedibility. And it is best to point out that fish dealers should not be trusted to cook anything. It will almost certainly be overseasoned and overcooked. Steamed molluscs should be consumed as soon as their shells open.

Crustaceans are often mistakenly overcooked. Lobsters in particular need only five to ten minutes to the pound, or until they turn bright red. Otherwise they will be thready and thoroughly unpalatable. Shrimps need only be brought to the boil, then drained immediately.

Nowadays there rarely is a chance to wander through open-air stalls in search of the freshest, perfect fish. The market has too often been replaced by prepackaged, precut, frozen or thawed seafood in supermarket cases. Yet for residents of fishing ports, in North America, Australasia, the Far East or Europe, the possibility exists to meet the incoming boats, haggle over a still-twitching prize and carry it home wrapped in newspaper. This, of course, means you must cope with gutting and cleaning the fish, a simple enough process if you provide yourself with heavy rubber gloves, a sharp knife and a space not irretrievably ruined by flying scales. For the squeamish, the fishseller can do the work, but preparation is part and parcel of cookery, and a good cook should at least know how to do it. The best way to learn is to watch an expert, your local fish dealer. There is absolutely no reason not to be able to fillet a bass or mackerel.

Once you have decided what to buy, have prepared it and have decided how to cook it, you have to get on with the job. Aluminum cookware has an unfortunate tendency to turn foods cooked with acid in them a peculiar, unappetizing gray. If the dish calls for wine or vinegar, use a glass, stainless steel, enameled iron or ceramic dish. Likewise, remember that any dish will continue to cook well after being removed from the stove, grill or oven if the utensil is one which retains heat, as do iron and to a lesser extent stainless steel. Glass and ceramic dishes that can go from oven to table are invaluable in seafood cookery and save on washing up also.

Since most fish and shellfish give up some liquid in cooking, serve them as simply as possible. A large platter, some wedges of lemon, perhaps a few sprigs of parsley for color are all that are needed. For some reason, restauranteurs insist on surrounding fish with slices of lemon. Pretty, no doubt, but of dubious value if you wish to squeeze the juice onto the fish. Likewise, serve the fish alone on dinner plates. Vegetables, salads and other side dishes are better served on separate plates. Otherwise, they may become watery and tasteless.

Elizabeth David believes that sorrel is the best accompaniment to plain grilled or baked fish. However, just as when she made this recommendation a generation ago, the chances of finding it are not much improved. Instead fresh spinach—very well-drained—boiled potatoes, grilled tomatoes, or a plain green salad will suffice. Certain dishes are traditionally served with rice, which must be cooked absolutely dry so as to absorb the savory juices from the fish.

With really good fish, drink the best white wine you can afford. With coarse fish try a light, dry white or even a light red wine. With helpings of fried fish or simple molluscs or shellfish, beer, either lager or ale, is recommended. One note of caution: sweet drinks make fish taste insipid.

Appetizers and Sauces

Artichokes with Sardines

serves 6

6 small artichokes
¼ cup lemon juice
¾ cup olive oil
salt to taste
1 egg
1 teaspoon Dijon-style mustard
1 teaspoon red wine vinegar
3 large boneless sardines, canned in
soy bean or olive oil
1 teaspoon black pepper
3 tablespoons coarsely chopped parsley
6 green olives, pitted

Discard the tough outer leaves of the artichokes. Trim the remaining leaves about ½ inch from the top. Remove the core of center thistles with a paring knife. Sprinkle half the lemon juice on the artichokes.

Bring a large saucepan of salted water to a boil and add ¼ cup of the olive oil and the remaining lemon juice. Stir with a wooden spoon and add the artichokes. Cook until tender, 15 to 20 minutes. Remove the artichokes from the boiling water and drain well.

Add the egg, vinegar, mustard and olive oil to a blender or food processor. Mix until a creamy smooth mayonnaise is formed.

In a small mixing bowl, put 2 tablespoons of the mayonnaise and the sardines. Mash together with a fork until smooth and velvety. Add the pepper and mix again.

Spoon equal amounts of the sardine mixture into the center of each artichoke. Top each artichoke with the remaining mayonnaise and garnish with parsley and an olive. Serve hot or cold.

ANCHOVIED MUSHROOMS

serves 6

6 large mushroom caps, stems removed
2 tablespoons melted butter
6 slices white bread, toasted and buttered
6 anchovy fillets, finely chopped
2 tablespoons sour cream
2 tablespoons chopped parsley

Preheat the broiler to high.

Brush each mushroom cap with butter and put them on a broiler pan. Grill for 5 minutes or until the mushrooms are tender.

While the mushrooms are cooking, combine the anchovies and sour cream in a small mixing bowl.

Remove the mushrooms from the broiler and place each mushroom cap on a piece of toast. Fill the caps with equal amounts of the anchovy mixture. Garnish with the parsley. Serve warm.

BAKED SHRIMP PARMESAN

serves 4

1 pound medium-sized shrimp
2 garlic cloves, finely chopped
1 teaspoon Dijon-style mustard
1 cup heavy cream
salt
black pepper
6 hard-cooked eggs, chopped
½ cup freshly grated Parmesan cheese
2 tablespoons butter

In a large pot, bring 2 quarts of water to a boil over high heat. Add the shrimp to the pot. When the water returns to a boil, reduce the heat and simmer the shrimp for 5 minutes.

Drain the shrimp, remove the shells and veins. Wash the shrimp, then put them on paper towels to dry.

Grease four individual ovenproof dishes with butter. Preheat the oven to 400°F.
In a medium-sized mixing bowl, combine the garlic, mustard, cream and salt and pepper to taste. Mix well.

Put the shrimp into a large mixing bowl. Add the chopped eggs and mix gently but thoroughly.

Divide the shrimp mixture among the ovenproof dishes.

Stir the cream mixture again, then divide it among the four dishes. Sprinkle one-quarter of the Parmesan cheese over each dish, then dot each dish with one-quarter of the butter.

Bake until the cheese melts and turns golden brown. Serve immediately.

BROILED HERRING BITS

serves 4

4 salt herrings cut into bite-size pieces
5 tablespoons chopped coriander leaves
1 tablespoon chopped fresh marjoram
or 1 teaspoon dried marjoram
¼ teaspoon salt
¼ teaspoon black pepper
1 large pimento, finely chopped
1 tablespoon chopped parsley
1 cup finely chopped onion

Place the herring pieces in a large glass or ceramic (not metal) baking dish. Cover the herring pieces with the coriander, marjoram, salt, pepper, pimento, parsley and onion. Cover the dish and marinate in the refrigerator for 6 hours.

Preheat the oven to broil.

Remove the herring pieces from the marinade and place them in an oven-proof glass or ceramic (not metal) dish. Broil the herring pieces until they are lightly browned, about 15 minutes.

CAVIAR CANAPÉS

serves 4

4 thin slices white bread
½ cup lumpfish caviar
3 tablespoons lemon juice
1 tablespoon finely chopped onion
4 tablespoons chopped
hard-cooked egg

Trim the crusts from the bread. Lightly toast the bread. Cut each slice into 4 squares.

Mix the caviar with the lemon juice and the onion. Spread the mixture on the bread squares. Sprinkle the chopped egg over the top and serve.

Deviled Clams

serves 4

½ cup diced onion
½ cup diced celery
½ cup finely chopped green pepper
4 tablespoons butter
2 tablespoons flour
1 tablespoon freshly grated Romano cheese
⅛ teaspoon salt
⅛ teaspoon white pepper
½ teaspoon Worcestershire sauce
1 dash Tabasco sauce
2 dozen plain crackers, crushed
1 6-ounce can minced clams

Melt the butter in a skillet. Add the onion, celery and green pepper and sauté until the onion is transparent but not browned.

Stir in the flour, cheese, salt, white pepper, Worcestershire sauce and Tabasco sauce, stirring vigorously to blend to an even consistency.

Add ½ cup of the cracker crumbs and mix.

Add the minced clams with their juice, and cook slowly until the mixture thickens.

Preheat the oven to 350°F.

Spoon the mixture into clam shells (real or ceramic) or small ovenproof bowls.

Melt another tablespoon of butter in the skillet and stir in the remaining bread crumbs. Sprinkle the crumbs over the filled shells or bowls. Bake until lightly browned, about 15 minutes.

Deviled Eggs with Crabmeat

serves 8

8 hard-cooked eggs, shelled and halved lengthwise
6 tablespoons crabmeat, flaked
2 tablespoons chopped, pitted black olives
¼ cup chopped pimento
5 anchovies
1 garlic clove, minced
1 tablespoon drained capers
½ cup sour cream
2 tablespoons chopped parsley
¼ teaspoon hot pepper sauce
6 tablespoons mayonnaise

Scoop out the yolks from the hard-cooked eggs and set them aside. Put the crabmeat, olives and pimento in the container of a food processor or blender and purée. Add the anchovies, garlic, capers, sour cream, parsley and hot pepper sauce. Blend the ingredients until well mixed. Add the mayonnaise and egg yolks. Blend again. Stuff the egg white halves with the filling and serve.

CRAB DIP

makes 3 cups

6 ounces cream cheese, softened
2 tablespoons very finely chopped onion
1 teaspoon Worcestershire sauce
1 teaspoon Tabasco sauce
salt to taste
black pepper to taste
4 tablespoons mayonnaise
1 pound cooked crabmeat, flaked

In a bowl combine the cream cheese, onion, Worcestershire sauce, Tabasco sauce, salt, pepper and mayonnaise. Mix well. Add the crabmeat and mix again.

CRAB PUFFS

serves 4

4 slices white bread
2 egg whites
½ pound flaked crabmeat
1 cup mayonnaise
1 tablespoon finely chopped parsley
1 tablespoon lemon juice
1 tablespoon paprika

Trim the crusts from the bread. Toast the bread. Cut each slice into 4 pieces. Set aside.

Preheat the broiler.

Whip the egg whites until they are stiff. Fold in the crabmeat, mayonnaise, parsley and lemon juice.

Put the 16 bread squares on the broiler pan. Spread each square with the crab mixture annd sprinkle with the paprika.

Broil for 2 minutes 6 inches from the heat source. Serve hot.

CRABMEAT SPREAD

makes 2 cups

1 cup sour cream
1 teaspoon curry powder
1 tablespoon finely chopped onion
¼ teaspoon black pepper
salt to taste
½ cup unsweetened shredded coconut
¼ pound cooked crabmeat, flaked

In a bowl combine the sour cream, curry, onion, pepper, salt and coconut. Mix well. Add the crabmeat and mix again.

CRAB SOUFFLÉS

serves 6

2 pounds crab legs
2 tablespoons butter
2 tablespoons flour
salt to taste
black pepper to taste
1 cup milk
2 eggs, separated
1 cup heavy cream, whipped

Shell the crab legs and remove the cartilage from the meat. Wash and dry the crabmeat, then break it up and put it into a large mixing bowl. Preheat the oven to 350°F. Butter six individual soufflé dishes.

In a saucepan, melt the butter over low heat. Add the flour and salt and pepper to taste. Blend well. Gradually add the milk, stirring constantly. Cook until the mixture thickens. Remove the pan from the heat.

In a large mixing bowl, beat the egg yolks. Stirring constantly, slowly add the butter mixture to the yolks. Add the crabmeat to the mixture, then fold in the whipped cream. In a separate bowl, beat the egg whites until they are stiff. Fold the egg whites into the crab mixture.

Divide the mixture among the six individual soufflé dishes. Set the dishes in a large baking pan. Add water to the pan so that it comes halfway up the sides of the soufflé dishes. Bake for 40 minutes, or until the soufflés are firm. Serve immediately.

ESCABÈCHE WITH LIME

serves 6

1 pound halibut or sole, thinly sliced
1 ½ cups or more fresh lime juice
1 green pepper, seeded and diced
2 bay leaves, crumbled
1 teaspoon crushed hot red pepper flakes
3 tablespoons olive oil
1 onion, minced
2 garlic cloves, minced
3 tablespoons minced fresh parsley
1 teaspoon salt
1 teaspoon black pepper

Put the fish in a large bowl and set aside.

Put the lime juice, green pepper, bay leaves, crushed red pepper, olive oil, onion, garlic, parsley, salt and pepper into jar with a tightly fitting lid. Cover the jar and shake vigorously until the salt dissolves. Pour the lime mixture over the fish, making sure that the fish is completely covered. Add more lime if needed to cover the fish. Cover the bowl and marinate the fish in the refrigerator for 24 hours. Drain the fish and serve on thin slices of dark bread.

ESCABÈCHE

serves 6 to 8

1 ½ pounds fresh fish fillets, at least ½ inch
thick
½ cup flour
½ teaspoon salt
freshly ground black pepper
½ cup olive oil
2 garlic cloves, crushed
⅛ teaspoon hot red pepper flakes
3 bay leaves
2 tablespoons vinegar
1 medium-sized sweet onion, thinly sliced
½ lemon, thinly sliced

Dust the fish fillets with the flour and black pepper to taste.

Heat the oil in a large, heavy skillet. When the oil is very hot, add the fish fillets and sauté on both sides until the fish is firm and flakes easily with a fork, about 5 minutes on each side. Remove the fish from the skillet, drain on paper towels and put into a serving bowl. Use a fork to break the fish into chunks.

Add the black pepper, salt, garlic, red pepper flakes, bay leaves and vinegar to the skillet. Bring to a boil and cook for 1 minute. Pour the marinade over the fish.

Marinate the fish in the refrigerator for at least 4 hours and preferably overnight, mixing occasionally.

Serve garnished with lemon and onion slices.

FISHKABOBS

serves 4

16 jumbo shrimp, shelled and deveined
1 lobster tail, shelled and cut into 4 chunks
8 sea scallops
8 large straw mushrooms
16 pineapple chunks
8 sweet red pepper chunks
8 green pepper chunks
6 tablespoons butter
2 tablespoons lemon juice
1 teaspoon oregano
½ teaspoon salt
½ teaspoon black pepper
½ teaspoon cayenne pepper

On each of the four 12-inch long skewers, spear in the following order: 1 straw mushroom, 1 shrimp, 1 pineapple chunk, 1 green pepper chunk, 1 scallop, 1 red pepper chunk, 1 pineapple chunk, 1 shrimp, 1 green pepper chunk, 1 red pepper chunk, 1 lobster chunk, 1 red pepper chunk, 1 green pepper chunk, 1 shrimp, 1 pineapple chunk, 1 red pepper chunk, 1 scallop, 1 green pepper chunk, 1 pineapple chunk, 1 shrimp and 1 mushroom.

Preheat the broiler. Melt the butter in a small saucepan. Blend in the lemon juice, oregano, salt, pepper and cayenne pepper.

Put the fishkabobs on a rack in the broiler pan and brush them with the butter mixture. Put them under the broiler and turn and brush with the butter mixture every minute for 8 minutes, or until the fish is cooked. Serve hot.

FISH CROQUETTES

makes 50 croquettes

2 tablespoons butter
¼ cup flour
1 teaspoon salt
½ teaspoon black pepper
1 cup light cream
3 cups flaked cooked fish
1 egg yolk, beaten
2 eggs, slightly beaten
1 cup unflavored breadcrumbs
oil for deep frying

Fill a deep frying pan or electric deep-fryer with oil until it is halfway to two-thirds full. Heat the oil to 350°F on a deep-fat thermometer.

Melt the butter in a saucepan. Over low heat, stir in the flour, salt, and pepper. Mix until well blended. Heat the mixture until it begins to bubble. Slowly add the cream, stirring constantly. Cook over medium heat until the mixture thickens, stirring constantly. Remove the saucepan from the heat and let the mixture cool.

Add the flaked fish to the cooled mixture. Add the beaten egg yolk. Stir well. Shape the mixture into 1-inch balls.

Dip the fish croquettes into the beaten eggs. Roll them in the breadcrumbs coating them evenly.

Carefully place the croquettes into the hot oil. Fry as many at a time as will fit easily in one layer. Do not crowd. Fry the croquettes turning often, until they are lightly browned, about 2 minutes.

Remove the croquettes from the oil with a slotted spoon and drain them on paper towels. Serve with tartar sauce.

FRIED MOZZARELLA WITH ANCHOVY SAUCE

serves 4

4 thick slices fresh mozzarella cheese
flour seasoned with salt and pepper,
for dredging
1 large egg, beaten
⅔ cup fine unflavored breadcrumbs
6 tablespoons butter
¼ cup drained capers
¼ cup rinsed and finely chopped anchovy
fillets
¼ cup dry white wine
4 thin lemon slices for garnish
watercress leaves for garnish

Put the seasoned flour, beaten egg, and breadcrumbs into separate small bowls.

Dip the mozzarella slices first in the flour and then in the egg. Roll the slices in the breadcrumbs to coat evenly. Put the coated slices on a rack.

Melt 2 tablespoons of the butter in a large skillet. When the butter is hot add the cheese slices and sauté over high heat until golden brown, about 1 to 2 minutes per side. Put the cooked slices onto individual serving plates.

Add the anchovies, capers, wine and remaining butter to the skillet. Cook over medium heat, stirring constantly, until the butter melts.

Spoon the sauce over the mozzarella slices. Garnish each plate with a slice of lemon and some watercress leaves, if desired. Serve warm.

GRILLED CHERRYSTONE CLAMS

serves 4 to 6

36 cherrystone clams
1 pound butter
6 tablespoons lemon juice
1 teaspoon salt
¼ cup minced fresh parsley

Melt the butter in a saucepan over a moderate heat. Stir in the lemon juice, salt and parsley. Remove the butter from the heat and pour it into 2 small bowls.

Scrub the clams thoroughly. Place the clams on a hot charcoal grill. Remove the clams when they pop open, after 2 to 3 minutes. (Discard any clams that do not open.) Pour some of the clam juice into the 2 bowls. Serve the clams in the shells. Remove the clams from their shells with small forks or toothpicks and dip them into the butter mixture.

ISLAND SHRIMP BALLS

serves 6

½ cup corn oil
2 cups chopped cooked shrimp
2 eggs, beaten
1 garlic clove, finely chopped
¼ cup breadcrumbs
¼ cup grated Parmesan cheese
1 tablespoon chopped parsley
¼ cup diced fresh pineapple
salt
black pepper

Pour the oil into a large, deep skillet and heat to 375°F.

While the oil is heating, in a large mixing bowl combine garlic, breadcrumbs, Parmesan cheese, parsley, pineapple and salt and pepper to taste. Mix well. Shape the mixture into balls with a diameter of 1 inch and put them into the oil as you form them.

Fry the balls until they are golden brown, turning them frequently. Remove the balls from the oil with a slotted spoon and drain them on paper towels. Serve hot.

JELLIED FISH

serves 6

2 pounds fish heads and trimmings
2 cups water
1 cup white wine
1 celery stalk, diced
1 bay leaf
½ cup coarsely chopped parsley
2 onions, quartered
½ teaspoon black pepper
2 tablespoons lemon juice
¼ teaspoon salt
2 tablespoons olive oil
2 pounds fish fillets

Place all the ingredients except the fish fillets in a medium-sized saucepan. Bring the liquid to a boil over high heat. Reduce the heat to medium, cover, and cook for 1 hour.

Strain the fish stock through a fine sieve into another saucepan. Discard any solids remaining in the sieve.

Add the fish fillets to the fish stock, cover, and simmer over low heat for 20 minutes.

Carefully remove the fish fillets and place them in a deep dish. Pour the stock over the fish and chill until the stock jellies. Serve cold.

KORTLAX

serves 6

2 pounds salmon (in one piece)
1 onion, quartered
2 carrots, peeled and quartered
1 celery stalk, quartered
1 garlic clove, chopped
1 bay leaf
1 tablespoon sugar
2 tablespoons salt
5 cups water
½ cup coarsely chopped fresh dill
1 teaspoon white peppercorns
½ cup white wine vinegar
½ cup sour cream
½ cup mayonnaise
½ teaspoon sugar
½ teaspoon salt
2 tablespoons prepared mustard
2 tablespoons lemon juice
2 tablespoons prepared white horseradish

Put the onion, carrots, celery, garlic, bay leaf, sugar, salt and ¼ cup chopped dill into a large saucepan with 2 cups of the water. Bring to a boil and cook for 30 minutes. Strain the broth through a sieve and set aside. Discard the solids remaining in the sieve.

Place the salmon in a deep skillet or fish poacher. Add the broth, vinegar and just enough of the water to cover the salmon. Poach over moderate heat for 30 to 40 minutes. Remove the skillet or poacher from the heat and let the salmon cool in the liquid for 40 minutes.

Remove the salmon from the broth and skin it. Put the salmon on a serving dish, cover and chill for 3 hours. Discard the poaching liquid or save it for another use.

In a mixing bowl combine the sour cream, mayonnaise, remaining dill, sugar, salt, mustard, lemon juice and horseradish. Mix until the sauce is smooth.

Serve the salmon with the sauce in a separate serving bowl.

Marinated Bluefish

serves 8

2 large bluefish fillets, boned and scaled
but with the skin
1½ tablespoons coarse salt
1½ tablespoons sugar
2 teaspoons crushed whole black
peppercorns
2 tablespoons dried rosemary
¼ teaspoon whole cloves
¼ teaspoon ground mace
½ teaspoon freshly grated nutmeg
Horseradish Cream

Rinse the bluefish fillets and gently pat them dry.

In a small bowl combine the salt, sugar, peppercorns, rosemary, cloves, mace and nutmeg.

Place one fish fillet, skin-side down, on a large piece of plastic wrap inside a long, shallow dish. Sprinkle the fillet with the salt and spices mixture. Place the second fillet on top, skin-side up, to form a "sandwich." Wrap the fish tightly in the plastic and weight it down with a large heavy plate or some heavy cans.

Marinate the fish in the refrigerator for at leat three full days. Three or four times a day, unwrap the plastic and baste the fish with the liquid that has accumulated in the dish. This is best done with a bulb baster. Re-wrap the fish tightly and replace the weights each time.

The bluefish has marinated long enough when the fillets become translucent. Unwrap the fish and gently scrape away and discard the spices. Place the fillets skin-side down and gently slice them on the diagonal, taking care not to cut through the skin. Lift the slices off the skin and arrange on serving plates. Serve with Horseradish Cream if desired.

Clam Guacamole

makes 1½ cups

1 large ripe avocado
1 garlic clove, finely chopped
½ teaspoon salt
½ teaspoon chili powder
1 teaspoon lime juice
½ cup chopped cooked clams

Peel the avocado and remove the pit. Mash the avocado and garlic together in a mixing bowl. Add the salt, chili powder, lime juice and clams. Mix well. Cover the bowl and chill for 1 hour before serving.

PICKLED MUSSELS

serves 8

2 quarts cooked mussels, in liquid
2 large onions, thinly sliced
4 garlic cloves, finely chopped
1 teaspoon dried dill
1 teaspoon dried oregano
1 cup white wine vinegar
2 teaspoons salt
2 teaspoons black pepper

Put the mussels into a large pot and add enough cold water to fill the pot to a depth of 3 inches. Cover the pot and steam the mussels over high heat until they open, about 5 to 8 minutes. Discard any mussels that do not open.

Drain the mussels and reserve the liquid. Remove the mussels from their shells. Rinse the mussels and arrange them in layers with the onion in a large glass jar.

Mix ½ cup of the mussel liquid with the garlic, oregano, dill, wine vinegar, salt and pepper. Stir thoroughly.

Pour the liquid mixture over the mussels, cover the jar and place it in the refrigerator for 3 days. Shake the jar twice a day.

PORTUGUESE CLAMS

serves 4

1 small onion, chopped
3 garlic cloves, chopped
¼ cup olive oil
2 pounds fresh small clams (or mussels), well scrubbed
1 tablespoon dry sherry
2 tablespoons fresh lemon juice
½ cup chopped fresh parsley
2 lemons, cut into wedges

Heat the olive oil in a deep skillet. Add the onions and garlic and sauté until the garlic is golden Add the clams and sherry to the skillet, cover tightly and steam over moderate heat until the clams open, about 5 to 10 minutes. Discard any clams that have not opened after 10 minutes. Add the lemon juice and parsley and shake the skillet to redistribute the clams. Simmer the clams over low heat for 2 minutes longer. Place the clams and broth in a serving bowl and serve with crusty French bread.

PICKLED SALMON

serves 6

1 cup distilled white vinegar
1 cup water
¼ cup lemon juice
3 tablespoons olive oil
1 onion, thinly sliced
1 bay leaf
1 teaspoon mustard seeds, or
1 teaspoon dry mustard
1 teaspoon whole cloves
1 teaspoon white peppercorns
1 teaspoon black peppercorns
2½ pounds fresh salmon, boned, skinned
and cubed
1½ teaspoons salt

In a large skillet, combine the vinegar, water, lemon juice, olive oil, onion slices, bay leaf, mustard, cloves, white peppercorns and black peppercorns. Bring to a boil over high heat. Reduce the heat and simmer for 45 minutes.

While the liquid is simmering, put the salmon cubes on a large platter and sprinkle with the salt. Set aside for 30 minutes, then put the salmon cubes into a colander and rinse thoroughly with cold water. Drain well. Pat the salmon cubes dry with paper towels.

Put the salmon cubes into glass jars. Pour the hot vinegar mixture over the salmon, a little at a time. Allow the liquid to settle at the bottom before adding more. Cool to room temperature. Cover the jars tightly and refrigerate for 24 hours before serving.

CLAM DIP

makes 2½ cups

1 cup chopped cooked clams
6 ounces cream cheese, softened
1 tablespoon lemon juice
1 teaspoon Worcestershire sauce
¼ teaspoon black pepper
1 tablespoon mayonnaise
1 tablespoon chopped parsley
½ teaspoon dry mustard
2 tablespoons chopped onion

In a bowl combine the cream cheese, clams, lemon juice, Worcestershire sauce, pepper, mayonnaise, parsley, mustard and onion. Mix well.

CLAMS CASINO

serves 6

30 small clams
10 bacon slices
4 tablespoons butter
4 tablespoons olive oil
2 garlic cloves, chopped
2 tablespoons chopped parsley
2 teaspoons lemon juice
1 teaspoon oregano
½ cup unflavored breadcrumbs

Preheat the oven to 425°F.

Scrub the clams and open them. Discard the top shells and pour off some of the liquid from each clam. Arrange the clams on a baking sheet.

Cut the bacon strips into thirds and set aside.

Heat the butter and olive oil in a saucepan. Add the garlic, parsley, lemon juice, oregano and breadcrumbs. Mix well.

Top each clam with some of the breadcrumb mixture. Cover each clam with a piece of bacon. Bake for 12 to 15 minutes, or until the bacon is crisp.

PICKLED MACKEREL

serves 8

4 small mackerel, cleaned
4 cups water
½ cup cider vinegar
¼ cup salt
4 bay leaves
12 black peppercorns
1 small dried hot red pepper

Preheat the oven to 250°F.

Combine the water, vinegar and salt in a mixing bowl. Stir until the salt dissolves.

Place the mackerel in a shallow baking dish. Pour the salt mixture over the fish. Add the bay leaves, peppercorns and hot red pepper.

Bake the fish for 45 minutes. Remove the dish from the oven and let the fish cool in the liquid.

Remove the fish from the liquid. Remove the skin and bones and serve.

Scallop Brochettes

serves 4

2 tablespoons finely grated onion
2 tablespoons lemon juice
salt to taste
black pepper to taste
1 pound sea scallops
4 small onions, halved
8 bacon slices, cut in half
8 white mushroom caps
3 tablespoons melted butter
lemon slices

Put the grated onion, lemon juice and a dusting of salt and pepper in a bowl. Add the scallops, toss and let marinate for 40 minutes at room temperature.

Drain the scallops, reserving the marinade. Thread the scallops alternately with the mushrooms, bacon and onion onto 8 metal skewers.

Preheat the broiler to high.

Broil the brochettes, basting them with the melted butter and reserved marinade until the bacon is crisp and the scallops white and firm, about 10 minutes. Turn the brochettes often to cook on all sides. Serve garnished with slices of lemon.

Smoked Salmon Canapés

serves 6

8 ounces smoked salmon, thinly sliced
2 tablespoons sweet butter, softened
1 teaspoon drained white prepared horseradish
1 tablespoon finely chopped parsley
dash Tabasco sauce
8 thin slices of pumpernickel bread
64 capers, drained

In a small mixing bowl combine the butter, horseradish, parsley and Tabasco sauce. Spread a thin layer of the mixture on each slice of bread.

Cover each slice of bread with a single layer of the smoked salmon. Cut each slice of bread into quarters. Garnish each bread square with two capers and serve.

SEAFOOD MOUSSE

makes 4 cups

¼ pound shrimp, shelled and deveined
¼ pound haddock fillet, skinned
¼ pound cooked and picked crabmeat
½ pound cream cheese
¼ cup minced scallions
2 tablespoons minced dill
2 tablespoons lemon juice
2 tablespoons vodka
½ teaspoon salt
1 teaspon black pepper
½ teaspoon Tabasco sauce
4 tablespoons drained capers

Cook the shrimp in a large pot of boiling water until they are pink, about 5 minutes. Drain well.

Bring 1½ cups water to the boil in a small skillet. Add the haddock fillet and poach until the fish flakes easily, about 5 to 8 minutes. Drain well.

Put the shrimp, haddock, crabmeat, cream cheese, scallions, dill, lemon juice, vodka, salt, pepper and Tabasco sauce into the container of a food processor or blender. Blend until the ingredients are a smooth purée.

Spoon the mousse into a serving dish. Smooth the top of the mousse, cover and chill for 1 hour or more. Serve with toast or crackers, with the capers on the side.

SMOKED WHITEFISH APPETIZER

serves 12

2 pounds smoked whitefish
1 cup mayonnaise
1 tablespoon dry mustard
1 tablespoon chopped chives
1 large tomato, seeded and diced
1 tablespoon dry sherry
black pepper to taste

Skin, bone and flake the fish. Put the meat into a mixing bowl, cover and chill for at least 4 hours.

In another mixing bowl combine the mayonnaise with the mustard, chive and tomato. Add the fish, sherry and black pepper. Mix gently but well.

SHRIMP CROQUETTES

serves 4

2 tablespoons butter
¼ cup flour
1 cup milk
1¼ cup cooked small shrimp, coarsely
chopped
2 tablespoons minced parsley
1 teaspoon salt
⅛ teaspoon cayenne pepper
1 teaspoon black pepper
2 tablespoons lemon juice
1 teaspoon Worcestershire sauce
1 cup unflavored breadcrumbs
2 egg whites, lightly beaten
oil for deep frying

Melt the butter in a medium-sized saucepan. Gradually stir in the flour and milk over moderate heat until the sauce thickens. Stir in the shrimp, parsley, salt, cayenne, pepper, lemon juice and Worcestershire sauce. Pour the mixture into a shallow dish and refrigerate until the mixture becomes firm.

Form the shrimp mixture into 4 rolls about 4 inches in length. Spread the breadcrumbs out on a flat surface and roll the cylinders in them until they are covered with the breadcrumbs. Pour the egg whites out on a plate and roll the breaded cylinders in the egg whites.

Heat the oil for deep frying in a large skillet or deep-fryer. When the oil is very hot, add the croquettes and fry for 4 minutes or until brown. Put the croquettes on paper towel and drain. Serve hot.

SHRIMP OR CRAB COCKTAIL

serves 6

2 pounds cooked shrimp or flaked
crabmeat
3 tablespoons lemon juice
2 tablespoons chopped parsley
2 cups Cocktail Sauce
2 lemons, quartered

Put the seafood into a bowl and sprinkle with the lemon juice. Add the parsley and mix well. Divide the fish into six serving bowls. Pour the cocktail sauce over the fish. Serve with the lemon wedges.

SEVICHE

serves 8

2 pounds fresh trout or any other firm
white fish or scallops
juice of 3 limes
juice of 3 lemons
1 large sweet red pepper
1 large red onion, thinly sliced and
separated into rings
2 canned jalapeño peppers, seeded and
diced
salt to taste
black pepper to taste
¾ cup olive oil

Slice the fish into strips approximately 4 × ½ inch in size. Put the strips into a shallow dish and cover with the lime and lemon juice. Mix well, cover, and refrigerate for 4 hours.

Place the red pepper on a broiler pan and broil, turning often, until the pepper is blackened all over. Put the pepper into a paper bag and fold the bag closed. Let the pepper cool for 8 to 10 minutes. Remove it from the bag and rub off the skin, using your fingers. Seed and stem the pepper and cut it into thin strips.

Remove the fish from the refrigerator and discard the marinade. In a bowl (preferably glass) make layers of the fish, red onion rings, red pepper strips and jalapeño peppers. Salt and pepper each layer heavily.

Pour the olive oil over the bowl, cover, and chill. Serve as an appetizer or first course with thinly sliced bread.

SHRIMP-STUFFED TOMATOES

serves 6 to 8

30 cherry tomatoes
½ pound shelled, cooked shrimp
½ teaspoon crushed hot red pepper flakes
2 scallions, minced
½ garlic clove, minced
2 teaspoons soy sauce
4 black olives, pitted and chopped

Halve each cherry tomato vertically and scoop out the pulp. Turn the tomatoes upside down and drain on paper towels for 20 to 30 minutes.

Put the shrimp, red pepper flakes, scallion, olives, garlic and soy sauce into a food processor or blender and blend until a lumpy, granular paste is formed. Stuff the shrimp mixture into the tomato shells and refrigerate until ready to serve.

SHRIMP FRITTERS

serves 6

½ cup corn oil
1 cup flour
1 teaspoon baking powder
salt to taste
black pepper to taste
2 eggs, beaten
½ cup light cream
1 small onion, finely chopped
1 teaspoon Tabasco sauce
1 pound cooked shrimp, chopped

Heat the oil in a deep skillet until it is 375°F.

While the oil is heating, in a large mixing bowl combine the flour, baking powder and salt and pepper to taste. Add the eggs and cream and mix well. Add the onions, Tabasco sauce and shrimp. Mix thoroughly.

Drop the batter, by the teaspoonful, into the oil and cook for 2 minutes. Remove the fritters with a slotted spoon, drain on paper towels and serve hot.

SPICY FISH APPETIZER

serves 8

1½ pounds flounder fillets, cut into very small cubes
1 cup lime juice
2 teaspoons Worcestershire sauce
1 teaspoon Tabasco sauce
1 tablespoon salt
6 tomatoes, seeded and coarsely chopped
1 cup unsweetened shredded coconut
1 head soft lettuce

Put the fish cubes into a large glass or ceramic (not metal) mixing bowl. Add the lime juice, Worcestershire sauce, Tabasco sauce, salt and half the tomatoes. Mix well. Cover the bowl and refrigerate for at least 12 hours.

Two hours before serving the appetizer, pour off the marinade. Add the remaining tomatoes and the coconut to the bowl. Mix well. Cover the bowl and refrigerate for 2 hours.

Shred the lettuce leaves and add them to the appetizer just before serving. Drain off any excess liquid before serving.

Stuffed Cherry Tomatoes

serves 6

4 cups large cherry tomatoes
¼ pound smoked salmon, chopped
1 onion, finely chopped
½ teaspoon dried dill
½ teaspoon black pepper

Wash the tomatoes and carefully cut off the tops. Scoop out the tomato pulp and the seeds and reserve. Set the tomatoes aside.

In a bowl combine the smoked salmon, onion, dill, pepper, and tomato pulp. Mix until thoroughly combined.

Carefully fill the tomatoes with the salmon mixture. Chill for at least 1 hour before serving.

Stuffed Clams

serves 4

24 medium-sized clams, in shells
4 large mushrooms, diced
2 scallions, diced
2 tablespoons garlic-flavored
breadcrumbs
6 tablespoons butter, softened
1 tablespoon chopped parsley
salt
black pepper
½ cup grated Parmesan cheese
1 tablespoon paprika
2 lemons, quartered

Carefully open the clam shells and remove the clams. Wash the shells and set aside.

Preheat the oven to 350°F.

Rinse the clams and chop them.

In a large bowl, combine the chopped clams with the mushrooms, scallions, breadcrumbs, butter, parsley and salt and pepper to taste.

Put the clam shells on a large baking sheet. Fill the shells with the clam mixture, sprinkle with the Parmesan cheese and the paprika. Bake for 15 minutes. Transfer the shells to a serving platter, garnish with the lemon wedges and serve.

STUFFED GIANT SHRIMP

serves 4

½ pound lean ground pork
12 very large shrimp, shelled and deveined
but with the tails
3 tablespoons chopped scallions
2 tablespoons minced mushrooms
½ teaspoon salt
1 teaspoon black pepper
12 egg roll wrappers (available in Oriental
groceries and specialty shops)
vegetable oil for deep frying

Sauté the pork in a skillet until it is browned. Drain off the fat. Combine the pork, scallions, mushrooms, salt and pepper in a mixing bowl.

Cook the shrimp in a large pot of boiling water for 3 minutes. Drain well. When the shrimp are cool enough to handle, enlarge the slit where the vein was removed with a sharp knife.

Insert some of the pork mixture into the opening of each shrimp. Roll each stuffed shrimp in an egg roll wrapper, tucking in the ends.

Put enough oil into a large heavy skillet to fill it a depth of 2 inches. Heat the oil to 350°F. Add the wrapped shrimp and fry, turning occasionally, until the wrappers are golden brown. Serve hot.

TUNA CREPES

serves 6

2 6½-ounce cans Italian tuna, drained
2 ounces drained anchovies
2 tablespoons chopped parsley
½ teaspoon salt
6 eggs, beaten
1 cup flour
1 cup cold water
2 teaspoons finely chopped onion
2 tablespoons vegetable oil

In a medium-sized mixing bowl, combine the tuna, anchovies, parsley, salt and pepper. Flake with a fork and mix until evenly blended. Set the filling aside.

In another mixing bowl, combine the eggs, flour, water and onions. Mix the batter thoroughly.

Lightly grease a large heavy skillet with the vegetable oil. Ladle 3 tablespoons of the batter at a time into the skillet, spreading it evenly, and cook for 3 to 5 minutes, or until the crêpe is solid but still slightly moist. Place 1 tablespoon of the tuna filling on the crêpe and fold it over. Remove from pan and set aside on large baking sheet. Repeat the process until all the batter and filling are used up.

Preheat the oven to 450°F.

Place the baking sheet in the oven and bake for 8 minutes. Serve hot.

STUFFED SARDINES

serves 6

2½ pounds fresh sardines, cleaned and
heads removed
1¼ cups olive oil
6 tablespoons soft unflavored
breadcrumbs
½ cup seedless white raisins
½ cup pine nuts
2 teaspoons sugar
6 anchovy fillets, rinsed and chopped
1 teaspoon black pepper
¼ cup chopped parsley
¼ cup chopped scallions
2 tablespoons olive oil
2 bay leaves, torn into strips
4 tablespoons lemon juice

Preheat the oven to 375°F.

Slit the sardines open at the bottom or stomach and carefully remove the backbone, but do not cut the sardines completely in half. Rinse the sardines in salted water and pat them dry with paper towels.

Heat the olive oil in a small skillet. Add the breadcrumbs and sauté, stirring constantly until golden brown. Put the breadcrumbs in a mixing bowl and add the raisins, pine nuts, and sugar. Add the anchovies, pepper, parsley and scallions. Mix until the ingredients are combined.

Stuff each sardine with the breadcrumb mixture and firmly close each sardine, using a toothpick if needed.

Rub the inside of a baking pan with olive oil and arrange the sardines in one layer on the bottom. Sprinkle the sardines with the bay leaves and cover with any remaining breadcrumb mixture. Bake for 30 minutes, or until the sardines are baked through. Sprinkle with lemon juice and serve.

TUNA SPINACH PÂTÉ

serves 8

1¼ pounds fresh spinach
boiling water
¾ cup heavy cream
3 large eggs
4 ounces tuna fish packed in olive oil,
drained and flaked
4 flat anchovy fillets, drained
½ cup finely chopped scallions
1 tablespoon lemon juice
⅓ cup soft unflavored breadcrumbs
½ teaspoon salt
¼ teaspoon black pepper

Preheat the oven to 375°F.

Generously butter the bottom of an 8½ × 4½-inch loaf pan. Line the bottom with waxed paper or parchment paper cut to size. Butter the paper.

Wash the spinach carefully to remove all grit. Discard any tough stems and discolored leaves. Place the spinach into a large saucepan and cover. Cook over medium heat for 3 to 4 minutes, or until the spinach is bright green and tender. Do not add water to the saucepan; the spinach will steam in the water clinging to its leaves from the washing.

Drain the spinach well. Squeeze it with your hands to remove as much moisture as possible. Chop the spinach coarsely and set aside in a large mixing bowl.

Put the heavy cream, eggs, tuna, anchovies, scallions and lemon juice into the container of a food processor or blender. Purée until the mixture is smooth. Transfer the mixture to the mixing bowl with the spinach and add the breadcrumbs, salt and pepper. Mix well.

Turn the mixture into the prepared loaf pan and cover it with a piece of aluminum foil. Place the loaf pan into a larger baking dish. Pour the boiling water into the baking dish until there is enough to come halfway up the sides of the loaf pan.

Bake in the center of the oven for 1 hour or until a knife inserted into the center of the pâté comes out clean but not dry. Remove the pan from the oven and from the water bath. Place the loaf pan on a rack and cool to room temperature.

Refrigerate the pâté, covered, for 3 to 4 hours, or until it is well chilled. To serve, carefully unmold the pâté onto a serving plate and slice it thinly.

ALMOND SAUCE

makes 1½ cups

2 tablespoons butter
2 tablespoons flour
½ cup milk
½ cup sour cream
½ cup almond slivers
4 tablespoons chopped scallions
2 teaspoons lemon juice

Preheat the oven to 375°F.

Melt the butter in a saucepan. Add the flour, stirring until it is well blended. Still stirring, gradually add the milk. When the sauce thickens, remove from the heat and blend in the sour cream

Put the almond slivers on a baking sheet and bake for 5 minutes or until the almonds are lightly toasted.

Blend the almonds and the scallions into the sauce, then stir in the lemon juice.

APRICOT SAUCE

makes 2 cups

¾ pound apricots, peeled, pitted and diced
2 cups water
4 tablespoons sugar

Put the apricots into a large skillet. Add the water and simmer over low heat for 30 minutes. Remove the skillet from the heat and stir in the sugar. Blend thoroughly. Pour the sauce into a bowl, when it is cool cover the bowl. Chill before serving.

BUTTER GARLIC SAUCE

makes ½ cup

¼ pound butter
4 garlic cloves, finely chopped
½ small onion, finely chopped
¼ cup parsley, finely chopped
salt to taste
black pepper to taste
½ teaspoon oregano

Melt the butter in a saucepan. Mix in the rest of the ingredients.

CLAM SAUCE FOR PASTA

serves 4

12 large clams
8 tablespoons butter
3 garlic cloves, crushed
1 teaspoon oregano
salt to taste
black pepper to taste
¾ cup dry white wine

Scrub the clams well. Put them into a large pot and add enough cold water to cover. Bring the water to a boil and cook until the clams open, about 5 minutes. Discard any clams that do not open.

Drain the clams well. Open the shells and remove the meat. Coarsely chop the clam meat.

Melt the butter in a saucepan over low heat. Add the garlic and sauté until the garlic is lightly browned. Remove the garlic and discard. Add the chopped clams, oregano, salt and pepper. Cook over low heat for 5 minutes, stirring often. Add the wine and heat until the liquid just boils. Serve hot over pasta.

CLARIFIED BUTTER

makes ¾ cup

1 cup sweet butter, cut into small pieces

Melt the butter in a small saucepan over low heat. Remove the saucepan from the heat and let the white milk solids settle to the bottom. Skim the foam from the top of the butter with a spoon.

Line a fine mesh sieve with a double layer of cheesecloth. Strain the yellow liquid in the saucepan through the sieve into a container with a tightly fitting lid. Discard any solids that remain in the sieve. Cover the container tightly and refrigerate until needed. It will keep almost indefinitely if kept tightly covered and well chilled.

COCKTAIL SAUCE
makes 1½ cups

½ cup chili sauce
½ cup catsup
¼ cup prepared horseradish
¼ cup lemon juice
2 teaspoons Worcestershire sauce
salt to taste
¼ teaspoon Tabasco sauce

Mix all the ingredients together thoroughly. Chill well before using.

DILL SAUCE
makes 1 cup

yolk of 1 hard-cooked egg
½ cup vegetable oil
1½ teaspoons cider vinegar
¼ teaspoon Worcestershire sauce
½ teaspoon dry mustard
½ teaspoon sugar
¼ teaspoon salt
¼ teaspoon black pepper
¼ teaspoon dried dill or 1 teaspoon
chopped fresh dill
¼ cup heavy cream

Press the egg yolk through a sieve into a bowl. Beat in the vegetable oil. Add the vinegar, Worcestershire sauce, mustard, sugar, salt, pepper and dill. Beat until well combined.

Whip the heavy cream until it is thick and holds it shape. Fold the whipped cream into the egg yolk mixture. Combine thoroughly and refrigerate until ready to use.

GREEN PEPPERCORN BUTTER
makes ½ cup

8 tablespoons softened sweet butter
¼ cup finely chopped fresh parsley
1 tablespoon green peppercorns, drained
1 teaspoon fresh lemon juice
½ teaspoon Dijon-style mustard
½ teaspoon Worcestershire sauce
salt to taste

Combine the butter, parsley, green peppercorns, lemon juice, mustard, Worcestershire sauce and salt in the container of a blender or food processor. Process until the mixture is smooth and well combined.

Transfer the mixture to a bowl or crock and cover. Refrigerate for at least 1½ to 2 hours before using.

HORSERADISH CREAM

makes 2¼ cups

1 cup chilled heavy cream
2 teaspoons sugar
½ teaspoon salt
3 tablespoons drained white
horseradish

Combine the cream, sugar and salt in a well-chilled bowl. Beat until the cream forms stiff peaks.

Fold in the horseradish.

LEMON BUTTER SAUCE

makes ½ cup

¼ pound butter
4 tablespoons lemon juice
½ teaspoon salt
½ teaspoon black pepper
½ teaspoon oregano

Melt the butter in a saucepan. Blend in the rest of the ingredients.

SALMON DILL BUTTER

makes ¾ cup

8 tablespoons softened sweet butter
3 ounces smoked salmon, finely chopped
1 teaspoon finely chopped fresh dill
1 teaspoon fresh lemon juice
½ teaspoon onion juice

Cream the butter in a mixing bowl until it is light and fluffy. Add the salmon, dill, lemon juice and onion juice. Stir with a wooden spoon until well mixed.

Put the mixture onto a large piece of plastic wrap. With the help of the plastic wrap, form the butter into a thick cylinder. To serve, unwrap the butter and slice it into pats.

SOUTHERN–STYLE TARTAR SAUCE

makes 1½ cups

1 teaspoon dry mustard
⅛ teaspoon cayenne pepper
¼ cup finely chopped dill pickle
6 shallots, finely chopped
1 tablespoon chopped chives
1 tablespoon chopped parsley
1 teaspoon finely chopped capers
1 cup mayonnaise
2 tablespoons tarragon vinegar

In a bowl combine the vinegar and cayenne pepper and whisk well. Add the pickles, shallots, chives, parsley and capers. Stir well. Beat in the mayonnaise and mustard.

Cover and refrigerate for 3 hours before serving. This sauce will keep for up to 2 days in the refrigerator.

TARTAR SAUCE

makes 1½ cups

1 cup mayonnaise
2 tablespoons lemon juice
½ teaspoon Tabasco sauce
½ teaspoon Dijon-style mustard
3 tablespoons drained pickle relish
1 tablespoon finely chopped parsley

Mix the ingredients together thoroughly. Refrigerate.

VINAIGRETTE

makes 2 cups

1½ cups olive oil
⅓ cup white wine vinegar
⅓ cup dark rum
1 teaspoon sugar
salt to taste
1 teaspoon black pepper
1 teaspoon paprika
¼ cup finely chopped coriander

Combine all the ingredients in a blender and blend thoroughly. Chill.

SOUPS

BASIC FISH STOCK
makes 3 quarts

5 pounds fresh fish bones and heads
3 quarts water
2 cups white wine
2 carrots, peeled and quartered
4 bay leaves
2 teaspoons dried thyme
2 garlic cloves, crushed
1 large sweet onion, sliced
6 parsley sprigs
1 tablespoon whole black peppercorns
1 teaspoon salt
2 tablespoons anise-flavored liqueur
(optional)

Put the fish, water, wine, carrots, bay leaves, thyme, garlic, onion, parsley, salt and peppercorns into a large heavy pot. Bring to a boil, partially cover the pot, reduce the heat, and simmer gently for 30 minutes. Skim the top occasionally as the stock cooks.

Strain the stock, discarding the solids. Return the stock to the pot and add the anise-flavored liqueur. Simmer for 30 minutes more. Cool. Store well covered in the refrigerator or freeze for future use.

CRAB BISQUE

serves 8

1 tablespoon lemon juice
2 pounds cooked crabmeat
4 cups fish stock
1 cup unflavored breadcrumbs
1 onion, thinly sliced
2 parsley sprigs
1 bay leaf
½ teaspoon oregano
2 tablespoons butter, softened
1 cup heavy cream
½ teaspoon salt
½ teaspoon black pepper
½ teaspoon cayenne pepper
4 tablespoons cooked and chopped
shrimp
1 tablespoon sweet butter

Pour the lemon juice over the crabmeat. Chop the crabmeat very fine.

In a large saucepan, combine the crabmeat, fish stock, breadcrumbs, onion, parsley and bay leaf. Bring to a boil. Lower the heat and simmer for 20 minutes.

Add the softened butter and heat just to the boiling point. Add the cream and season with the salt, pepper and cayenne pepper. Heat the soup, but do not boil.

Just before serving, stir in the shrimp and butter. Serve hot.

CODFISH CHOWDER

serves 6

3 pounds fresh codfish
3 onions, finely chopped
1 carrot
3 parsley sprigs
1 bay leaf
1 whole clove
1½ teaspoons salt
2 pounds potatoes
2 tablespoons butter
black pepper to taste
salt to taste
2 cups milk
1 tablespoon chopped parsley
½ cup shredded lettuce

Trim the skin and bones from the codfish and place the trimmings in a large pot. Add water to cover and add one-third of the onions, the carrot, parsley sprigs, bay leaf, salt, and clove. Bring to a boil and cook for 15 minutes.

Dice the codfish fillets and the potatoes into small pieces about ½-inch square.

Melt the butter in a deep saucepan and sauté the remaining onions until lightly browned. Strain the fish broth over the onions. Add the diced codfish and potatoes. Cook just below the boiling point for about 30 minutes, or until the potatoes are soft.

Add black pepper to taste, the milk, chopped parsley, and lettuce. Heat thoroughly and serve at once.

COLD SHRIMP SOUP

serves 6

¾ pound cooked shrimp, shelled,
deveined and coarsely chopped
1 medium-sized cucumber, peeled
1 tablespoon chopped fresh dill or
1 teaspoon dried dill
1 tablespoon Dijon-style mustard
½ teaspoon salt
4 cups buttermilk

Cut the cucumber in half lengthwise. Scoop out and discard the seeds. Chop the cucumber finely.

Combine the cucumber, shrimp, dill, mustard, salt and buttermilk in a large bowl. Stir well. Cover the bowl and chill for at least 2 hours. Stir again before serving.

CORN AND SHRIMP CHOWDER

serves 6

3 tablespoons butter
¼ cup chopped scallions
1 garlic clove, finely minced
¼ teaspoon black pepper
1½ cups light cream
½ cup water
2 potatoes, peeled and diced
¼ teaspoon salt
½ teaspoon dried parsley
2 cups milk
3 ounces cream cheese
1 cup whole kernel corn, drained
1½ pounds shrimp, shelled, deveined and
chopped

Melt the butter in a large heavy pot or Dutch oven. Add the scallions, garlic and pepper and sauté over low heat until the scallions are tender but not browned.

Add the cream, water, potatoes, salt, parsley and milk. Simmer for 15 to 20 minutes, or until the potatoes are soft. Stir frequently so the cream and milk do not form a skin. Do not allow the mixture to come to a boil.

Soften the cream cheese with a fork, then stir it into the soup. When the cream cheese is fully blended, add the corn and shrimp. Bring the soup slowly to a boil, then immediately reduce the heat and simmer for 5 to 10 minutes, or until the shrimp are white and tender. Serve the chowder piping hot.

DEEP SEA CHOWDER

serves 4

2 cups water
12 oysters
12 clams
12 mussels
12 medium-sized shrimp
¼ pound butter
1 celery stalk, chopped
1 onion, chopped
2 leeks, finely chopped
3 medium-sized potatoes, diced
½ teaspoon salt
1 teaspoon black pepper
1 teaspoon cayenne pepper
2 cups milk
1 cup light cream
3 egg yolks
3 tablespoons lemon juice

In a large saucepan, bring the water to a boil. Put the oysters, clams, mussels and shrimp into a steamer basket and place in the saucepan. Steam the seafood until all the shells open. Drain the seafood and reserve the liquid in the saucepan.

In the top of a double boiler, over briskly boiling water, melt the butter. Blend in the salt, pepper and cayenne pepper. Add the celery, onion, leeks and potatoes, and cook, stirring frequently, until the vegetables are tender.

While the vegetables are cooking, shell all the seafood and pour the lemon juice over them. Beat the eggs and blend in the milk and cream. Pour the egg mixture over the vegetables and stir in the seafood and reserved liquid, simmer for 10 minutes and serve.

DOWN-EAST HADDOCK CHOWDER

serves 6

⅓ cup diced salt pork
1 onion, quartered and sliced
3 potatoes, peeled and cubed
2 pounds haddock fillets, cut into cubes
1 quart water
1 small celery stalk with leaves, chopped
⅛ teaspoon ground mace
2½ cups milk
½ cup heavy cream

Sauté the salt pork in a large pot until the pieces are crisp at the edges and tender. Remove the pieces and reserve.

In the pork fat left in the pot, sauté the onion until the pieces are translucent but not brown. Add the potatoes, fish, water, celery, salt, pepper and mace and bring to a boil. Reduce the heat and simmer for about 15 minutes, or until the potatoes are tender and the fish flaky.

Stir in the milk, cream and salt pork pieces and slowly bring back to a boil. Serve over crackers or toasted bread rounds.

FISH SOUP WITH ONIONS, CUCUMBERS AND TOMATOES

serves 8

1½ cups white onions, finely chopped
¼ teaspoon finely grated lemon rind
1 pound halibut steaks, cut into pieces
1 pound swordfish steaks, cut into pieces
1 bay leaf
1 garlic clove, crushed
¼ teaspoon black pepper
¼ teaspoon white pepper
7 cups water
2 large cucumbers, peeled and cut into slices
2 cups fresh tomatoes, peeled, seeded, and cut into pieces
½ cup heavy cream
2 teaspoons finely chopped fresh parsley
1 cup white wine
½ cup pitted black olives, halved

In a very large soup pot, combine the 7 cups water with onions, parsley, lemon rind, bay leaf and black pepper. Bring the liquid to a boil, then reduce the heat to medium. Simmer for 2 minutes.

Add the fish to the pot and simmer for 5 minutes. Reduce the heat to low and simmer 5 minutes longer.

Add the cream, white wine, white pepper, garlic clove, cucumbers and tomatoes to the pot. Simmer over low heat for 5 minutes. Do not let the soup boil.

Remove the pot from the heat. Stir in the olives. Let stand for 30 seconds. Stir again and serve.

HALIBUT SOUP

serves 6

1 cup dry white wine
4 cups water
2 tablespoons lemon juice
1 garlic clove, finely chopped
2 tablespoons olive oil
½ teaspoon salt
1 teaspoon black pepper
2 pounds fresh halibut, cleaned, skinned, boned and cut into small pieces
3 ounces grated Parmesan cheese

In a large pot combine the white wine, water, lemon juice, garlic, olive oil, salt and pepper. Bring to a boil over high heat.

Reduce the heat to medium-low and stir in the halibut. Simmer for 30 minutes.

Ladle the soup into individual soup bowls. Sprinkle each serving with some of the Parmesan cheese and serve.

LOBSTER BISQUE

serves 6

2 cups milk
2 cups heavy cream
4 tablespoons butter
1 large onion, finely chopped
2 celery stalks, finely chopped
2 tablespoons flour
½ teaspoon paprika
1 teaspoon salt
½ teaspoon black pepper
2 cups cooked lobster meat
1 teaspoon lemon juice
¼ cup dry sherry

In a large mixing bowl, whisk together the milk and cream. Set aside.

In a large saucepan melt the butter. Add the onion and the celery. Cook over medium heat, stirring constantly, for 5 minutes, or until the vegetables are tender, but not brown. Stir in the flour, paprika, salt and pepper.

Still stirring, pour the milk and cream mixture into the saucepan in a slow but steady stream. Quickly bring the sauce to a boil. Stir constantly to make sure the soup is smooth. Reduce the heat and simmer for 3 minutes.

Put the lobster meat into a bowl. Add the lemon juice and mix well. Add the lobster to the soup. Stir in the sherry. Simmer the soup for 5 more minutes stirring frequently. Pour the soup into serving bowls and serve immediately.

MANHATTAN CLAM CHOWDER

serves 6

24 clams
¼ pound bacon, chopped
3 large onions, chopped
4 cups water
6 large, ripe tomatoes, skinned, seeded
and chopped
4 celery stalks, chopped
5 tablespoons chopped parsley
1 bay leaf
½ teaspoon dried thyme
1 teaspoon oregano
3 small potatoes, peeled and diced
2 tablespoons lemon juice
2 teaspoons black pepper

Scrub the clam shells. Open the shells and remove the clams. Reserve the liquid.

Put the bacon into a large pot and cook over medium heat, stirring frequently until brown. Add the onions and cook over low heat, stirring frequently, for 10 minutes, or until the onions are translucent.

Add the water, tomatoes, celery, parsley, bay leaf, oregano, thyme, potatoes, lemon juice. Cover the pot and simmer for 2 hours.

Add the clams and their liquid. Season with the pepper and simmer for 15 more minutes. Serve hot.

NEW ENGLAND CLAM CHOWDER
serves 6

24 clams
½ pound salt pork, diced
3 onions, finely chopped
2 cups boiling water
2 tablespoons lemon juice
3 potatoes, peeled and finely diced
3 cups milk
2 cups heavy cream
1 teaspoon salt
2 teaspoons black pepper

Scrub the clams and open the shells. Remove the clams and reserve their liquid. Chop the clams.

Put the salt pork into a large pot and cook over high heat, stirring constantly, until the pork is half done, about 8 to 10 minutes. Pour off most of the fat and add the onions. Cook over high heat, stirring constantly, until the onions are brown.

Add the boiling water, lemon juice, potatoes, salt and pepper. Cover and simmer for 10 minutes. Add the reserved clam liquid and simmer for 10 minutes.

Add the clams, milk and cream to the pot. Cook over a low heat for 15 more minutes stirring frequently. Be careful not to let the soup boil. Serve immediately.

MUSSEL SOUP
serves 6

50 mussels, about 4 pounds
4 cups water
1 large onion, coarsely chopped
2 bay leaves
3 tablespoons olive oil
2 tablespoons lemon juice
1 teaspoon salt
1 teaspoon black pepper
½ teaspoon oregano
1 leek (white part only), finely chopped
½ pound rice

Scrub, debeard and rinse the mussels. Put them into a large pot and add the water, onions and bay leaves. Cover the pot and cook over medium heat for 5 minutes, or until the mussels open. Remove the mussels with a slotted spoon and discard any that have not opened. Strain and reserve the broth. Remove the mussels from the shells and set aside. Discard the shells.

In a large saucepan, heat the olive oil. Stir in the lemon juice, salt, pepper and oregano. Add the leeks and cook over medium high heat, stirring constantly, until they are golden brown.

Add the mussel broth and the rice. Stir once and simmer over medium heat for about 20 minutes, or until the rice is tender.

Stir in the mussels and the tomato. Bring to a boil for 1 minute.

Remove the bay leaves, ladle the soup into serving bowls and serve.

CREAMY MUSSEL SOUP

serves 4

2 pounds mussels, scrubbed and
debearded
2 small onions, quartered
3 shallots, chopped
3 parsley sprigs
¼ teaspoon cayenne pepper
salt to taste
black pepper to taste
1 cup dry white wine
3 tablespoons butter
1 bay leaf
½ teaspoon thyme
2½ cups heavy cream

Put the mussels into a large pot and add enough cold water to cover. Add the onions, shallots, parsley, cayenne pepper, salt, pepper, wine, butter, bay leaf and thyme. Cover the pot and bring the liquid to a boil. Simmer until the mussels open. Discard any mussels that do not open.

Strain the cooking liquid through a double thickness of clean cheesecloth into a saucepan. Remove the mussels from their shells and divide them among four individual deep soup bowls.

Bring the cooking liquid to a boil and add the cream. Reduce the heat and cook until the soup begins to thicken. Ladle the soup over the mussels in the soup bowls and serve.

OYSTER SOUP

serves 4

2 tablespoons olive oil
1 green pepper, chopped
1 whole leek, chopped
1 medium-sized onion, chopped
3 cups fish stock
½ cup dry white wine
1 tablespoon lemon juice
1 pint (about 2½ cups) shucked oysters
with their liquid
½ teaspoon dried thyme
½ teaspoon salt
⅛ teaspoon hot red pepper flakes
1 small carrot, peeled and julienned

Heat the oil in a skillet. Add the green pepper, leek, and onion. Sauté over medium heat until the vegetables are soft.

With a slotted spoon, transfer the vegetables to a large pot. Add the fish stock, wine and lemon juice. Bring the mixture to a boil. Reduce the heat and simmer, uncovered, until the flavors are well blended, about 7 minutes.

Add the oysters and their liquid, the thyme, salt and the red pepper flakes. Continue to simmer until the edges of the oysters are slightly curled, about 5 minutes.

With a slotted spoon, remove the oysters and put them into four individual soup bowls. Spoon the broth over the oysters. Garnish with the julienned carrots.

SCALLOP AND ARTICHOKE SOUP

serves 6

½ pound thawed frozen artichoke hearts
4 tablespoons butter
2 tablespoons flour
2 cups chicken broth
½ pound sea scallops, coarsely chopped
salt to taste
1 cup heavy cream

Melt the butter in a saucepan and add the artichoke hearts. Sauté for 3 minutes. Add the flour and blend well. Add the chicken broth, stir well, and simmer until the artichokes are tender, about 5 minutes.

Purée the artichoke mixture in a blender or food processor. Pour the mixture back into the saucepan and cook over low heat for 1 minute. Add the scallops and cook gently until the scallops are white, about 3 minutes.

Add the cream and lemon juice and cook until the mixture is hot. Do not let the soup boil.

SHELLFISH SOUP

serves 6

7 tablespoons butter
1 tablespoon flour
2 cups milk
2 cups light cream
½ pound crabmeat, cooked and flaked
½ pound lobster tail, cooked and chopped
½ pound shrimp, cooked and peeled
1 tablespoon lemon juice
1 teaspoon grated lemon rind
½ teaspoon salt
1 teaspoon black pepper
3 tablespoons dry sherry
1 teaspoon parsley

In the top of a double broiler, over briskly boiling water, melt the butter. Blend in the flour. Stirring constantly, gradually add the milk and the cream.

In a large mixing bowl mix together the crabmeat, lobster and shrimp. Add the lemon juice and mix well.

Add the shellfish and the lemon rind to the soup. Stir well and continue to cook for 20 minutes.

Season the soup with the salt and pepper and stir in the sherry.

Ladle the soup into individual bowls, sprinkle with parsley and serve.

SHRIMP AND RICE SOUP

serves 4

2 tablespoons olive oil
2 tablespoons butter
1 cup raw rice
3 large ripe tomatoes, skinned and
chopped
½ onion, chopped
2 cups water
1 cup white wine
1 teaspoon salt
1 teaspoon paprika
1 teaspoon black pepper
1 teaspoon Tabasco sauce
3 tablespoons lemon juice
1 cup cooked shrimp

Heat the olive oil and the butter in a large saucepan. When the butter has melted, add the rice and cook, stirring constantly, until it turns golden brown.

Add the tomatoes, onion, water, wine, salt, pepper, paprika and Tabasco. Stir well. Cover the pan and simmer over low heat for 10 minutes.

Mix the lemon juice with the shrimp. Add the shrimp to the soup. Simmer for 10 more minutes and serve.

SHE-CRAB SOUP

serves 6 to 8

1 pound crabmeat and roe (if possible),
cleaned
6 tablespoons butter
1 tablespoon flour
2 cups milk
2 cups light cream
1 teaspoon grated lemon rind
¼ teaspoon ground mace
1 teaspoon salt
¼ teaspoon pepper
3 tablespoons dry sherry
1 teaspoon finely chopped parsley

In the top of a double broiler over briskly boiling water, melt the butter. When melted, add the flour and blend well. Pour in the milk and light cream. Stir constantly. Add the grated lemon rind, mace and crabmeat and roe. Stir well and continue cooking for 20 minutes. Add the salt and pepper.

Remove the mixture from the heat and allow it to stand over the hot water for 15 minutes. Stir in the sherry and serve. Garnish each bowl with chopped parsley.

The soup need not be made with female crabs and their roe; any crabmeat will do.

STEWS AND CASSEROLES

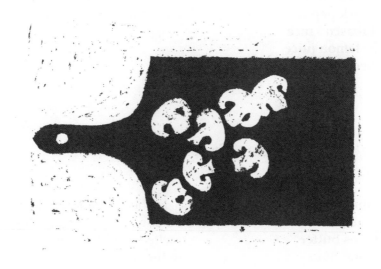

CREOLE SALPICON

serves 6

meat from 24 crawfish, diced
3 tomatoes, peeled, seeded and finely chopped
12 mushrooms, chopped
2 tablespoons butter
3 tablespoons flour
2 cups boiling milk
salt to taste
1 teaspoon grated nutmeg
12 black peppercorns
1 herb bouquet (1 bay leaf, ¼ teaspoon cloves, 1 parsley sprig tied in a cheesecloth bag)

Melt the butter in a saucepan. Add the flour and cook for 5 minutes, stirring constantly.

Gradually whisk in the boiling milk. Add the nutmeg, salt to taste, and peppercorns. Drop in the herb bouquet and cook over medium heat for 15 minutes.

Remove the saucepan from the heat. Discard the herb bouquet. Strain the milk mixture through a sieve and return it to the saucepan. Add the tomatoes, crawfish meat and mushrooms. Return the mixture to the heat and cook for 5 minutes. Serve hot with rice.

CRAB STEW

serves 4

3 pounds crab legs
2 tablespoons butter
1 small onion, chopped
2 cups thinly sliced mushrooms
2 tomatoes, peeled and chopped
¼ teaspoon cayenne pepper
1 cup heavy cream
½ cup light cream
salt
2 tablespoons finely chopped parsley
1 teaspoon finely chopped chives
¼ cup brandy

In a large pot, bring 3 quarts of water to a boil over high heat. Add the crab legs. When the water returns to a boil, reduce the heat to low and simmer the crab legs for 10 minutes.

While the crab legs are cooking, in a large skillet melt the butter. Add the onion and cook, stirring constantly, over medium heat for 2 minutes. Add the mushrooms and continue to cook, stirring frequently, for 2 minutes more. Add the tomatoes and cook, stirring frequently, for 5 minutes more. Reduce the heat to low and let the mixture simmer gently.

Drain the crab legs. Shell the crabmeat and remove the cartilage. Break the crabmeat into small pieces and add to the large skillet. Increase the heat to medium.

Stir in the cayenne pepper, heavy cream, light cream and salt to taste. Continue to stir until the mixture comes to a boil.

Remove the skillet from the heat and stir in the parsley, chives and brandy. Serve the stew hot over rice.

FISHERMAN'S STEW WITH ROUILLE

serves 10

2 pounds halibut steaks
1 2-pound red snapper, cleaned
1 2-pound striped bass, cleaned
2 pounds haddock steaks
2 pounds codfish steaks
1 2-pound whitefish, cleaned
9 tablespoons olive oil
2 cups coarsely chopped onions
1 cup thinly sliced leeks
6 garlic cloves, finely chopped
2 cups white wine
3 pounds tomatoes, peeled, seeded and
coarsely chopped
1 teaspoon grated orange rind
1 teaspoon dried thyme
1 bay leaf
¼ teaspoon saffron threads
½ teaspoon salt
½ teaspoon black pepper
2 green peppers, coarsely chopped
½ teaspoon Tabasco sauce
½ cup chopped pimentos
3 tablespoons unflavored breadcrumbs
5 cups cooked rice

Trim the skin and bones from the fish steaks. Fillet the whole fish. Cut the fish steaks and fillets into 1-inch cubes. Reserve the trimmings, heads and bones.

Heat 3 tablespoons of the olive oil in a large, 6-quart pot. Add the onions, leeks and 2 chopped garlic cloves. Cook over low heat, stirring occasionally, for 5 minutes.

Add 6 cups of water and the white wine and reserved fish trimmings to the pot. Cover and simmer over low heat for 5 minutes.

Add the tomatoes, orange rind, thyme, parsley, bay leaf, saffron, salt and pepper. Raise the heat slightly and simmer for 10 minutes longer.

While the fish stock is simmering, prepare the rouille. Combine the remaining garlic with the green peppers, Tabasco sauce, pimentos, remaining olive oil and breadcrumbs in a small mixing bowl. Mix well.

Put the rouille mixture into a saucepan and add 1 cup water. Simmer over moderate heat for 10 minutes. Put the rouille into a small serving bowl and set aside.

When the fish stock is ready, strain it through a cheesecloth into another pot. Discard the solids remaining in the cheesecloth.

Bring the strained stock to a boil over medium heat. Add the fish pieces and cook for 10 minutes. Reduce the heat to low and cook for 5 minutes longer.

Put ½ cup of the cooked rice into each individual soup bowl. Ladle the soup on top. Serve with rouille.

ITALIAN FISH STEW

serves 6

18 clams, in shells
2 pounds bass fillets
1 pound shrimp, peeled and deveined
1 large lobster tail, shelled and deveined
1 pound crab legs, shelled and cartilage
removed
½ cup olive oil
1 large onion, chopped
1 green pepper, chopped
1 sweet red pepper, chopped
12 straw mushrooms
4 ripe tomatoes, peeled and chopped
4 garlic cloves, finely chopped
½ cup tomato purée
1 cup red wine
1 cup dry sherry
small bunch parsley, chopped
1 teaspoon sugar
½ teaspoon crushed red pepper
1 tablespoon oregano
salt
black pepper

Scrub the clams and set aside. Cut the bass fillets into serving-size pieces. Cut the lobster tail and the crab legs into pieces. Put the bass, lobster, crab and shrimp into a large pot. Set aside.

In a large skillet, heat the olive oil. Add the onion, red pepper, green pepper, garlic and mushrooms. Cook over low heat for 5 minutes, stirring frequently. Add the tomatoes, tomato purée, red wine, sugar, sherry, half the parsley, red pepper, oregano, and salt and pepper to taste. Cover the skillet and cook over low heat for 15 minutes. Carefully pour the sauce and vegetables into the pot with the fish. Mix well and simmer for 30 minutes.

Add the clams and continue to simmer until the clams open. Transfer the stew to a large serving bowl. Sprinkle with the remaining chopped parsley and serve.

MARDI GRAS SEAFOOD GUMBO

serves 8

¼ cup bacon drippings
3 pounds thinly sliced fresh okra
¼ cup vegetable oil
¼ cup flour
4 onions, diced
2 tablespoons tomato paste
¼ cup puréed tomatoes
4 cups cold water
½ pound oysters, shelled
1 pound crabmeat, picked and flaked
2 pounds medium-sized shrimp, shelled
and deveined
¾ pound diced baked ham
3 bay leaves
½ cup chopped parsley
2 garlic cloves, minced
1 shallot, chopped
salt to taste
black pepper to taste
1 teaspoon chili sauce

Heat the drippings in a skillet over low heat. Add the okra and sauté until the mixture thickens. Remove the skillet from the heat and set aside.

In a heavy pot or Dutch oven, heat the vegetable oil. Slowly blend in the flour, stirring constantly until a rich, brown gravy (roux) is formed.

Add the onions, tomato paste, puréed tomatoes and water and mix thoroughly. Then add the reserved okra and drippings, and the oysters, crabmeat, shrimp, ham, bay leaves, parsley, garlic, shallot, salt and pepper. Mix well.

Simmer the gumbo over medium heat for 45 minutes to 1 hour, or until the seafood is tender and opaque. Stir in the chili sauce just before removing the gumbo from the heat. Serve piping hot over saffron rice.

OYSTER STEW

serves 4

2 cups whole shelled oysters
4 cups milk, scalded
¼ cup butter
1½ teaspoons salt
¼ teaspoon black pepper
¼ teaspoon ground nutmeg
¼ teaspoon ground ginger

Strain the oysters through a cheesecloth or fine wire strainer, catching the oyster juice in a large pot. Wash the oysters in cold water, carefully checking for grit and pieces of shell.

Bring the oyster juice slowly to a boil. Add the washed oysters, bring the juice back to the boil for 30 seconds, and then simmer until the edges of the oysters curl, about 3 to 4 minutes. Remove the oysters with a spoon and cut them into halves, or if they're large, quarters.

Add the milk, butter, salt, pepper, nutmeg and ginger to the simmering oyster juice, and stir until evenly blended. Return the oysters to the stew and cook for 5 minutes over low heat. Serve immediately.

OYSTER STEW WITH SESAME SEEDS

serves 8

4 tablespoons sesame seeds
2 onions, thinly sliced
6 strips bacon or salt pork
3 tablespoons flour
2 cups oyster liquor or 1 cup water and
1 cup dry sherry
3 cups shelled oysters

Preheat the oven to 450°.

Spread the sesame seeds on a foil-covered backing sheet. Toast the seeds in the oven until they are browned. Set aside.

Fry the bacon and onion in a heavy stew pot until the bacon is cooked but not crisp. Remove the bacon and onion and set aside. Leave the drippings in the pot.

Reduce the heat a little and slowly stir in the flour, continuing to stir until the drippings become a rich brown gravy. Gradually stir in the oyster liquor until it is thoroughly blended. Simmer the mixture over medium heat, stirring constantly for about 5 minutes, or until the mixture has thickened and is very smooth.

Put the reserved sesame seeds into a small plastic bag. Seal the bag and crush the seeds with a rolling pin until they are a coarse powder. Add the powder to the stew and stir well.

Chop the reserved bacon strips into small pieces, and add them and the reserved onion to the stew. Add the oysters and cook about 5 to 10 minutes or until the edges of the oysters curl. Serve piping hot.

SEAFOOD STEW

serves 6

3 garlic cloves, finely chopped
3 small onions, chopped
vegetable oil
½ teaspoon dried thyme
¼ cup chopped parsley
¼ teaspoon caraway seeds
1 bay leaf
2 cups white wine
14 ounces whole, peeled plum tomatoes
¾ pound small squid
1½ pounds cod fillets
1 pound flounder fillets
1 pound striped bass fillets
¼ teaspoon salt
black pepper to taste
14 soft-shell clams, scrubbed and rinsed

Heat a thin layer of vegetable oil in a Dutch oven or deep pot over moderate heat. Add the garlic and onion and sauté until transparent but not browned. Add the thyme, parsley, caraway seeds, bay leaf and white wine. Raise the heat and bring the ingredients to a boil. Cover the pot, reduce the heat, and simmer for about 10 minutes.

Add the tomatoes, and lay the squid on top. Simmer, covered, for 10 more minutes.

Lay the cod, flounder and bass fillets over the squid, one at a time, and dust with the salt and pepper. Cover and let simmer for 12 minutes.

Spread the clams around the edges of the pot, cover, and simmer for 10 to 15 minutes, or until the clams open and are tender and opaque.

SCALLOP STEW

serves 4

2 pounds sea scallops
½ cup dry vermouth
2 garlic cloves, finely chopped
6 tablespoons olive oil
1 large red onion, thinly sliced and broken into rings
6 plum tomatoes, peeled and chopped
4 tablespoons butter
salt to taste
black pepper to taste
2 tablespoons chopped parsley

Wash the scallops, but do not dry them. Put them into a small bowl, add the vermouth and garlic, mix well and let stand for 30 minutes.

In a large skillet, heat the olive oil. Add the onion rings and cook, stirring constantly until they turn golden. Add the tomatoes, cover the skillet and cook until the tomatoes are soft. Add the butter, the scallops and the marinade and salt and pepper to taste. Simmer for 5 minutes, uncovered. Stir in the parsley. Transfer to a serving bowl and serve.

SHRIMP GUMBO

serves 6

8 tablespoons butter
2 garlic cloves, finely minced
2 small green peppers, coarsely chopped
2 small sweet red peppers, coarsely chopped
2 medium-sized onions, finely chopped
3 cups whole canned tomatoes
1 bay leaf
¼ teaspoon cayenne pepper
½ teaspoon Tabasco sauce
salt to taste
black pepper to taste
2 pounds medium-sized shrimp, shelled and deveined

In a large saucepan melt the butter over low heat. Add the garlic, red peppers and green peppers and mix well. Add the onions. Cook, stirring constantly, for 2 minutes. Add the tomatoes, bay leaf, cayenne pepper, Tabasco sauce and salt and pepper to taste. Stir gently but thoroughly. Half cover the saucepan and simmer for 25 minutes.

Add the shrimp to the mixture in the saucepan and cook for 5 minutes. Serve immediately with rice.

PICKEREL STEW

serves 4

2 pounds pickerel fillets, skin removed
3 cups water
¼ cup red wine vinegar
salt to taste
1 bay leaf
2 whole cloves
1½ cups milk
1½ cups light cream
2 tablespoons butter
1 tablespoon flour
4 medium-sized potatoes, boiled, peeled and cut into pieces
1 teaspoon finely chopped fresh dill

Wash and dry the fillets and cut each one into 3 or 4 pieces.

In a large pot combine the water, vinegar, salt, bay leaf and cloves. Bring to a boil. Add the fish. Cook over medium heat for 10 minutes. Remove the pot from the heat and set aside.

In a saucepan, combine the milk and cream and heat until lukewarm. Add to the fish mixture and stir gently.

In a small saucepan, melt the butter. Blend in the flour. When well blended, add to the fish mixture. Stir in the potatoes and dill. Cook the fish stew for 8 more minutes over medium heat.

SWORDFISH STEW

serves 4

1½ pounds swordfish steaks
4 cups fish stock
1 cup diced celery
2 tomatoes, seeded and chopped
1 tablespoon tomato paste
½ green pepper, chopped
1 onion, chopped
1 large carrot, chopped
½ teaspoon dried thyme
½ teaspoon dried basil
1 teaspoon salt
black pepper to taste
4 bacon slices, diced
2 potatoes, peeled and diced

Cut the swordfish steaks into 2-inch cubes.

Put the fish stock in a large pot and add the celery, tomatoes, tomato paste, green pepper, onion, carrot, thyme, basil, salt and pepper. Simmer over medium heat for 30 minutes.

Sauté the diced bacon until crisp. Add the bacon to the mixture in the pot. Add the potatoes and simmer for 10 minutes longer. Add the swordfish cubes and simmer for 20 minutes longer, or until the potatoes are tender. Serve hot.

CRAB CASSEROLE

serves 4

3 pounds crab legs
8 tablespoons butter
1½ cups coarse cracker crumbs
2 large onions, finely chopped
6 celery stalks, finely chopped
2 tablespoons finely chopped parsley
¼ cup heavy cream
¼ teaspoon cayenne pepper
1½ teaspoons dry mustard

Rinse the crab legs. Put them into a steamer basket and steam them over boiling water for 10 minutes. Drain the crab legs, shell them and remove any cartilage from the meat. Break up the crabmeat and put it into a large bowl.

Preheat the oven to 350°F. Grease a medium-sized casserole dish with butter.

In a small saucepan, melt the butter over low heat. Remove the pan from the heat and set aside to cool.

Add the cracker crumbs to the crabmeat and mix well. Then add the onion, celery and parsley. Mix well.

In a small bowl, combine the cooled melted butter, the cream, cayenne pepper and dry mustard. Mix thoroughly.

Add the cream mixture to the crab mixture and mix well. Carefully spoon the mixture into the casserole dish. Bake for 30 minutes. Serve immediately.

COLONIAL FISH POT

serves 6

1 tablespoon salt
1 tablespoon paprika
½ teaspoon white pepper
½ teaspoon dried thyme
¼ cup flour
1 pound thickly cut cod fillets
1 pound thickly cut haddock steaks
1 pound flounder fillets
6 bacon strips, diced
4 onions, sliced
6 tablespoons butter
12 white mushroom caps
2 leeks, sliced crosswise
¼ pound Edam or Gouda cheese, diced
3 cups milk
6 eggs, beaten
salt to taste

Mix the salt, paprika, pepper, thyme and flour together on a plate.

Dredge the cod, haddock and flounder in the flour mixture, coating all sides. Cut the fish into large chunks.

Cook the bacon in a large heavy pot until half done. Add the fish chunks and the onions to the drippings and sauté, stirring often with a wooden spoon, until the onions are tender and browned.

Preheat the oven to 325°F.

Use half the butter to grease a large casserole dish. Pour in the fish, bacon, and onions, and add the mushrooms and leeks.

Mix the diced cheese, milk and beaten eggs in a bowl and pour over the fish in the casserole.

Bake for 40 minutes. Remove the dish from the oven and dot the casserole with the remaining butter. Bake again for 5 minutes.

FISH AND POTATO HASH

serves 4

1 pound fish fillets
salt to taste
black pepper to taste
¼ cup flour
4 tablespoons butter or olive oil
½ pound potatoes, peeled and diced
1 large onion, coarsely chopped
1 garlic clove, crushed

Cut the fish fillets into strips. Sprinkle them with salt and pepper and dredge them in the flour.

Heat the butter or olive oil in a large heavy skillet. Add the potatoes and sauté until they are browned on all sides. Add the onion and garlic clove and sauté until the onions are transparent.

Push the potatoes and onions to the sides of the skillet. Add the fish strips to the center of the skillet and sauté until they are browned on all sides. Serve hot.

OYSTER CASSEROLE

serves 6

1 quart fresh oysters, shelled
2 tablespoons finely chopped parsley
1 small onion, diced
2 tablespoons finely minced shallots
½ teaspoon salt
¼ teaspoon cayenne pepper
1 tablespoon lemon or lime juice
plain soda crackers
3 cups light cream
butter
garlic powder
dry mustard

Grease a casserole dish with butter, and spread a layer of oysters on the bottom. Spread some of the parsley, onion and shallots on top of the oysters, and dust with half the salt and pepper. Sprinkle with half the lemon juice, then make a layer of soda crackers on top of the oysters. Spread another layer of oysters on top of the crackers, and repeat the layering as before.

Preheat the oven to 325°F.

Pour the cream over the casserole. Top with thin pats of butter all over the surface. Dust with garlic powder and mustard to taste. Bake for about 30 minutes, or until the cream is thickened and bubbly.

SMOKED SALMON CASSEROLE

serves 4

1 tablespoon butter, softened
4 medium potatoes, thinly sliced
1 small white onion, finely chopped
1 pound smoked salmon, thinly sliced
1½ cups light cream
4 tablespoons butter, melted
3 tablespoons chopped parsley
1 teaspoon black pepper
½ teaspoon grated nutmeg

Preheat the oven to 325°F. Grease a medium-sized casserole dish with the softened butter.

Arrange one-third of the potatoes on the bottom of the casserole. Sprinkle half the chopped onion over the potatoes. Arrange half the salmon on top of the potatoes. Then make another layer of one-third of the potatoes and sprinkle with the remaining onion. Arrange the remaining salmon slices and cover with the rest of the potatoes.

Pour the cream around the side of the casserole. Pour the melted butter over the top. Sprinkle with the parsley, pepper and nutmeg. Bake for 1 hour. Serve hot.

Shrimp and Corn Soufflé

serves 6

6 ears corn
2 pounds small shrimp
3 eggs, separated
2 teaspoons sugar
1 tablespoon cream
1 tablespoon butter, melted

In a large pot, bring 3 quarts of water to a boil over high heat. Add the shrimp. When the water returns to a boil, reduce the heat and simmer the shrimp for 5 minutes. Drain the shrimp, remove the shells and veins. Wash the shrimp and dry them. Put them into a large bowl.

Preheat the oven to 300°F. Grease a 2-quart soufflé dish.

Shuck the corn and remove the silk. Cut the kernels off the cob. Mix the corn kernels with the shrimp.

In a large mixing bowl, beat the egg yolks. Stir in the sugar, cream and melted butter. Add the corn and shrimp. Mix well.

In another bowl, beat the egg whites until they are stiff. Fold the egg whites into the shrimp mixture.

Spoon the mixture into the prepared soufflé dish. Cover the dish with aluminum foil and set it in a pan of hot water. (The water should come about three-quarters up the side of the soufflé dish.) Bake for 45 minutes.

Remove the foil from the dish and bake for 15 minutes more, or until the top is golden brown. Serve immediately.

CAVIAR ITALIANO

serves 4

1 pound linguini
4 tablespoons sweet butter
4 tablespoons fresh ricotta cheese
3 tablespoons heavy cream
2 teaspoons black pepper
⅓ cup lumpfish caviar
1 tablespoon finely chopped parsley

In a large pot of boiling water cook the linguini until it is almost completely cooked. Drain the linguini. Reserve 2 tablespoons of the water in which it cooked.

While the linguini is cooking, in a large skillet melt the butter. Add the ricotta, cream and pepper and cook over low heat, stirring constantly, for 3 minutes. Add the caviar to the cream mixture and stir until smooth.

Add the drained linguini, the reserved water and the parsley to the skillet and continue to cook, stirring constantly, for 2 minutes more. Transfer to a serving dish and serve immediately.

CURRIED SHELLFISH WITH SPINACH

serves 6

12 large shrimp
12 sea scallops
12 crab legs
1 large lobster tail
8 tablespoons butter
1 small onion, chopped
1 sweet red pepper, sliced into rings
1 green pepper, sliced into rings
4 garlic cloves, finely chopped
12 straw or small white mushrooms
2 scallions, chopped
4 teaspoons curry powder
½ teaspoon cayenne pepper
½ teaspoon Tabasco sauce
salt to taste
2 cups dry white wine
½ pound fresh spinach, very well rinsed

Put the shrimp, scallops, crab legs and lobster tail into a steamer basket. Steam the seafood over boiling water for 5 minutes. Remove the seafood from the steamer and let cool. Shell and devein the shrimp. Shell the crab legs and break the meat into chunks. Shell the lobster tail and cut the meat into chunks. Set the seafood aside.

Melt the butter in a large skillet. Add the onions, red pepper, green pepper and garlic. Cook over low heat, stirring constantly, until the vegetables are tender. Add the mushrooms, scallions, curry powder, cayenne pepper, Tabasco sauce and salt to taste. Stir well. Add the reserved shellfish and stir again. Cook over low heat, stirring constantly, for 5 minutes.

Add the wine to the skillet and bring the liquid to a boil over medium heat. Remove the skillet from the heat and add the spinach leaves. Stir gently for 3 minutes, or until the spinach is wilted and bright green. Transfer the curry to a serving bowl and serve hot.

Codfish Pie

serves 4

¾ pound fresh codfish, cubed
¼ pound thickly sliced salt pork or bacon
1 onion, finely chopped
3 tablespoons flour
freshly ground black pepper to taste
2½ cups milk
1 cup diced cooked potatoes
1½ cups flour
2 teaspoons baking powder
¼ teaspoon salt
6 tablespoons melted shortening
light cream

Put the codfish in a large kettle and add enough cold water to cover. Bring the water quickly to a boil, then reduce the heat, cover and simmer for about 15 minutes, until the fish is tender and easily flaked.

Drain the codfish well and flake it with a fork. Set aside.

Put the salt pork or bacon in a skillet and cook over medium heat until the pieces are brown and crisp. Remove the pieces from the skillet and save. Spoon off and discard half the drippings. Add the onion to the skillet and sauté until tender. Then sprinkle in the 3 tablespoons of flour, stirring constantly with a wooden spoon, until all the flour is evenly blended. While continuing to stir, add the pepper and gradually blend in the milk. Cook until the mixture begins to thicken. Stir in the codfish, pork or bacon pieces and potatoes and cook for about 2 minutes, or until all the ingredients are thoroughly blended. Turn off the heat and let the skillet cool.

In a mixing bowl, combine the flour, baking powder and salt. Stir in the shortening and enough light cream to make the dough soft and workable.

Knead the dough for about a minute, then roll it out into a ¼-inch crust.

Preheat the oven to 400°F.

Pour the codfish mixture into a deep, butter-greased baking dish. Lay the crust over the top of the baking dish, trim and seal the edges.

Bake the pie for about 25 minutes, or until the crust is golden brown and flaky.

HADDOCK PUDDING

serves 4

½ cup unflavored breadcrumbs
1 pound haddock fillets, skinned and
ground
8 tablespoons butter, softened
1 tablespoon anchovy paste
salt to taste
black pepper to taste
4 eggs, separated
3 tablespoons flour
1 cup light cream
1 cup heavy cream

Preheat the oven to 325°F. Butter a 2-quart baking dish. Spread the breadcrumbs over the bottom of the dish and set aside.

In a small bowl, combine the ground haddock, butter, anchovy paste and salt and pepper to taste. Set aside. In a medium-sized bowl beat the egg yolks with the flour and light cream. Add the fish mixture to the egg mixture and beat for 30 seconds.

In a third bowl, beat the heavy cream until it is thick and holds its shape.

In a fourth bowl, beat the egg whites until they are stiff but not dry.

Fold the heavy cream and the egg whites into the fish mixture. Mix gently.

Turn the mixture into the baking dish and bake for 1 hour, or until a knife inserted into the center comes out clean. Remove the pudding from the oven and let stand for 5 minutes.

Place a serving dish over the top of the baking dish. Turn the pudding over onto the serving dish. Serve hot.

SCALLOPED TUNA

serves 4

2 tablespoons butter
4 tablespoons flour
1 cup milk
2 cups drained canned tuna
2 eggs, beaten
black pepper to taste
1 tablespoon lemon juice
1 scallion, chopped
1 tablespoon chopped parsley
1 tablespoon chopped pimento
2 tablespoons chopped black olives
½ cup unflavored breadcrumbs

Preheat the oven to 375°F. Butter a large baking dish.

Melt the butter in a saucepan over medium heat. Stir in the flour. Gradually stir in the milk and simmer until the mixture thickens.

Remove the saucepan from the heat and stir in the tuna, eggs, pepper, lemon juice, scallion, parsley, pimento and olives. Pour the mixture into the baking dish. Sprinkle the breadcrumbs over the top and bake for 25 minutes. Serve hot from the baking dish.

SHRIMP AND EGG BAKE

serves 4

6 hard-boiled eggs, chopped
2 tablespoons butter
½ teaspoon dried chervil
1 teaspoon Dijon-style mustard
1 teaspoon salt
½ teaspoon black pepper
½ cup chopped cooked shrimp
1 cup heavy cream
½ cup grated Parmesan cheese
butter

Preheat the oven to 400°F.

Divide the eggs and shrimp among 4 small, buttered ovenproof dishes.

Mix the chervil, mustard, salt and pepper with the cream and spoon evenly over the egg-shrimp mixture. Sprinkle with grated cheese, dot with butter, and bake until cheese melts and turns golden brown.

SWEET AND SOUR SALMON

serves 6

3 onions, sliced
3 lemons, sliced
½ cup honey
⅓ cup seedless raisins
1 bay leaf
8 thin salmon steaks
1 teaspoon salt
3 cups water
8 crushed gingersnaps
½ cup cider vinegar
½ cup sliced blanched almonds

Combine the onions, lemon slices, honey, raisins, bay leaf, fish, salt and water in a large saucepan. Cover and cook over low heat for 30 minutes. Remove the fish.

Add the gingersnaps, vinegar and almonds to the fish stock. Cook over low heat. Stir until smooth. Serve the sauce over the fish, either warm or cold.

SALADS

ANDALUSIAN MUSSEL SALAD

serves 6

1 hard-cooked egg yolk
¼ cup olive oil
1 garlic clove, finely chopped
4 tablespoons white wine vinegar
1 tablespoon chopped fresh parsley
½ teaspoon salt
½ teaspoon black pepper
½ cup chopped green pepper
½ cup chopped sweet red pepper
1 medium-sized onion, thinly sliced to form rings
1½ cups cooked fresh mussels, well drained
6 coarsely chopped pimento-stuffed green olives
6 black olives

In a small bowl, mash the egg yolk with 2 tablespoons of the olive oil and the garlic. Add the remaining olive oil and the vinegar. Stir well. Add the parsley, salt and pepper. Stir until well blended.

In a serving bowl, put the green and red peppers, onion, mussels and chopped green olives. Toss gently. Pour the egg dressing over the salad and toss gently again. Cover the bowl and refrigerate for 30 minutes.

Remove the salad from the refrigerator, garnish with the black olives and serve.

Avocado Shrimp Boats

serves 6

¼ cup olive oil
¼ cup white wine vinegar
4 tablespoons finely chopped scallions
½ teaspoon Tabasco sauce
½ teaspoon oregano
2 cups chopped cooked shrimp
2 large tomatoes, peeled, seeded and diced
1 cucumber, peeled and diced
2 tablespoons coarsely chopped
pimento-stuffed olives
3 tablespoons chopped pimentos
salt to taste
black pepper to taste
3 large avocados
1 tablespoon lemon juice
6 romaine lettuce leaves
3 tablespoons chopped parsley

Combine the olive oil, vinegar, scallions, Tabasco sauce and oregano in a jar that has a tight-fitting lid. Cover the jar tightly and shake until the marinade is well blended.

Put the shrimp into a bowl and pour the marinade over them. Toss well. Cover the bowl and let stand at room temperature for 1 hour.

Add the tomatoes, cucumber, olives, pimentos and salt and pepper to taste to the shrimp. Toss well.

Halve the avocados and remove the pits. Sprinkle the avocados with the lemon juice. Put 1 lettuce leaf on each of six serving plates. Put an avocado half on each plate. Fill and cover each avocado half with the shrimp mixture. Sprinkle with parsley and serve.

Bean and Tuna Salad

serves 6

2 cups drained cooked cannelini or other
white beans
½ cup olive oil
3 tablespoons lemon juice
1 teaspoon salt
½ teaspoon black pepper
1 small onion, thinly sliced
8 black olives, pitted and halved
6 to 8 ounces canned tuna, drained
2 tablespoons chopped parsley
2 tablespoons chopped basil

Put the beans into a large salad bowl.

Put the olive oil, lemon juice, salt and pepper into a jar with a tightly fitting lid. Cover the jar securely and shake well. Pour the dressing over the beans.

Add the onion slices and black olives to the salad bowl and toss. Add the tuna and toss again. Sprinkle the parsley and basil over the salad and serve.

CLAM AND PASTA SALAD

serves 4 to 6

½ pound cooked pasta shapes
½ cup pure olive oil
½ pound minced cooked clams or mussels
3 tablespoons fresh lemon juice
1½ garlic cloves, finely chopped
3 tablespoons chopped fresh parsley
2 tablespoons chopped fresh basil
1 tablespoon chopped fresh mint
3 tablespoons grated Parmesan cheese
1 teaspoon salt
1 teaspoon black pepper

In a large salad bowl, put the pasta and 1 tablespoon of the olive oil. Lightly toss. Add the minced clams and toss again.

Put the remaining olive oil, lemon juice and garlic into a jar with a tightly fitting lid. Cover tightly and shake until blended. Add the parsley, basil, mint, Parmesan cheese, salt and pepper. Shake again until well mixed. Pour the dressing over the pasta and clams. Toss well. Cover the bowl and chill for 2 hours. Toss well before serving.

CRAB SALAD WITH HOT CAPER DRESSING

serves 4

½ cup olive oil
3 tablespoons red wine vinegar
1 tablespoon lemon juice
2 garlic cloves, finely chopped
3 tablespoons drained capers
½ teaspoon salt
½ teaspoon black pepper
½ teaspoon oregano
½ teaspoon paprika
½ head romaine lettuce, torn into small pieces
1½ cups flaked cooked crabmeat
1 tomato, peeled, seeded and diced
3 scallions, chopped

In a saucepan, combine the olive oil, vinegar, lemon juice, garlic, capers, salt, pepper, oregano and paprika. Cook over medium-low heat until the dressing is almost boiling.

While the sauce is heating, in a large serving bowl combine the lettuce, crabmeat, tomato and scallions. Toss well.

When the sauce is ready, pour it over the salad and toss again. Serve immediately.

CRAB AND FRUIT SALAD

serves 4

1 pound cooked crabmeat, picked and
flaked
1 navel orange, peeled, sectioned and
chopped
½ cup drained mandarin orange slices
½ cup chopped celery
½ cup seedless white grapes, cut in half
½ teaspoon dried dill
salt to taste
black pepper to taste
½ cup mayonnaise
slivered almonds

Mix the crabmeat, orange pieces, mandarin orange sections, celery, grapes, and dill in a large salad bowl. Mix in the mayonnaise, a little at a time, until it lightly coats all the ingredients in the bowl. Season with salt and pepper. Sprinkle the almond slivers on top and serve chilled.

MINT COD SALAD

serves 8

2 cups water
1 pound cod, cut into chunks
1 cup thinly sliced radishes
1 small cucumber, thinly sliced
4 tablespoons finely chopped fresh mint
1 small red onion, thinly sliced and
broken into rings
2 scallions, thinly sliced
5 tablespoons water
1 tablespoon lemon juice
3 tablespoons olive oil
2 tablespoons red wine vinegar
1 teaspoon sugar

Bring the water to a boil in a saucepan. Add the cod and cook for 2 to 3 minutes, or until the fish flakes easily. Drain the fish well and put it in a bowl. Add all remaining ingredients and toss well but carefully. Cover and refrigerate for 1 hour before serving.

HERRING SALAD

serves 4

2 cups diced, pickled herring
2 potatoes, boiled, peeled and diced
2 carrots, diced
1 onion, chopped
4 tablespoons sweet pickle relish,
drained
2 large cooked beets, diced
1 cup sour cream
2 tablespoons white wine vinegar
2 hard-cooked eggs, chopped
2 tablespoons Dijon-style mustard
1 teaspoon sugar

Put the herring, potatoes, carrots, onion, relish and beets into a large mixing bowl and toss gently.

Combine the sour cream, vinegar, eggs, mustard and sugar in a small bowl and blend thoroughly.

Pour the dressing over the herring mixture and mix until the ingredients are well coated. Cover the bowl and chill before serving.

SALT HERRING SALAD

serves 4 to 6

2 salt herrings
2 small apples, peeled, cored, and cut into
small pieces
2 cups finely chopped cooked beets
½ cup chopped onion
¼ cup chopped dill pickle
2 hard-cooked eggs, chopped
olive oil
cider vinegar
lettuce leaves

Place the salt herrings in a large bowl. Add enough cold water to cover and soak for 2 hours. Drain the herrings and carefully flake the meat. Discard the skin and bones.

Place the herring meat in a mixing bowl. Add the apples, beets, onions, and pickle. Add oil and vinegar to taste. Toss well and chill for 2 hours.

Remove the salad from the refrigerator 45 minutes before serving. Toss it again, sprinkle with the chopped eggs, and serve on a bed of lettuce leaves.

Lobster Salad
serves 6

3 cups cooked lobster meat, cut into
bite-sized pieces
1 cup diced celery
1 whole scallion, chopped
1 teaspoon salt
¼ teaspoon paprika
2 tablespoons French dressing
1 tablespoon olive oil
4 pimento-stuffed green olives, sliced
lettuce leaves
1 hard-cooked egg, sliced
capers

Put the lobster meat, celery, scallion, salt, paprika, French dressing, olive oil and sliced olives in a bowl and mix until the ingredients are well-blended.

Arrange the lettuce leaves on a serving platter. Spoon the lobster salad onto the lettuce and garnish with slices of hard-cooked egg and capers.

Lobster Salad with Cranberries
serves 4

1 pound coarsely chopped cooked lobster
½ pound fresh mushrooms, sliced
½ pound fresh cranberries
2 tablespoons lemon juice
6 tablespoons olive oil
2 tablespoons red wine vinegar
2 tablespoons Dijon-style mustard
2 tablespoons unflavored yogurt
1 teaspoon crushed dried mint
salt
black pepper
4 lettuce leaves

Combine the lobster, mushrooms, cranberries and lemon juice in a large bowl. Mix well. Chill for 1 hour.

In a small bowl combine the olive oil, vinegar, mustard, yogurt, mint and salt and pepper to taste. Blend thoroughly.

Place a lettuce leaf on each of the four serving plates. Top each leaf with a portion of the lobster mixture. Pour the sauce over the salad and serve.

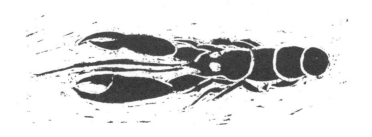

FRUIT AND MUSSEL SALAD

serves 4

40 mussels, scrubbed, rinsed and
debearded
½ cup water
½ cup dry white wine

DRESSING:
1 hard-cooked egg, finely chopped
1 egg yolk
3 tablespoons Dijon-style mustard
1 tablespoon finely chopped onion
2 teaspoons minced shallot
2 teaspoons chopped fresh basil or
1 teaspoon dried basil
2 teaspoons chopped fresh oregano or
1 teaspoon dried oregano
1 garlic clove, finely chopped
½ teaspoon salt
black pepper to taste
3 tablespoons dry white wine
3 tablespoons white wine vinegar
1 cup olive oil
2 small heads soft lettuce, washed and
dried
2 ripe pears, peeled, cored and halved
watercress for garnish (optional)

Combine the water and white wine in a large pot. Bring to a boil and add the mussels. Cover the pot and cook, shaking the pot occasionally, until the mussels open, about 5 minutes. Remove the pot from the heat and cool. When the mussels are cool enough to handle, remove them from their shells. Remove the black rims if desired. Put the mussels into a large mixing bowl and set aside.

In a small bowl combine the hard-cooked egg, egg yolk, mustard, onion, shallot, basil, oregano, garlic, salt and pepper. Add the wine and vinegar. Whisk until well blended. In a slow, steady stream, whisk in the olive oil. Continue to whisk until the dressing is smooth and well blended.

Pour the dressing over the mussels and toss until well coated.

Line four individual serving plates with the lettuce leaves. Put half a pear on each plate. Spoon the mussels over the pears and serve. Garnish with watercress if desired.

MARINATED MUSSEL SALAD
serves 6

1 hard-cooked egg yolk
¼ cup olive oil
2 garlic cloves, finely chopped
4 tablespoons white wine vinegar
1 tablespoon lemon juice
1 tablespoon chopped parsley
salt to taste
black pepper to taste
1 green pepper, chopped
1 sweet red pepper, chopped
1 medium-sized onion, thinly sliced
and broken into rings
2 cups (about 4 pounds unshelled)
cooked mussels, rinsed and drained
6 pimento-stuffed green olives,
chopped

First make the marinade. In a small bowl, mash the egg yolk with half the olive oil. Blend in the garlic, the rest of the olive oil, the vinegar, lemon juice, parsley and salt and pepper to taste.

In a large mixing bowl combine the green pepper, red pepper, onion, mussels and olives. Add the marinade and mix well. Refrigerate, covered, for at least 2 hours. Serve cold.

SALMON SALAD

serves 4

6 tablespoons red wine vinegar
2 scallions chopped
¾ cup olive oil
salt to taste
black pepper to taste
4 tablespoons butter
1 pound salmon fillet, skinned and sliced
very thinly
1 head soft lettuce, washed and dried

Combine the vinegar and the scallions in a bowl and whisk in the olive oil. Add salt and pepper to taste and set aside.

Arrange the lettuce leaves on a serving platter and set aside.

Melt the butter in a large skillet. Add the salmon slices and cook for 10 seconds on each side.

Arrange the salmon slices on the lettuce.

Whisk the dressing once again and pour it over the salmon. Serve immediately.

SALMON SALAD WITH VINAIGRETTE

serves 4

2 cups drained canned salmon
½ cup diced celery
½ cup shredded cabbage
¼ cup finely chopped green pepper
1 scallion, chopped
¼ teaspoon paprika
Vinaigrette
black pepper to taste
1 head soft lettuce
4 hard-cooked eggs, sliced

Break the salmon into pieces. Remove any bones. Put the salmon into a mixing bowl. Add the celery, cabbage, green pepper, scallion, paprika, vinaigrette dressing and black pepper to taste. Toss gently but well.

Arrange lettuce leaves on each of four individual serving plates. Top the leaves with some of the salmon salad. Garnish each serving with a sliced egg.

SCALLOP SALAD

serves 4

1 cup lemon juice
1 cup lime juice
1 cup olive oil
2 tablespoons crushed red pepper
2 garlic cloves, finely chopped
2 pounds sea scallops, coarsely chopped
2 tomatoes, peeled, seeded and chopped
1 avocado, peeled, pitted and diced
4 scallions, chopped
salt to taste
black pepper to taste
1 teaspoon chopped parsley
1 head soft lettuce, torn into pieces

In a large mixing bowl, combine the lemon juice, lime juice, olive oil, red pepper, garlic and scallops and mix thoroughly. Cover the bowl and refrigerate for 2 hours.

In a large mixing bowl, combine the tomatoes, avocado, scallions, and salt and pepper to taste. Toss gently. Drain the scallops, reserving half the marinade. Add the scallops and the reserve marinade to the tomato mixture. Toss well and let stand at room temperature for 30 minutes.

Divide the lettuce among four large bowls. Using a slotted spoon, add a portion of the scallop mixture to each bowl. Serve immediately.

SCALLOPS CEVICHE

serves 6

1 cup fresh lemon juice
1 cup fresh lime juice
3 tablespoons crushed hot red pepper flakes
1 large garlic clove, minced
2 pounds raw scallops, coarsely chopped
2 large tomatoes, seeded and chopped
1 avocado, peeled and diced
¼ cup minced scallions
½ teaspoon salt
½ teaspoon black pepper
1 head romaine lettuce, torn into bite-sized pieces

Put the lemon and lime juice into a large mixing bowl. Add the red pepper and garlic. Stir.

Add the scallops. If there is not enough of the lemon/lime juice to cover the scallops, add more juice until they are covered. Stir well. Refrigerate for 3 hours. The scallops will turn white from "cooking" in the marinade.

Put the tomatoes, avocado, green onion, salt and pepper into a large mixing bowl. Toss.

Drain the scallops, reserving ¼ cup of the marinade. Add the scallops to the tomatoes and avocado mixture. Add the reserved marinade to the salad and toss. Let stand at room temperature for 30 minutes, tossing occasionally.

Make a bed of the romaine lettuce on a serving platter. Drain the salad and arrange it on the lettuce. Serve.

Warm Scallop Salad

serves 4

2 ripe tomatoes
⅓ cup olive oil
2 shallots, finely chopped
2 tablespoons fresh lime juice
½ teaspoon salt
½ teaspoon black pepper
2 tablespoons finely chopped fresh
basil or ½ teaspoon dried basil
1 pound sea scallops
2 tablespoons olive oil
salt to taste
black pepper to taste
2 bunches arugala, tough stems removed

Peel, halve, and seed the tomato. Chop it finely and set aside.

Heat ⅓ cup olive oil in a skillet over medium heat. Add the shallots and sauté until soft, about 2 to 3 minutes. Stir in the lime juice, salt and pepper. Remove the skillet from the heat and add the tomato and basil. Stir well and set the dressing aside.

Rinse and gently dry the scallops. Cut very large scallops in half.

Heat 2 tablespoons olive oil in another skillet over moderately high heat. Add the scallops and sauté, turning frequently, for 3 to 5 minutes. Remove the skillet from the heat and put the scallops into a large mixing bowl.

Add half the dressing to the warm scallops. Season with additional salt and pepper and toss well.

Distribute the arugala evenly among four individual serving plates. Top each plate with a portion of the warm scallops. Drizzle additional dressing over each portion and serve.

Seafood Salad in Papaya

serves 4

1 cup chopped cooked shrimp
1 cup flaked cooked crabmeat
4 finely chopped celery stalks
1 cup mayonnaise
½ teaspoon curry powder
2 ripe papayas, chilled
2 tablespoons lime juice
1 lime, quartered

In a mixing bowl combine the shrimp, crab, celery, mayonnaise and curry powder and mix well.

Cut the papayas in halves and scoop out the seeds. Put each papaya half on a serving plate. Fill each papaya with one-fourth of the seafood mixture. Sprinkle with the lime juice and serve garnished with lime wedges.

SEAFOOD PASTA SALAD

serves 6

1 pound small pasta shells
½ cup plus 2 tablespoons olive oil
½ pound snow peas, trimmed
1 sweet red pepper, thinly sliced
1 pound cooked shrimp, shelled and
deveined
1 pound cooked crabmeat, flaked
1 small red onion, thinly sliced
1 cup pitted whole black olives
1½ teaspoons dried dill
2 garlic cloves, finely chopped
½ cup lemon juice
salt to taste
black pepper to taste

Cook the pasta shells in boiling water. When they are almost cooked, add the snow peas and the red pepper. Cook for 2 minutes. Drain well.

Put the pasta and vegetables into a large serving bowl. Add the 2 tablespoons of olive oil and mix well.

Add to the pasta mixture the shrimp, crabmeat, red onion and olives. Mix thoroughly.

In a small bowl combine the dill, garlic, lemon juice, ½ cup of olive oil and salt and pepper to taste. Mix well. When the dressing is blended, pour it over the seafood mixture. Toss gently but thoroughly. Serve immediately.

SHELLFISH AND GRAPEFRUIT SALAD

serves 4

1 cup cooked shrimp
½ cup chopped cooked lobster
½ cup flaked cooked crabmeat
½ cup cooked scallops
½ grapefruit, peeled and broken into
sections
½ cup black or green olives
½ cup olive oil
2 tablespoons red wine vinegar
1 teaspoon Dijon-style mustard
salt to taste
black pepper to taste

Chill all the seafood.

Just before serving, in a large serving bowl mix the shrimp, lobster, crabmeat and scallops with the olives and grapefruit sections.

In a small bowl combine the olive oil, vinegar, mustard and salt and pepper to taste. Mix well and pour over the salad. Toss and serve.

SHRIMP AND CAULIFLOWER SALAD

serves 6

1 cup cold cooked rice
1 pound cooked shrimp, shelled and
deveined
½ teaspoon salt
1 tablespoon lemon juice
1 tablespoon chopped scallion
2 tablespoons Vinaigrette
1 tablespoon chopped green olive
1 cup diced cooked cauliflower
⅓ cup mayonnaise

Combine all the ingredients in a large serving bowl. Toss well. Cover and refrigerate for at least 1 hour. Toss well again before serving.

SHRIMP SALAD WITH MELON BALLS

serves 6

2 pounds cooked shrimp, shelled and
deveined
2 tablespoons lemon juice
2 teaspoons finely chopped onion
1½ cups chopped celery
1 teaspoon salt
1 cup mayonnaise
1½ tablespoons curry powder
6 tablespoons sour cream
1 large honeydew melon, scooped into
balls
1 large cantaloupe, scooped into balls
1 head soft lettuce

In a serving bowl combine the shrimp, lemon juice, onion, celery, salt and mayonnaise.

In a small bowl combine the curry powder with the mayonnaise. Add the mixture to the shrimp and toss well. Cover the bowl and chill for at least 3 hours.

Add the melon balls before serving. Toss well. Serve on a bed of lettuce.

SHRIMP AND THREE-BEAN SALAD

serves 4

1 cup drained cooked red kidney beans
1 cup drained cooked white kidney beans
1 cup drained cooked green beans
½ green pepper, chopped
½ sweet red pepper, chopped
2 teaspoons chopped onion
1 tablespoon chopped pimento
1 pound cooked shrimp, shelled and
deveined
2 tablespoons lemon juice
½ cup olive oil
¼ cup white wine vinegar
½ teaspoon cayenne pepper
salt to taste
black pepper to taste

If canned beans are being used, rinse and drain them well. In a mixing bowl combine the beans with the green and red pepper, onion, pimento and shrimp. Toss well and set aside.

In a blender combine the lemon juice, olive oil, vinegar, cayenne pepper and salt and black pepper to taste. Blend at the lowest speed for 1 minute.

Pour the dressing over the salad. Toss well. Chill for 1 hour before serving.

SQUID SALAD

serves 4 to 6

1½ pounds cleaned fresh small squid
2 small baking potatoes, peeled and cut into ½-inch slices
1 large celery stalk, cut into 3-inch pieces
¼ cup dry white wine or dry vermouth
salt to taste
black pepper to taste
3 tablespoons fresh lemon juice
⅓ cup olive oil
½ cup finely chopped celery leaves and ribs
¼ cup julienned sweet red pepper
1 head soft lettuce, washed and dried

Cut off the tentacles from the squid just below the eyes, and set aside for another use. Discard the quill from inside the body sac. Rinse the sac thoroughly. Carefully peel off and discard the purple membrane covering the sac. Carefully remove the back flaps from the sac and set them aside for another use. Cut the sac into ½-inch rings. Set aside.

Put the potato slices into a saucepan with enough water to cover. Bring the water to a boil over moderately high heat. Cook, uncovered, until the potatoes are soft, about 12 to 15 minutes. Drain well and put the slices into a large mixing bowl.

Bring a large saucepan of boiling salted water to a boil. Add the celery stalk and wine and boil, uncovered, for 10 minutes. Lower the heat and add the squid. Simmer until the rings are tender and opaque, about 4 minutes. Be careful not to overcook. Drain the squid well and add to the bowl with the potatoes. Discard the celery stalk.

In a small mixing bowl combine the salt, pepper and lemon juice. Whisk until well blended. In a slow, steady stream, whisk in the olive oil. Continue to whisk until the dressing is smooth and well blended. Stir in the chopped celery and the sweet red pepper.

Pour the dressing over the squid and potato mixture. Toss gently until ingredients are well coated. Serve on individual plates lined with soft lettuce leaves.

MARINATED SQUID WITH GINGER

serves 4

1½ pounds cleaned squid
2 teaspoons cornstarch
3 tablespoons dry sherry
2 tablespoons plus 1 teaspoon
vegetable oil
2 tablespoons fresh ginger, finely sliced
1 cup peas
1½ cups sliced celery
¾ cup clam juice
1½ cups thickly sliced scallions

Rinse and gently pat dry the squid. Depending on their size, quarter or halve the tentacles lengthwise. Cut the body sac in half lengthwise and then crosswise into ¼ inch strips.

In a bowl combine the cornstarch, sherry and 1 teaspoon vegetable oil. Mix well and add the squid. Marinate at room temperature, turning occasionally, for 1 to 2 hours.

Heat the remaining oil in a large skillet. Add the ginger, peas and celery. Cook briefly, stirring constantly, for 30 to 40 seconds. Stir in the clam juice and bring the mixture to a simmer. Cover and simmer until the celery is just tender, about 3 to 4 minutes.

Add the squid, the marinade and the scallions. Cook over moderate heat, stirring constantly, until the squid is opaque about 2 minutes. Remove from the heat, transfer to a serving platter, and serve.

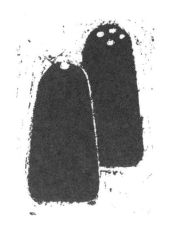

SWORDFISH SALAD

serves 6

1½ cups water
1 teaspoon oregano
1 bay leaf
6 peppercorns
1 small onion, thinly sliced and broken
into rings
3 tablespoons olive oil
salt to taste
black pepper to taste
2 pounds swordfish fillets
6 lemon slices
2 egg yolks
1 tablespoon lemon juice
½ teaspoon cayenne pepper
½ cup sour cream
1 head soft lettuce, torn into pieces
2 tomatoes, diced
4 scallions, chopped
1 cup chopped cooked shrimp
12 Greek *calamata* or black olives

In a large mixing bowl combine the water, oregano, bay leaf, peppercorns, onion, olive oil, and salt and pepper to taste. Mix well.

Put the swordfish fillets into a large skillet. Pour the sauce over them. Cover the fillets with the lemon slices. Bring to a boil, reduce the heat to low and simmer for 10 minutes.

Remove the skillet from the heat and let the fish cool for 10 minutes.

Transfer the fish to a plate and cover. When the fish is completely cool put the plate into the refrigerator.

Strain the liquid into a saucepan. Cook over medium heat until it is reduced to ½ cup.

In a mixing bowl beat the egg yolks. Blend in the lemon juice and the cayenne pepper. Gradually add the warm fish stock, stirring constantly, and beat until well blended. Transfer the mixture to the top of a double boiler. Cook over boiling water, stirring constantly, until the sauce thickens, then remove the top half of the boiler. When the egg yolk mixture is cool, slowly blend in the sour cream. Pour the dressing into a bowl and refrigerate for 1 hour.

In a large serving bowl, combine the lettuce, tomatoes, scallions, shrimp and olives. Remove the swordfish from the refrigerator. Flake the fish into the bowl. Add the sauce and mix well. Serve immediately.

New England Clam Chowder

Shrimp and Three-Bean Salad

Stuffed Clams

Flounder with Cider Sauce

Lobster Salad

Shrimp with Zucchini

Salmon with Lime and Walnut Oil

Crab Casserole

TARAMA SALAD

serves 4 to 6

3 large all-purpose potatoes
3 tablespoons milk
4 ounces red caviar or red roe
6 tablespoons water
¼ cup fresh lemon juice
1 small onion, minced
¾ cup olive oil

Peel the potatoes. Cook them in boiling water until very soft, about 20 minutes.

Drain the potatoes and put them into a mixing bowl. By hand or with an electric beater, mash the potatoes, slowly adding the milk, until smooth. Add the caviar and water to the potatoes. Mix well. Add the lemon juice and onion to the mixture and mix briefly. Slowly beat in the olive oil. Continue to beat until a smooth paste is formed.

FANCY TUNA SALAD

serves 4

1 head soft lettuce, torn into pieces
14 ounces canned tuna, drained and flaked
1 green pepper, thinly sliced
1 sweet red pepper, thinly sliced
1 small red onion, thinly sliced into rings
2 large tomatoes, cut into wedges
2 hard-cooked eggs, pushed through a wire sieve
2 tablespoons chopped green olives
8 anchovy fillets
1 tablespoon chopped parsley
1 cup French or any other salad dressing

Divide the lettuce among four large salad bowls. Place one-quarter of the tuna flakes in the center of the lettuce bed in each bowl.

Arrange one-quarter of the green bell pepper, red bell pepper, red onion, tomatoes, crumbled eggs, olives, and anchovy fillets around each portion of tuna. Sprinkle with the parsley and serve with the dressing on the side.

FRESH TUNA SALAD

serves 4

1 pound tuna, cooked and flaked
1 tablespoon lemon juice
3 scallions, chopped
1 cup mayonnaise
1 tablespoon Dijon-style mustard
5 tablespoons pickle relish, drained
4 hard-cooked eggs, sliced
2 lemons, quartered
2 medium-sized tomatoes, quartered

Put the tuna into a large mixing bowl and sprinkle with the lemon juice. Add the scallions, mayonnaise, mustard and relish and mix well.

Put a large scoop of tuna salad on each of four serving dishes (on a leaf of lettuce if desired). Garnish with the hard-cooked egg slices, tomato and lemon wedges and serve.

FRESH TUNA SALAD WITH CHICKPEAS

serves 6 to 8

1 cup white wine vinegar
2 garlic cloves, crushed
1 tablespoon hot red pepper flakes
1 tablespoon black pepper
1½ cups olive oil
1 onion, thinly sliced
2 bay leaves
2 pounds fresh tuna, cubed
2 cups canned chickpeas, rinsed and drained
20 brine-cured black olives

Combine the vinegar, garlic, red pepper flakes, and pepper in a mixing bowl. Slowly whisk in 1 cup of the olive oil. Continue whisking until the dressing is well blended.

Add the onion, bay leaves, and tuna cubes. Stir well, cover the bowl and marinate overnight in the refrigerator. Stir occasionally.

To serve, drain the tuna and reserve the marinade. Remove the bay leaves and discard. Combine the tuna and chickpeas in a serving bowl.

In a small bowl combine ¼ cup of the reserved marinade. Whisk in the remaining ½ cup olive oil until the mixture is well blended. Season to taste with salt and pepper.

Pour the dressing over the tuna mixture and toss well. Garnish with the olives. Serve at once.

TOFU TUNA SALAD

serves 4

6½ ounces drained canned tuna
1 tofu cake (bean curd)
2 tablespoons chopped onion
4 scallions, minced
1 medium-sized green pepper, coarsely chopped
¼ cup mayonnaise
½ teaspoon salt

Put the tuna, tofu, onion, scallion and pepper into a bowl. Stir with a wooden spoon until blended. Add the mayonnaise and stir again. Serve.

WHITEFISH SALAD

serves 4

3 large smoked whitefish, cleaned and sliced open
1½ cups sour cream
1 large red onion, chopped
1 tablespoon chopped fresh dill or
1 teaspoon dried dill
1 tablespoon vodka
salt to taste
black pepper to taste
1 cup chopped watercress

With a fork, break apart two of the fish into large meaty chunks. Put the pieces into a mixing bowl.

Add the sour cream, onion and dill. Mix until thoroughly blended. Add the vodka, salt and pepper and mix again.

Stuff some of the salad into the cavity of the remaining fish. Arrange the remaining stuffing around the fish. Garnish with watercress and serve.

FISH

BROILED FISH STEAKS WITH GREEN PEPPERCORNS

serves 4

4 8-ounce fish steaks, about 1 inch thick
1 tablespoon green peppercorns
1 tablespoon vegetable oil
½ teaspoon salt
3 tablespoons lemon juice
lemon wedges

Rinse the green peppercorns in cold water and drain well. Put them into a small bowl and add the oil and salt. With the back of a spoon, crush the green peppercorns into the oil. Add the lemon juice and mix well.

Put the fish steaks into a shallow dish. Pour the green peppercorn sauce over the steaks and marinate at room temperature for 30 to 60 minutes, turning occasionally.

Preheat the broiler to high. Brush the broiler pan lightly with oil.

Broil the fish steaks 4 inches from the heat, brushing often with the leftover marinade, until cooked through and opaque white in the center and golden brown on top, about 10 minutes. The steaks do not need to be turned. Serve garnished with lemon wedges.

SAUCY CREOLE FISH

serves 6

4 tablespoons butter
2 tablespoons chopped onion
4 tablespoons chopped celery
2 tablespoons chopped sweet red pepper
2 tablespoons flour
½ cup light cream
½ cup fine unflavored breadcrumbs
¼ teaspoon dried rosemary
1 cup cooked crabmeat
1 cup coarsely chopped cooked shrimp
¼ cup chopped parsley
¼ teaspoon salt
¼ teaspoon black pepper
1½ teaspoons Worcestershire sauce
½ teaspoon Tabasco sauce
6 fillets of sole or flounder
3 tablespoons melted butter

CREOLE SAUCE:
4 cups canned tomatoes
2 tablespoons butter
2 garlic cloves, chopped
1 bay leaf
1 teaspoon salt
¼ teaspoon black pepper
⅛ teaspoon cayenne pepper
1 tablespoon flour

Preheat the oven to 350°F.

In a saucepan melt the butter. Add the onion, celery, and red pepper and cook gently until tender, about 5 to 8 minutes. Carefully stir in the flour. Stir until the mixture is smooth. Add the light cream and continue cooking, stirring often, until the mixture has thickened.

Remove the saucepan from the heat. Stir in the breadcrumbs, rosemary, crabmeat, shrimp, parsley, salt, pepper, Worcestershire sauce and Tabasco sauce.

Place the 6 fillets flat on a work surface. Place a heaping tablespoon of the filling on the wide end of each fillet. Roll up the fillets and secure them closed with toothpicks.

Arrange the fillets in a baking dish. Brush them with the melted butter and sprinkle them with salt. Bake for 15 minutes. Pour the Creole sauce (see below) over the fish. Reduce the oven temperature to 325° and bake for 30 minutes longer.

To prepare the Creole sauce, in a saucepan combine the tomatoes, 1 tablespoon of butter, garlic, bay leaf, salt, black pepper, and cayenne pepper. Cook over moderate heat, stirring occasionally, until the mixture is reduced to about half, about 20 to 30 minutes.

In a small saucepan, melt the remaining butter. Stir in the flour and continue cooking until the mixture is lightly browned.

Add the flour mixture to the tomatoes. Cook for 2 to 3 minutes. Remove the sauce from the heat and strain it through a sieve. Pour the sauce over the fish and continue baking.

ESCABÈCHE

serves 4

1½ pounds fresh fish fillets, at least
½ inch thick
½ cup flour
½ cup olive oil
2 crushed garlic cloves
⅛ teaspoon hot red pepper flakes
3 bay leaves
½ teaspoon salt
2 tablespoons vinegar
1 medium-sized sweet onion, thinly sliced
½ lemon, thinly sliced

Dust the fish fillets with the flour. Shake off excess.

Heat the oil in a large, heavy skillet. When very hot, add the fish fillets and sauté on both sides until fish is firm and flakes easily with a fork, about 5 minutes on each side. Remove the fish from the skillet and place in a serving bowl.

Add the garlic, red pepper flakes, bay leaves, salt and vinegar to the skillet. Bring to a boil and pour the marinade over the fish.

Marinate the fish in the refrigerator for at least 4 hours and preferably overnight, turning occasionally. Serve garnished with the lemon and onion slices.

FISH WITH AVOCADO MAYONNAISE

serves 4

2 tablespoons butter
2 pounds fish fillets
6 tablespoons lemon juice
2 teaspoons salt
2 ripe avocados
2 tablespoons olive oil
3 tablespoons finely chopped onion
½ teaspoon black pepper

Melt the butter in a large skillet. Add the fish fillets, 4 tablespoons lemon juice and 1 teaspoon salt. Cover the skillet and cook over low heat for 20 minutes.

To make the avocado mayonnaise, purée the avocado flesh in a blender or food processor. With the motor running, gradually add the remaining salt, lemon juice, olive oil, onion and pepper. Blend until mixture is smooth.

Arrange the fish fillets on a serving platter. Serve the avocado mayonnaise on the side.

FISH AND EGGS

serves 6

3 medium-sized boiled potatoes, peeled
and sliced
6 hard-cooked eggs, sliced
1 cup cooked fish, flaked
1 tablespoon butter
2 cups light cream
salt to taste
black pepper to taste
¼ teaspoon dried rosemary
¼ cup chopped scallions

Preheat the oven to 350°F. Butter a large baking dish.

Arrange a layer of sliced potatoes in the bottom of the baking dish. Top the layer with a layer of the fish. Top the fish layer with a layer of sliced eggs. Repeat the layering until the ingredients are used up.

Melt the butter in a saucepan over low heat. Add the cream, rosemary, scallions and salt and pepper to taste. Heat the mixture until it just simmers.

Pour the cream mixture over the layers in the baking dish. Bake for 20 minutes. Serve hot from the dish.

GRILLED FISH WITH FRESH FRUITS

serves 6

vegetable oil
3 tablespoons butter
2 cups small cubes fresh pineapple
1 cup peeled, thinly sliced nectarine
1 tablespoon grated lemon rind
1½ pounds fresh fish fillets

Preheat the broiler to high. Brush the broiler pan with vegetable oil.

Melt the butter in a skillet over low heat. Add the pineapple, nectarine and lemon rind. Cook, stirring frequently, until the fruit is thoroughly warmed. Remove the skillet from the heat.

Broil the fish for 1½ to 2 minutes per side. Serve with the warm fruit.

FISH IN PARCHMENT

serves 4

4 8-ounce fish steaks
½ cup dry white wine
4 tablespoons butter
½ cup thinly sliced onion
1 peeled and julienned carrot
½ cup thinly sliced scallions
½ cup finely chopped dill
black pepper to taste

Preheat the oven to 350°F.

Put the fish in a shallow bowl. Pour the wine over the fish and let marinate, turning occasionally, until needed.

Melt the butter in a skillet over medium heat. Add the onion, carrot and scallions. Cook, stirring occasionally, until soft, about 5 minutes. Remove the skillet from the heat.

Prepare four pieces of kitchen parchment paper or heavy aluminum foil large enough to fold around a single steak, a little more than twice the size of each steak.

Place 1 teaspoon of liquid from the skillet onto the center of each piece of parchment or foil. Top each with a fish steak. Top each fish steak with one-quarter of the vegetable mixture and of the dill. Pour one-quarter of the remaining wine over each steak and top with any liquid remaining in the skillet.

Fold the edges of the parchment or foil tightly together to make a leak-proof seam. This is easier to do if you fold the long seam first and the ends next.

Place the fish packets on a baking sheet and bake for 30 to 35 minutes. To serve, place a packet on each plate. Open at the table with scissors or a sharp knife.

GLAZED WHOLE BAKED FISH

serves 4

1 2-pound whole firm-fleshed fish, cleaned, with head and tail
3 whole scallions, sliced lengthwise very thinly
1 tablespoon chopped ginger
2 garlic cloves, halved
2 tablespoons lemon juice
3 tablespoons chutney
2 tablespoons vegetable oil

Preheat the oven to 375°F.

Wash the fish and gently pat dry. Put the scallion, ginger and garlic into the cavity of the fish.

Coat the bottom of a baking dish with 1 tablespoon oil. Use a baking dish that is as close to the size of the fish as possible. Put the fish in the pan and sprinkle with the lemon juice. Coat the top of the fish with the chutney and then with the remaining oil.

Bake, basting occasionally with the pan drippings, until fish is firmly set inside and the skin is golden brown, about 25 minutes.

LEMON FRIED FISH

serves 6

2 pounds thinly sliced fish steaks
4 tablespoons flour
4 tablespoons olive oil
6 tablespoons lemon juice
4 tablespoons water
1 teaspoon salt
½ teaspoon black pepper
1 teaspoon ground coriander
1 teaspoon ground cumin
3 egg yolks

Dredge the fish steaks lightly in the flour. Shake off any excess.

Heat the olive oil in a large skillet over medium heat. Add the fish steaks and cook for 5 minutes. Turn the steaks and cook for 5 minutes longer. Cover the skillet and reduce the heat.

In a mixing bowl combine the lemon juice, water, salt, pepper, coriander and cumin. Mix well. Add the mixture to the skillet, cover and cook for 15 minutes.

Remove the skillet from the heat. Transfer the fish steaks to a serving platter and set aside in a warm place.

Beat the egg yolks in a mixing bowl. Pour the cooking liquid from the skillet over the egg yolks, beating constantly. Pour the egg mixture into the skillet and cook over medium heat until the mixture thickens. Do not let the mixture boil. Serve the sauce with the fish.

LIME-GRILLED FISH STEAKS

serves 4

4 8-ounce fish steaks, about 1 inch thick
2 tablespoons lime juice
2 tablespoons vegetable oil
1 teaspoon grated ginger
¼ teaspoon cayenne pepper
salt to taste
black pepper to taste

In a bowl, combine the lime juice, 1 tablespoon oil, ginger, cayenne, salt and black pepper to taste. Marinate the fish steaks for 30 to 60 minutes, turning occasionally.

Preheat the broiler to high. Brush the broiler pan with the remaining oil. If cooking outdoors, use white coals and brush the grill with the remaining oil.

Broil or grill the fish, brushing often with the leftover marinade, until cooked through and opaque white in the center, about 10 minutes. If cooking on a grill, turn the fish when half done. Do not turn the fish if cooking in a broiler.

POACHED FISH WITH ALMONDS

serves 4

½ cup vegetable oil
⅔ cup slivered, blanched almonds
¼ cup white wine *or* sherry *or* dry vermouth
¼ cup lemon juice
2 tablespoons fennel seeds
½ teaspoon salt
¼ teaspoon white pepper
1½ pounds fish fillets

Heat the oil in a large heavy skillet. Add the almonds and sauté, stirring often, until the almonds begin to turn golden. Remove the almonds and drain on paper towels. Set aside.

Add the wine, lemon juice, fennel seeds, salt and white pepper to the skillet. Stir well and bring to a simmer. Add the fish fillets and spoon the sauce over them.

Cover the skillet and gently poach the fillets until the fish flakes easily with a fork, about 7 to 8 minutes.

Place the fillets on a serving platter. Spoon the sauce over the fillets and sprinkle with the almonds. Serve at once.

ROAST WHOLE FISH

serves 4

1 4-pound whole fish, cleaned, with head
and tail
2 teaspoons olive oil
2 thinly sliced onions
1 peeled and thinly sliced carrot
1 green pepper, cut into thin rings
3 tablespoons lemon juice
1 teaspoon chopped fresh thyme *or*
½ teaspoon dried thyme
1 teaspoon chopped fresh rosemary *or*
½ teaspoon dried rosemary
½ cup chopped parsley
¼ cup chopped dill
salt to taste
black pepper to taste
2 tablespoons butter
½ teaspoon paprika
1 cup red *or* white wine

Preheat the oven to 375°F. Grease a roasting pan with the olive oil.

Place the onions, carrot, and green pepper in layers in the cavity of the fish. Sprinkle with the 1½ tablespoons of the lemon juice. Top the vegetables with the thyme, rosemary, parsley and dill. Add salt and black pepper to taste. Dot the stuffing with 1 tablespoon butter and close the cavity with string or skewers.

Put the fish into the roasting pan. Sprinkle the remaining lemon juice over the fish. Top with additional black pepper to taste and the paprika. Dot the top of the fish with the remaining butter. Pour the wine over the fish.

Roast the fish, basting often with the pan juices and adding more butter if necessary, until the flesh is firm to the touch, about 35 to 45 minutes.

SKILLET-STEAMED FISH

serves 4

1 tablespoon vegetable oil
1 onion, coarsely chopped
1 garlic clove, crushed
2 large tomatoes, seeded and coarsely
chopped
2 tablespoons wine *or* cider vinegar
¾ cup water
4 large fish fillets
salt to taste
black pepper to taste

Heat the oil in a large non-stick skillet over medium heat. Add the onion and garlic and cook until golden brown, about 5 minutes. Add the tomatoes. Stir well and cook until tomatoes are just heated through, about 2 minutes. Add the vinegar and stir well.

Push the tomato mixture to one side of the skillet. Add the water. When the liquid starts to simmer, add the fish and cover the skillet. Cook until the fish flakes easily, about 8 to 10 minutes.

Remove the fish and place on a serving platter. Add salt and pepper to taste to the tomato mixture and stir. Spoon the tomato mixture over the fish and serve hot.

STIR-FRIED FISH FILLETS

serves 4

4 tablespoons vegetable oil
1½ pounds fresh fish fillets, cut into 1-inch strips
2 large leeks, cut into thin, 2-inch strips
1 garlic clove, minced
½ teaspoon salt
1 tablespoon finely chopped fresh ginger
¼ teaspoon sugar
2 tablespoons wine vinegar
2 tablespoons chopped coriander

Heat 2 tablespoons of the oil in a wok or a large skillet over medium-high heat. When the oil is very hot, add the fish strips in small batches and cook, stirring constantly, until just cooked through, about 3 minutes per batch. Add additional oil if necessary. Remove each batch with a slotted spoon when done and set aside.

Add 2 tablespoons of the oil to the wok or skillet. When the oil is very hot, add the leeks, garlic, salt, ginger and sugar. Cook, stirring constantly, for 3 minutes. Add the vinegar and cook, stirring constantly, for 1 minute longer. Return the cooked fish to the wok or skillet and cook, stirring gently, until heated through.

Arrange the mixture on a serving platter, sprinkle with the chopped coriander, and serve immediately.

STUFFED FILLETS BAKED IN LETTUCE LEAVES

serves 4

8 to 10 large lettuce leaves
2 ¾-pound fresh fish fillets, each about ¾-inch thick
1 cup finely chopped fresh parsley
1 cup chopped onion
1 carrot, peeled and grated
½ teaspoon salt
freshly ground black pepper
½ cup white wine

Preheat the oven to 400°F.

Line the sides and bottom of a baking dish with the lettuce leaves. The leaves should hang over the edges of the dish.

Put one fillet into the dish. Cover it with the onion, carrot and parsley. Sprinkle with salt and black pepper to taste. Top with the remaining fillet. Fold the ends of the lettuce leaves over the top fillet. Add the wine to the dish.

Cover the dish with aluminum foil and bake for 15 minutes. Remove the foil, fold back the lettuce leaves, and serve the fish immediately. Serve the steamed lettuce separately.

SWEET AND SOUR FISH

serves 4

1 1½- to 2-pound whole cleaned fish, with head and tail
¼ teaspoon paprika
¼ cup flour
black pepper to taste
1 tablespoon vegetable oil
½ cup sweet red pepper strips
½ cup green pepper strips
1 peeled carrot, cut into 1-inch rounds
1 onion, diced
1 tablespoon slivered ginger root
1 cup orange *or* pineapple juice
1 cup peeled fresh peaches, cut into 1-inch pieces
2 tablespoons wine *or* cider vinegar
1 teaspoon cornstarch

Combine the flour, paprika and black pepper to taste in a large shallow dish. Dredge the whole fish on both sides in the mixture. Shake off the excess.

Heat the oil in a heavy skillet over high heat. When the oil starts to bubble, add the fish and lower the heat to medium. Brown the fish on both sides, about 5 minutes per side. Carefully remove the fish with a large spatula and place it on a platter lined with paper towels.

Pour off all but ½ teaspoon of oil from the skillet. Add the red pepper, green pepper, carrot, onion and ginger. Add the fruit juice and mix well. Cover the skillet and simmer until the vegetables are tender but still crisp, about 12 to 15 minutes.

Add the fruit and vinegar to the skillet. Stir gently and push the mixture to one side of the skillet. Return the fish to the skillet and cover. Cook until fish flakes easily with a fork, about 5 minutes per side.

Remove the fish from the skillet and put it on a serving platter. Spoon the fruit and vegetables over the fish and serve.

For a thicker sauce, remove ¼ cup liquid from the skillet and put it into a small bowl. Add 1 teaspoon cornstarch to the bowl and stir until dissolved. Pour the mixture back into the skillet and mix well. Cook over low heat until the sauce thickens, about 5 minutes. Pour the sauce over the fish and serve.

BASS IN ASPIC

serves 6

1 5- to 6-pound striped bass
1 cup diced onion
1 cup diced celery
½ cup sliced carrots
1 tablespoon lemon juice
½ teaspoon ground white pepper
½ teaspoon salt
3 cups cold water
1 cup mayonnaise

Clean and fillet the fish. Reserve the head and bones.

In a medium-sized pot, place the fish fillets, reserved head and bones, onion, celery, carrots, lemon juice, pepper, salt and water. Simmer over low heat for 20 minutes.

Carefully remove the pieces of fish fillets with a slotted spoon and place them in a deep medium-sized glass or ceramic (not metal) dish. Cover and chill in the refrigerator.

Strain the broth through a fine sieve. Discard the solids remaining in the sieve. Replace broth in pot and bring to a boil over high heat. Cook for 15 to 20 minutes, or until the liquid is reduced by about half.

Pour the broth over the fish pieces and chill for hours or more. The broth will gel as it chills. Serve cold with lemon wedges.

BAKED BASS WITH VERMOUTH SAUCE

serves 6

6 8-ounce bass fillets
1 cup dry vermouth
⅓ cup olive oil
1 cup finely chopped fresh mushrooms
3 scallions, finely chopped
2 tablespoons lemon juice
½ teaspoon cayenne pepper
½ teaspoon oregano
salt to taste

Wash and dry the bass fillets. Put them into a large casserole dish. Preheat the oven to 375°F.

In a large mixing bowl, combine the vermouth with the olive oil, mushrooms, scallions, lemon juice, cayenne pepper, oregano and salt to taste. Mix well. Pour the mixture over the bass fillets. Cover the casserole; use aluminum foil if it has no lid. Bake for 30 minutes. Serve immediately.

BASS WITH ANISETTE PEPPER SAUCE

serves 6

6 8-ounce striped bass fillets
1 tablespoon water
1 teaspoon paprika
2 tablespoons butter
3 small sweet red peppers, cut into strips
¼ cup anisette-flavored liqueur
1 cup heavy cream
¼ cup tomato sauce
¼ cup chopped parsley
salt to taste
black pepper to taste

Preheat the broiler. Wash and dry the fillets. Put the fillets on the broiler pan and sprinkle them with the water and paprika.

Broil the fillets for 6 minutes on each side.

While the fish is cooking, melt the butter in a small saucepan. Add the red pepper and cook, stirring constantly, until soft. Stir in the liqueur, cream and tomato sauce. Cook over medium heat until the sauce is reduced by half. Remove the pan from the heat and add the parsley and salt and pepper to taste.

Transfer the bass fillets to a serving platter. Pour the sauce over them and serve.

GRILLED BASS WITH HERBS

serves 6

6 8-ounce bass fillets
1 cup white wine or dry vermouth
⅓ cup olive oil
1 cup chopped fresh mushrooms
½ cup chopped scallions
2 tablespoons lemon juice
2 teaspoons salt
¼ teaspoon cayenne pepper
¼ teaspoon dried tarragon

Heat the coals in a barbecue until they are gray and very hot.

Cut 6 pieces of heavy aluminum foil (or doubled regular aluminum foil) into 18-inch squares. Lightly oil the foil.

In a large bowl combine the wine, olive oil, mushrooms, scallions, lemon juice, salt, pepper and tarragon. Mix well.

Place one fillet on each piece of foil. Pour the dressing over the pieces. Wrap the fish in the foil and seal carefully. Place the packages on the grill, about 6 inches from the coals.

Grill for 20 to 25 minutes or until the fish flakes easily when tested with a fork. Serve hot.

BASS BAKED WITH FENNEL

serves 8

**1 4- to 5-pound cleaned whole striped or
sea bass
1 tablespoon walnut oil
2 teaspoons coarse salt
5 small fennel bulbs
2 large onions, thickly sliced
2 large tomatoes, thickly sliced and seeded
1½ cups dry white wine or dry vermouth
2 cups heavy cream
4 tablespoons chilled sweet butter
2 tablespoons minced fennel fronds
salt to taste
lemon wedges for garnish
fennel fronds for garnish**

Trim the tough outer ribs from the fennel bulbs and discard. Peel the bulbs, halve them lengthwise, and trim. Reserve the trimmings and the fronds. Set aside.

Preheat the oven to 400°F.

Gently pat the fish dry. Rub it inside and out with the walnut oil and sprinkle inside and out with the coarse salt. Measure the thickness of the fish to determine its cooking time later. Stuff the cavity of the fish with the reserved fennel trimmings.

Line a large roasting pan with a piece of aluminum foil folded in half lengthwise. Put the fish on the foil. Arrange the onion slices on top of the fish; arrange the tomato slices on top of the onion slices. Hold the slices in place with wooden toothpicks.

Arrange the fennel bulbs around the fish and add the wine. Cover the pan securely with a piece of aluminum foil. Bake the fish for 9 minutes per inch of thickness, or until it is just opaque.

While the fish cooks, boil the cream in a saucepan until it is reduced to 1 cup. Remove from the heat.

Remove the fish from the oven. Remove the toothpicks and the tomatoes and onions. Discard the onions. Chop the tomatoes finely and set aside. Reserve the pan juices.

Using the edges of the foil as handles, transfer the fish to a serving platter and keep warm. Arrange the fennel bulbs around the fish.

Strain the pan juices through a sieve into a saucepan. Discard any solids remaining in the sieve. Bring the pan juices to a boil and continue to boil until the liquid is reduced to 1½ cups. Add the pan juices to the reduced cream. Bring the mixture to a boil and continue to boil until the sauce is reduced to about 1¾ cups.

Remove the sauce from the heat and whisk in the butter, ½ tablespoon at a time. Add the minced fennel fronds and stir to blend. Season with salt if desired and pour the sauce into a sauceboat.

Arrange the chopped tomatoes, lemon wedges and fennel fronds around the fish. Serve with the sauce on the side.

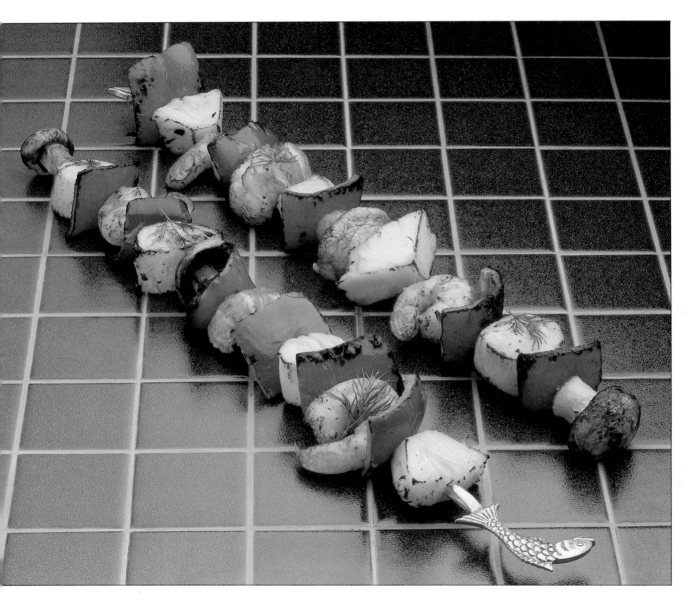

Fishkabobs

Baked Oysters (above)

Mackerel Stuffed with Berries (right above)

Broiled Cod in Lemon Butter Sauce (right below)

Bass à la Grecque

Broiled Halibut Steaks with Apricot Sauce

Shrimp on Tap

110

BASS WITH GOAT CHEESE AND WALNUT TOPPING

serves 4

4 8-ounce bass fillets
2 tablespoons butter, melted
coarse salt to taste
black pepper to taste
3 ounces goat or feta cheese, softened
6 tablespoons heavy cream
½ cup coarsely chopped walnuts
1 scallion, sliced
2 tablespoons chopped parsley
⅓ cup dry vermouth or white wine
⅓ cup chicken broth
2 teaspoons lemon juice

Preheat the broiler. Rinse and dry the fillets and put them on a rack in the broiler pan.

Brush the fillets with 1 tablespoon of the melted butter and sprinkle them with salt and black pepper to taste. Broil the fillets for 10 minutes without turning them.

While the fish broils, in a small bowl blend the goat cheese and the cream until smooth. Add the walnuts, scallions, parsley and the remaining melted butter. Mix well and set aside.

Remove the broiler pan from the broiler and carefully turn the fillets. Cover each fillet with some of the cheese mixture. Return the fillets to the broiler for 2 minutes.

In a small saucepan bring the vermouth and chicken broth to a boil. Continue to boil until the mixture is reduced by half. Remove the saucepan from the heat and stir in the lemon juice.

Transfer the fish to a serving platter. Pour the lemon sauce over the fillets and serve.

Barbecued Halibut

BASS STUFFED WITH SHRIMP AND CHESTNUTS

serves 4

1 whole sea bass, about 3 pounds
½ pound chestnuts
1 tablespoon fine unflavored breadcrumbs
1 teaspoon finely chopped parsley
½ cup tiny shrimp, cooked
½ teaspoon oregano
1 tablespoon grated lemon rind
3 tablespoons lemon juice
1 egg yolk, slightly beaten
salt to taste
1 teaspoon cayenne pepper
½ teaspoon black pepper
2 tablespoons olive oil

Clean, wash and dry the bass and remove the central bone. Preheat the oven to 375°F.

Fill a saucepan with water. Bring the water to a boil over high heat. Cut a slit in the shell of each chestnut. Put the chestnuts into the saucepan and boil for 20 minutes, or until they are tender. Drain the chestnuts, dry them with paper towels and shell them as soon as they are cool enough to handle.

Put the chestnuts into the blender and purée.

In a large mixing bowl, combine the chestnut purée with the breadcrumbs, parsley, shrimp, oregano, lemon rind, lemon juice, egg yolk, pepper, cayenne pepper and salt to taste.

Stuff the cavity of the bass with the chestnut mixture. Close the cavity with wooden toothpicks. Brush the fish with olive oil and put it into a baking dish. Bake for 30 minutes.

Transfer the fish to a serving platter, remove the toothpicks and serve.

Bass with Goat Cheese (*Chèvre*) Topping

serves 4

2 tablespoons sweet butter, melted
4 6- to 8-ounce sea bass or red snapper
fillets
coarse salt to taste
black pepper to taste
⅓ cup dry vermouth
⅓ cup chicken broth
2 teaspoons lemon juice

GOAT CHEESE TOPPING:
3 ounces Montrachet or other goat cheese,
at room temperature
6 tablespoons heavy cream
½ cup coarsely chopped walnuts
3 tablespoons sliced whole scallions
2 tablespoons finely chopped parsley
2 tablespoons finely chopped fresh
marjoram
or 1 teaspoon dried marjoram
coarse salt to taste
black pepper to taste

In a small bowl blend the softened goat cheese and the cream with a spoon until smooth. Add the walnuts, scallions, parsley, marjoram, salt and pepper. Blend well and set aside.

Preheat the oven to broil. Brush a broiling pan with 1 tablespoon of the melted butter.

Brush the fillets with the remaining butter. Season the fish on both sides with salt and pepper.

Grill the fillets 4 inches from the heat until the fish is not quite opaque in the center, about 9 to 10 minutes per inch of thickness.

Remove the pan and spread the topping evenly over the fish fillets. Return the pan and cook until the cheese begins to melt and the fish is opaque in the center, about 1 to 2 minutes longer. Remove the fillets from the pan and keep them warm on a plate.

Put the broiling pan over moderate heat and stir in the vermouth and chicken broth. Bring the mixture to a boil, stirring constantly to loosen the brown bits on the bottom of the pan. When the liquid comes to the boil, pour it into a small saucepan. Bring to the boil again. Continue to boil until the liquid is reduced to ⅓ cup. Stir in the lemon juice and season to taste with salt.

Spoon the sauce over the fish and serve.

STUFFED BASS WITH RAISIN SAUCE

serves 6

1 whole striped bass, about 5 pounds
6 ounces unflavored breadcrumbs
¼ cup hot water
2 tablespoons butter, melted
3 tablespoons finely chopped onion
1 tablespoon finely chopped parsley
1 egg beaten
salt to taste
black pepper to taste

RAISIN SAUCE:
2 tablespoons butter
2 tablespoons flour
¼ teaspoon black pepper
1 tablespoon brown sugar
1½ cups water
4 tablespoons chopped raisins
4 tablespoons chopped almonds
2 tablespoons grated horseradish
¼ cup fine unflavored breadcrumbs
3 tablespoons lemon juice

Clean, wash and dry the fish. Preheat the oven to 400°F.

Put the breadcrumbs in a large mixing bowl and add the hot water. Mix the breadcrumbs and water. Then turn the crumbs on to a clean kitchen towel and press dry. Return the breadcrumbs to the bowl and add the melted butter, onion, parsley, egg and salt and pepper to taste.

Stuff the cavity of the fish with the mixture. Close the cavity with wooden toothpicks.

Put the fish into a baking dish and bake for 50 minutes.

To make the raisin sauce, melt the butter in a saucepan. Blend in the flour, black pepper, brown sugar and water. Stir the mixture until it begins to boil. Add the raisins, almonds and horseradish. Heat thoroughly. Just before serving, stir in the fine breadcrumbs and the lemon juice.

Remove the fish from the oven and carefully transfer it to a serving platter. Remove the toothpicks. Pour the sauce over the fish and serve.

BROILED BLOWFISH

serves 6

6 large blowfish tails
6 tablespoons butter
2 teaspoons finely chopped parsley
1 teaspoon oregano
2 tablespoons lemon juice
½ teaspoon black pepper
¼ teaspoon paprika
2 lemons, quartered

Clean and wash the blowfish tails. Carefully skin the tails. Pat dry and set aside. Preheat the broiler.

In a saucepan, over very low heat, melt the butter. Stir in the parsley, oregano, lemon juice, pepper and paprika. Remove the pan from the heat.

Put the fish tails on the broiler pan. Brush the tails with some of the butter mixture. Broil the tails for 15 minutes, turning them and basting them with the butter mixture every 3 minutes.

Transfer the tails to a serving platter. Garnish with the lemon quarters and serve.

BROILED BLOWFISH WITH MAÎTRE d'HÔTEL SAUCE

serves 4 to 6

6 blowfish tails
melted butter

MAÎTRE d'HÔTEL SAUCE:
2 teaspoons chopped parsley
5 tablespoons softened butter
1 tablespoon lemon juice
salt to taste
black pepper to taste

Clean and wash the blowfish tails. Carefully remove the small fillets.

Place the fillets in a broiling pan and brush with melted butter. Broil until done, about 15 to 20 minutes.

To make the maître d'hôtel sauce, cream the parsley with the softened butter in a small bowl. Add the salt, pepper and lemon juice. Blend thoroughly.

Serve fish with maître d'hôtel sauce spread on it. This sauce is excellent for any broiled fish.

BAKED BLUEFISH

serves 4 to 6

**1 4- to 5-pound whole bluefish
salt to taste
black pepper to taste
4 tablespoons mayonnaise
2 lemons, sliced
4 scallions, chopped (including green part)**

Preheat the oven to 400°F.

Clean, wash and dry the fish. Rub it with salt and pepper inside and out. Coat the fish with the mayonnaise inside and out.

Place the fish in a baking dish that has been lined with aluminum foil. Arrange the lemon slices on top of the fish and sprinkle the fish with the chopped scallions.

Bake the fish for 40 to 50 minutes, or 10 minutes per pound. Serve in the baking dish.

BAKED BLUEFISH WITH SARDINES

serves 4

**1 4-pound bluefish, cleaned
1 small can sardines, drained
3 tablespoons butter
1 cup dry white wine
1 small onion, finely chopped
1 teaspoon chopped parsley
½ cup unflavored breadcrumbs**

Preheat the oven to 400°F.

Combine the sardines, butter, onion, parsley and breadcrumbs in a mixing bowl. Mix well. Fill the cavity of the bluefish with about one-third of the mixture.

Place the stuffed bluefish into a baking dish. Cover the top of the fish with the remaining sardine mixture. Add the wine to the dish.

Bake the fish for 30 to 40 minutes, basting occasionally with the pan juices. Serve hot.

BROILED BLUEFISH WITH SPICY SAUCE

serves 6

6 8-ounce bluefish fillets
2 tablespoons butter, melted
2 tablespoons olive oil
salt to taste
black pepper to taste
3 tablespoons chili sauce
1 tablespoon lemon juice
1 tablespoon Worcestershire sauce
1 tablespoon red wine vinegar
1 teaspoon finely chopped parsley
1 scallion, finely chopped
½ teaspoon cayenne pepper

Wash and dry the fillets and put them on the rack of a large broiler pan. Pre-heat the broiler.

In a small bowl, combine the butter and olive oil. Brush the top of the fillets with the mixture. Cook the fillets for 10 minutes on the first side.

While the fillets are broiling, in a small saucepan combine the chili sauce, lemon juice, Worcestershire sauce, vinegar, parsley, scallion, cayenne pepper and salt and pepper to taste.

Remove the pan from the broiler, baste the fillets with the sauce, then broil for 2 more minutes.

Turn the fish and baste with the sauce. Return to the broiler and cook for 5 more minutes. Heat the remaining sauce over low heat.

Transfer the fillets to a serving platter. Pour the sauce over them and serve.

MARINATED BLUEFISH WITH HORSERADISH

serves 6

6 8-ounce bluefish fillets
2 teaspoons oregano
2 tablespoons lemon juice
½ cup olive oil
1 tablespoon prepared horseradish, drained
1 teaspoon Worcestershire sauce
½ teaspoon paprika
½ teaspoon cinnamon
coarse salt to taste
black pepper to taste

Wash and dry the fillets and set aside.

In a large mixing bowl combine the oregano, lemon juice, olive oil, horseradish, Worcestershire sauce, paprika, cinnamon, and salt and pepper to taste.

Put the fillets into a shallow bowl in a single layer. Pour the marinade over the fish, cover the bowl and refrigerate for 4 hours.

Preheat the broiler.

Put the fillets on the rack of a large broiler pan. Baste with the marinade. Broil for 6 minutes on each side, basting every 2 minutes. Serve hot.

DEEP-FRIED PARMESAN BUTTERFISH

serves 4

2 pounds butterfish fillets
1 teaspoon salt
1 teaspoon black pepper
¼ cup yellow cornmeal
¼ cup cracker meal
¼ cup grated Parmesan cheese
1 egg, beaten
½ cup olive oil

Wash and dry the fillets. With a sharp knife, score the fleshy side of each fillet, making 3 slashes on each one. Season the fillets with the salt and pepper and set aside.

In a large, shallow dish, combine the cornmeal, cracker meal, and Parmesan cheese. In another shallow dish beat the egg. In a large skillet, heat the olive oil over medium heat.

Dip the fillets into the egg, then roll them in the cornmeal mixture. Cook them in the hot oil for 5 minutes. Carefully turn the fillets and cook for 3 minutes more. Drain the fillets on paper towels, arrange on a serving platter and serve.

CATFISH FRY

serves 4

2 pounds catfish fillets
½ cup flour
¼ cup cornmeal
¼ cup grated Parmesan cheese
1 teaspoon oregano
½ teaspoon cayenne pepper
1 egg
2 tablespoons water
salt to taste
black pepper to taste
½ cup olive oil

Wash and dry the fillets.

In a shallow bowl mix the flour with the cornmeal, Parmesan cheese, oregano, cayenne pepper and salt and pepper to taste. Set aside.

In another shallow bowl beat the egg and water together.

In a large skillet, heat the olive oil. While waiting for the oil to bubble, dip the fillets in the egg mixture and roll them in the flour mixture until they are well coated. Put the fillets into the olive oil and cook for 8 minutes on each side. Remove from the olive oil and drain well on paper towels. Serve accompanied by tartar sauce and lemon quarters.

OVEN-FRIED SHERRY CATFISH

serves 6

6 8-ounce catfish fillets
1 cup soft unflavored breadcrumbs
1 tablespoon finely chopped parsley
1 teaspoon paprika
1 teaspoon lemon juice
½ teaspoon white pepper
salt to taste
¼ cup olive oil
1 cup dry sherry
2 lemons, quartered

Wash and dry the catfish fillets and set aside. Preheat the oven to 450°F. Grease a baking dish large enough to hold the fillets in one layer.

Put the breadcrumbs into a baking dish and toast them in the oven for 1 minute.

On a plate, combine the breadcrumbs with the parsley, paprika, lemon juice, white pepper and salt to taste. Pour the olive oil into one shallow bowl and the sherry into another. Rub the fillets with the olive oil, then dip them into the sherry. Next roll them in the breadcrumb mixture. Arrange the fillets in the baking dish.

Bake the fish for 10 minutes on each side, sprinkling the fillets with some of the sherry every few minutes.

Serve the fish garnished with the lemon quarters.

SOUTHERN-FRIED CATFISH

serves 4

2 pounds catfish fillets
salt to taste
black pepper to taste
¼ cup bacon drippings
3 tablespoons lemon juice
4 tablespoons chopped parsley
1 teaspoon paprika

Wash and dry the fish and season with salt and pepper.

In a large skillet, heat the bacon drippings. When the drippings are hot, put the fish into the skillet and cook over medium heat for 8 minutes on each side.

Drain the fish on paper towels. Sprinkle with the lemon juice, parsley and paprika. Serve immediately.

PASTA WITH RICOTTA AND CAVIAR

serves 4

4 tablespoons sweet butter
2 tablespoons fresh ricotta cheese
2 tablespoons heavy cream
black pepper to taste
¾ pound linguini
¼ cup caviar

Melt the butter in a large skillet. Add the ricotta, cream and a very generous amount of black pepper. Stir and cook over moderately low heat for 2 minutes.

Cook the linguini in a large pot of boiling salted water until it is *al dente*. Drain well, reserving 2 tablespoons of the cooking water.

Add the caviar to the cream mixture in the skillet. Stir well until smooth.

Add the drained linguini to the skillet. Add the reserved cooking water and cook, stirring constantly, for 1 minute.

Transfer to a serving dish and serve at once.

BARBECUED COD

serves 4

4 8-ounce cod fillets
2 tablespoons lemon juice
4 tablespoons chili sauce
2 tablespoons olive oil
2 tablespoons Worcestershire sauce
1 tablespoon drained prepared horseradish
1 tablespoon chopped parsley
½ cup finely minced onion
2 garlic cloves finely minced
½ teaspoon salt
1 teaspoon black pepper
1 teaspoon sugar
4 tablespoons butter

Place the fillets in a shallow dish.

Combine the lemon juice, chili sauce, olive oil, Worcestershire sauce, horseradish, onion, parsley, garlic, salt, pepper and sugar in a bowl. Mix well and pour over the fillets. Cover and refrigerate for 2 hours.

Preheat the oven to 325°F.

Place the butter in four pats in a baking dish. Lay the fillets over the butter and pour the marinade over the fillets. Cover the dish and bake for 25 minutes. Cool slightly before serving.

BROILED COD IN LEMON BUTTER SAUCE

serves 4

4 8-ounce cod fillets
6 tablespoons butter, melted
4 tablespoons lemon juice
1 teaspoon oregano
salt to taste
black pepper to taste
2 tablespoons garlic-flavored breadcrumbs

Wash and dry the fillets. Set aside. Preheat the broiler.

In a shallow baking dish mix the butter, lemon juice, oregano and salt and pepper to taste. (If the broiler is gas, be sure the baking dish is flameproof.) Put the fillets into the dish and turn them once or twice to completely coat them.

Put the baking dish under the broiler and cook for 5 minutes. Remove the dish from the broiler, turn the fillets and sprinkle them with the breadcrumbs. Broil for 5 more minutes.

Transfer the fillets to a serving platter, pour over them any sauce remaining in the baking dish and serve.

FRIED EEL

serves 4

4 medium-sized eels
1 cup lemon juice
½ cup flour
¼ cup grated Parmesan cheese
¼ cup cracker meal
½ teaspoon salt
½ teaspoon black pepper
½ teaspoon oregano
½ teaspoon finely chopped parsley
2 garlic cloves, finely chopped
¼ cup olive oil

Skin, wash and dry the eels. Put them in a large bowl. Add to the bowl the lemon juice and enough water to cover the eels. Cover the bowl and set aside for 30 minutes.

In a large shallow bowl mix the flour, Parmesan cheese, cracker meal, salt, pepper, oregano, parsley and garlic. Remove the eels from the bowl. Cut them into 2½-inch pieces. Dredge the pieces in the flour mixture.

In a large skillet heat the olive oil over medium heat. Add the eels to the skillet and fry them for 10 minutes, constantly and carefully turning them.

Drain the eels on paper towels, transfer to a serving platter and serve.

FLOUNDER WITH CIDER SAUCE

serves 6

6 8-ounce flounder fillets
salt to taste
pepper to taste
4 tablespoons chopped scallions
2 cups cider
4 tablespoons butter
1½ tablespoons flour
1 tablespoon finely chopped parsley

Preheat the oven to 375°F. Wash and dry the fillets.

Put the fillets into a buttered baking dish. Sprinkle with salt and pepper and the scallions. Add just enough cider to cover the fillets. Cover the dish and bake for 20 minutes.

Transfer the fillets to a serving platter. Turn the oven off and put the platter into the oven to keep the fillets warm.

Pour the juices from the baking dish into a saucepan. Add the butter and cook over low heat. Blend in the flour. Stir until the sauce begins to thicken, then cook for 5 minutes more, stirring occasionally. Add the parsley, pour the sauce over the fillets and serve.

FLOUNDER WITH GARLIC AND TOMATOES

serves 4

3 tablespoons olive oil
1 tablespoon butter
2 teaspoons finely chopped garlic
4 6- to 8-ounce flounder fillets
3 medium-sized ripe tomatoes, seeded and coarsely chopped
1 teaspoon salt
¼ teaspoon black pepper
2 tablespoons finely chopped parsley

Place the butter and oil in a large skillet and heat until the butter melts. Add the fillets and sauté them for about 2 minutes per side. Transfer the fish to a serving plate.

Pour off all but 1 tablespoon of the butter and oil from the skillet. Reduce the heat. Add the garlic and sauté for 2 to 3 minutes or until soft. Stir in the tomatoes and raise the heat. Cook, stirring often, until the tomatoes are thick and almost all the liquid has evaporated. Add the salt, pepper, and parsley. Stir well.

Return the fish to the skillet. Cover the skillet and reduce the heat. Cook just long enough to heat the fish through, about 3 minutes. Remove the fish to a serving platter. Pour the sauce over the fish and serve immediately.

FLOUNDER WITH GRAPES

serves 6

6 8-ounce flounder fillets
1 cup white wine
¼ cup water
5 tablespoons butter
1 tablespoon flour
½ cup milk
salt to taste
black pepper to taste
2 egg yolks, beaten
1 cup seedless grapes

Preheat the oven to 375°F. Wash and dry the fillets.

Roll up each fillet and fasten it with string. Put the fillets into a buttered baking dish. Add the wine and water. Cover the dish and bake for 20 minutes.

While the fish is cooking, in a saucepan melt the butter over low heat. Blend in the flour. Slowly stir in the milk. Season with salt and pepper to taste. Simmer for 10 minutes. Remove the pan from the heat and set aside for 2 minutes.

Put the egg yolks into a mixing bowl. In a steady stream, stirring constantly, add the sauce to the egg yolks. Stir in 3 tablespoons of liquid from the baking dish. Blend thoroughly.

Remove the fish from the oven. Take the strings off the fish rolls. Arrange the grapes in the baking dish with the fish and pour the sauce over the top. Return the dish to the oven and cook uncovered for 5 more minutes. Serve hot in the baking dish.

FLOUNDER IN MUSTARD SAUCE

serves 6

6 8-ounce flounder fillets
½ cup wine vinegar
1 teaspoon salt
2 tablespoons butter
2 tablespoons white wine
1 teaspoon chopped parsley
1 teaspoon lemon juice
2 teaspoons Dijon-style mustard
1 egg yolk, beaten

Place the fillets in a large skillet and add the vinegar and salt. Cover the skillet and simmer over low heat for 10 minutes. Pour off the liquid and remove the fillets from the skillet. Arrange the fish on a serving platter and set aside in a warm place.

Melt the butter in a skillet. Add the wine, parsley, lemon juice and mustard. Stir well and cook for 1 minute. Reduce the heat to low and stir in the egg yolk. Cook gently for 3 minutes, stirring constantly. Do not let the sauce boil. Pour the sauce over the fish and serve.

FLOUNDER WITH SHRIMP AND CLAM SAUCE

serves 6

6 8-ounce flounder fillets
1 cup white wine
1 cup water
2 bay leaves
2 tablespoons butter
1 onion, finely chopped
½ cup chopped mushrooms
1 tablespoon flour
1 cup milk
1 egg yolk, beaten
¼ teaspoon black pepper
¼ teaspoon nutmeg
¼ teaspoon ground allspice
4 whole cloves
1 cup chopped cooked clams
12 medium-sized cooked shrimp, shelled, deveined and chopped

Preheat the oven to 350°F.

Arrange the fillets in a large buttered baking dish. Add the white wine, water and bay leaves. Cover the dish and bake for 12 minutes.

To make the sauce, melt the butter in a large skillet. Add the onion and sauté for 3 minutes. Add the mushrooms and sauté for 3 minutes more. Sprinkle the mixture with the flour and stir well. Add the milk, egg yolk, pepper, nutmeg, allspice, cloves, clam and shrimp. Stir well until the sauce thickens.

Pour off the liquid from the baking dish. Pour the sauce over the fish, cover the dish and bake for 10 minutes longer.

SPICED FLOUNDER

serves 6

3 pounds flounder fillets
¼ cup lemon juice
½ teaspoon ground ginger
½ teaspoon finely chopped garlic
¼ teaspoon ground cumin
½ teaspoon paprika
¼ teaspoon cayenne pepper
¼ teaspoon ground tumeric
½ teaspoon salt
1 cup white wine

In a small mixing bowl, combine all the ingredients except the flounder fillets. Mix well.

Preheat the oven to 375°F.

Arrange the fish in a large baking dish and pour the sauce over the fish. Bake for 15 minutes. Serve hot.

POACHED FLOUNDER WITH SAFFRON

serves 4

½ teaspoon dried thyme
½ teaspoon white peppercorns
10 parsley sprigs
1 cup water
1 cup white wine
2 bay leaves
1 medium-sized onion, quartered
4 8-ounce flounder fillets
¼ teaspoon hot red pepper flakes
8 ounces tomato purée
½ teaspoon salt
¼ teaspoon saffron
½ lemon, thinly sliced

Put the thyme, white peppercorns and parsley into the center of a 3-inch square of cheesecloth. Tie the cheesecloth closed to form a bag, a *bouquet garni.*

Put the *bouquet garni,* water, white wine, bay leaves and onion into a large skillet. Bring to a simmer over medium heat and add the fish fillets. Cover the skillet and continue to simmer until the fish is firm and flakes easily with a fork, about 7 to 10 minutes. Remove the fish with a slotted spoon, put it on a serving platter, and set aside in a warm place. Remove the *bouquet garni,* bay leaves and onion and discard.

Add the tomato purée, hot red pepper flakes and salt to the liquid in the skillet. Mix well and bring to the boil. Continue to boil until the liquid is reduced by half, about 10 minutes. Add the saffron and half the lemon slices and boil for 1 minute longer.

Spoon the sauce over the fish fillets. Garnish with the remaining lemon slices and serve hot.

HADDOCK DIANE

serves 6

1 cup sweet butter, softened
1½ pounds mushrooms, sliced
4 tablespoons diced scallions
4 tablespoons chopped parsley
½ cup sherry
2 pounds haddock, cubed
¼ cup brandy
1½ cups fish or chicken broth
1 tablespoon flour
1 tablespoon lemon juice
1 tablespoon mint jelly
1 tablespoon Worcestershire sauce
½ teaspoon salt
1 teaspoon black pepper

Melt the butter in a large skillet. Add the mushrooms, scallions and parsley and sauté for 2 minutes. Add the sherry and cook for 1 minute longer. Add the haddock and cook, turning once, for 3 minutes.

Pour the brandy over the fish and carefully ignite. When the flame dies out, add the broth, flour, lemon juice, mint jelly, Worcestershire sauce, salt and pepper. Stir well and simmer for 5 minutes. Serve hot over rice.

STUFFED HADDOCK

serves 4

4 1-pound haddock fillets
2 onions, finely chopped
2 celery stalks, finely chopped
4 tablespoons butter
2 eggs
1 cup milk
3 tablespoons lemon juice
3 cups garlic-flavored breadcrumbs
1 pound cooked crabmeat, flaked
1 tablespoon chopped parsley
½ teaspoon salt
1 teaspoon cayenne pepper
½ cup melted butter

Prehat the oven to 375°F.

Melt the butter in a skillet. Add the onions and celery and sauté for 3 minutes.

Beat the eggs in a bowl. Stir in the milk, lemon juice and breadcrumbs. Stir in the onions and celery. Add the crabmeat, parsley, salt and cayenne pepper to the bowl.

Lay the fillets flat on a working surface. Place one-quarter of the crab mixture on each fillet. Roll up the fillets and fasten them closed with wooden toothpicks.

Bake for 30 minutes, basting with the melted butter every 5 minutes. Serve hot.

HADDOCK STUFFED WITH CRABMEAT

serves 4

1 haddock, about 3 pounds
1½ pounds crabmeat, cooked and flaked
2 celery stalks, finely chopped
1 green apple, finely chopped
1 tablespoon chopped sweet red pepper
1 tablespoon chopped green pepper
1 cup garlic-flavored breadcrumbs
1 egg, beaten
2 tablespoons melted butter
1 tablespoon lemon juice
salt to taste
black pepper to taste
¼ teaspoon paprika
1 lime, sliced
parsley sprigs

Clean, wash and dry the haddock. Set aside. Preheat the oven to 400°F. Butter a baking dish large enough to hold the fish.

In a large mixing bowl, combine the crabmeat, celery, green apple, red pepper, green pepper, breadcrumbs, egg, butter, lemon juice and salt and pepper to taste. Mix well.

Stuff the cavity of the haddock with the mixture. Close the cavity with wooden toothpicks.

Put the fish into the baking dish. Bake for 30 minutes. Remove the toothpicks, garnish with the lime slices and parsley sprigs and serve.

BAKED HALIBUT

serves 4

4 8-ounce halibut steaks
12 tablespoons butter
4 tablespoons lemon juice
6 scallions, chopped
4 tablespoons chopped parsley
salt to taste
black pepper to taste

Wash and dry the halibut steaks. Preheat the oven to 350°F.

Melt the butter in a saucepan over low heat. Stir in the lemon juice, scallions, parsley, and salt and pepper to taste.

Pour half of the butter mixture into a casserole dish. Put the steaks into the dish. Pour the remaining butter mixture over the steaks. Cover the dish. Bake for 20 minutes, or until the fish flakes easily when touched with a fork. Serve hot.

HALIBUT STEAKS WITH ALMOND SAUCE

serves 4

½ cup slivered almonds
4 8-ounce halibut steaks
4 tablespoons butter
salt to taste
black pepper to taste
2 tablespoons flour
½ cup milk
½ cup sour cream
4 tablespoons chopped scallions
2 teaspoons lemon juice

Preheat the oven to 450°F. With butter, lightly grease a shallow baking dish large enough to hold the halibut steaks in one layer.

Spread the almond slivers on a baking sheet. Toast the almonds in the oven for 5 minutes. Set aside to cool. Reduce the oven temperature to 375°F.

Wash and dry the halibut steaks. Put them into the baking dish.

In a small saucepan, melt half the butter. Brush the steaks with the melted butter and sprinkle them with salt and pepper to taste. Bake for 20 minutes.

In a medium-sized saucepan, melt the remaining butter over medium heat. Add the flour and cook, stirring constantly, for 2 minutes. Gradually add the milk and continue to stir until the mixture thickens. Remove the saucepan from the heat and stir in the sour cream, the scallions, lemon juice and the toasted almond slivers.

Transfer the halibut steaks to a serving platter. Pour the sauce over the steaks and serve.

BROILED HALIBUT STEAKS WITH APRICOT SAUCE

serves 6

¾ pound fresh apricots, peeled, pitted and halved
4 tablespoons sugar
6 8-ounce halibut steaks
2 tablespoons olive oil
2 teaspoons oregano
1 teaspoon black pepper
3 tablespoons lemon juice
1 tablespoon paprika
1 tablespoon finely chopped fresh mint

Put the apricots in a bowl and add 2 cups warm water. Let soak for 3 to 4 hours.

Transfer the apricots and the soaking liquid to a large skillet. Simmer over low heat for 30 minutes. Pour the apricot mixture into a bowl and stir in the sugar. Set aside.

Put the halibut steaks into a large baking dish and set aside.

In a small mixing bowl combine the olive oil, oregano, pepper, mint and lemon juice. Pour the mixture over the fish steaks. Cover the dish and marinate the steaks for 30 minutes.

Preheat the broiler.

Put the halibut steaks on a rack in the broiler pan. Reserve the marinade. Sprinkle the steaks with the paprika.

Broil the fish for 10 minutes, basting the steaks with the reserved marinade every 2 minutes. Carefully turn the steaks and cook for 6 minutes more, continuing to baste every 2 minutes.

Transfer the steaks to a serving platter and sprinkle with the mint. Put the apricot sauce into a serving bowl. Serve the steaks immediately with the sauce on the side.

HALIBUT STEAKS WITH RED AND GREEN TOPPING

serves 4

2 teaspoons sweet butter
½ cup pecan halves
4 8-ounce halibut steaks
salt to taste
black pepper to taste
flour for dredging
4 tablespoons butter
3 tablespoons vegetable oil
2 peeled celery stalks, cut into
1½×¼-inch strips
1 sweet red pepper, cut into
1½×¼-inch strips

Melt the 2 teaspoons butter in a skillet over moderately low heat. Add the pecans and the salt. Cook, stirring often, until the nuts are lightly toasted, about 2 minutes. Remove from the heat and set aside.

Season the halibut steaks on both sides with salt and pepper. Dredge the steaks in the flour and shake off any excess.

Melt the vegetable oil and 2 tablespoons of the butter in a large skillet over moderately high heat. Add the fish steaks and cook until lightly browned, about 4 minutes per side. Arrange the steaks on a serving platter large enough to hold them all in a single layer. Keep warm.

In another skillet, melt the remaining butter over low heat. Add the celery and red pepper strips and cook, stirring constantly, until tender, about 5 to 6 minutes.

Spoon the celery and red pepper over the halibut steaks. Sprinkle with the toasted pecans and serve at once.

PECAN HALIBUT STEAKS

serves 4

4 8-ounce halibut steaks
1 teaspoon salt
1 teaspoon black pepper
4 tablespoons flour
5 tablespoons butter
4 tablespoons corn oil
2 tablespoons lemon juice
½ cup pecan halves
2 celery stalks, peeled and slivered
1 sweet red pepper, slivered

Wash and dry the halibut steaks. Preheat the oven to the lowest setting.

On a plate, combine 1 teaspoon of salt and 1 teaspoon of black pepper with the flour.

In a large skillet, over low heat, melt 2 tablespoons of the butter and heat the corn oil.

While the oil is heating, rub the steaks with the lemon juice. Dredge each steak in the flour, shake off the excess and put it into the skillet. Cook the steaks for 5 minutes on each side. Drain them well on paper towels. Gently pat them dry with more towels, then transfer the steaks to a serving platter. Put the platter into the oven.

To the same skillet, add the remaining butter, the pecan halves, celery, red pepper and salt to taste. Cook over medium heat for 8 minutes, stirring constantly.

Remove the platter from the oven and, using a slotted spoon, cover the halibut steaks with the pecan and vegetable mixture. Serve at once.

BARBECUED HALIBUT

serves 4

4 8-ounce halibut steaks
⅓ cup brandy
⅓ cup lemon juice
¼ teaspoon dried dill
1 bay leaf
1 medium-sized red onion, thinly sliced
½ lemon, thinly sliced
⅓ cup chili sauce
2 tablespoons melted butter

Combine the brandy, lemon juice, dill and bay leaf in a shallow bowl. Add the halibut steaks to the bowl and top with the lemon and onion slices. Cover and refrigerate for 1 hour.

Remove the bowl from the refrigerator. Drain the steaks, reserving the marinade. Discard the onion and lemon slices. Place the steaks on a well-oiled grill over hot coals.

In a small bowl combine the chili sauce, butter, and reserved marinade. Baste the steaks every 2 minutes with the mixture as they cook. Grill the steaks 5 to 6 minutes on each side.

BROILED MACKEREL

serves 6

6 mackerel fillets, about 8 ounces each,
with the skin left on
salt to taste
black pepper to taste
¼ teaspoon cayenne pepper
4 tablespoons lime juice
2 tablespoons dry sherry
1 tablespoon Dijon-style mustard
¼ teaspoon ground fennel seeds

Wash and dry the fillets. Place them skin side down on a lightly buttered baking dish. Preheat the broiler. (If the broiler is gas, be sure the baking dish is flameproof.)

Brush the fillets with 2 tablespoons of melted butter and season with cayenne pepper and salt and pepper to taste. Broil for 5 minutes.

In a small bowl, combine the remaining 4 tablespoons of melted butter, the lime juice, sherry, mustard and fennel. Mix thoroughly.

Turn the fillets carefully, pour the sauce over them and broil for 5 more minutes. Serve hot.

BROILED SPICED MACKEREL

serves 6

6 large mackerel fillets
2 tablespoons very coarsely ground black
pepper
1 large onion, chopped
1½ tablespoons salt
½ teaspoon dried dill
1½ cups white wine vinegar
2 tablespoons butter

Arrange 3 fillets in a large deep baking dish. Sprinkle them with half the pepper, onion, salt and dill. Top with the remaining fillets. Sprinkle with the remaining seasonings. Pour the vinegar over the fillets. Cover the dish and let stand overnight at room temperature.

To broil the mackerel, remove the fillets from the dish, reserving the marinade. Preheat the broiler. Pat the fish dry with paper towels. Arrange the fillets on a broiling pan and broil for 7 minutes without turning.

Pour the reserved marinade and the broiling pan juices into a saucepan. Cook over high heat until the liquid is reduced by half. Add the butter and stir until it melts. Pour the sauce over the fish and serve.

MACKEREL STUFFED WITH CRANBERRIES

serves 4

2 mackerel, about 1½ pounds each
½ pound cranberries
5 tablespoons unflavored breadcrumbs
5 tablespoons butter, softened
1 tablespoon lemon juice
1 tablespoon dry sherry
1 teaspoon anchovy paste
¼ teaspoon cayenne pepper
salt to taste
black pepper to taste

Clean the mackerel. Remove the heads and tails. Split the fish down the spine and remove the bones. Set the fish aside. Preheat the oven to 350°F. Lightly butter a baking dish large enough to hold both fish.

Chop the cranberries coarsely. In a mixing bowl combine the berries with the breadcrumbs, butter, lemon juice, sherry, anchovy paste, cayenne pepper, and salt and pepper to taste.

Stuff each mackerel with half the berry mixture. Wrap each fish in aluminum foil.

Put the fish into the baking dish and bake for 30 minutes.

Remove the foil carefully and serve.

MONKFISH CATALÁN

serves 4

4 8-ounce monkfish fillets
olive oil
2 tablespoons lemon juice

TOMATO and ONION SAUCE:
2 tablespoons olive oil
1 large garlic clove, minced
4 tablespoons chopped parsley
1 medium-sized onion, chopped
½ cup white wine
2 large ripe tomatoes, seeded and chopped
½ teaspoon salt
black pepper to taste

Preheat the broiler to high. Brush the fillets with olive oil and sprinkle them with the lemon juice.

Broil the fillets until they are firm to the touch and flake easily, about 7 minutes per side. When done, transfer the fillets to a serving platter and keep warm.

Heat the olive oil in a heavy skillet over medium heat. Add the garlic, parsley and onion. Cook, stirring frequently, until the onions are soft and golden brown. Add the white wine, lower the heat, and simmer for 5 minutes. Add the tomatoes and salt and cook only until the tomato pieces are hot but still firm. Season to taste with black pepper.

Spoon the sauce over the monkfish fillets. Serve immediately.

MONKFISH IN CREAM SAUCE

serves 4

4 8-ounce monkfish fillets
1 cup brandy
1 teaspoon oregano
1 tablespoon chopped parsley
½ teaspoon salt
½ teaspoon cayenne pepper
1 teaspoon paprika
1 cup light cream

Place the fillets in a shallow dish.

Combine the cognac, oregano, parsley, salt, cayenne pepper and paprika in a bowl. Pour the mixture over the fish fillets. Cover the dish and refrigerate for 2 hours.

Preheat the oven to 325°F. Remove the fillets from the marinade and place them in a baking dish. Set aside. Pour the marinade into a saucepan. Cook the marinade gently over low heat.

Beat the cream in a bowl until it is almost stiff. Add the hot marinade, 1 tablespoon at a time, to the cream, stirring constantly. Pour the sauce over the fish and bake for 7 minutes. Serve hot.

BAKED PERCH

serves 6

8 large perch fillets
¼ teaspoon salt
¼ teaspoon black pepper
1 cup coarsely chopped onions
3 tablespoons coarsely chopped parsley
¼ cup olive oil
¼ cup lemon juice
½ cup white wine

Preheat the oven to 375°F.

In a large baking pan, arrange the perch fillets skin-side down. Sprinkle with the salt and pepper and top with the onions.

Combine the parsley, wine, lemon juice and olive oil in a small mixing bowl. Mix thoroughly.

Pour half the olive oil mixture over the fish and bake for 10 minutes. Baste the fish with the remaining olive oil mixture and bake for 10 minutes longer. Serve immediately.

BREADED PERCH

serves 4

4 8-ounce perch fillets
1 egg, beaten with 1 teaspoon of water
½ cup fine unflavored breadcrumbs
3 tablespoons olive oil
6 tablespoons butter
3 tomatoes, peeled
½ cup sliced mushrooms
1 tablespoon finely chopped scallions
1 tablespoon finely chopped parsley
3 tablespoons flour
1¼ cups beef broth
1 tablespoon tomato paste
1 teaspoon oregano
salt to taste
black pepper to taste

Wash and dry the perch fillets and cut each one in half. Butter a large baking dish. Preheat the oven to 350°F.

Put the beaten egg in one shallow bowl and the breadcrumbs in another. Dip each piece of fish in the egg mixture and then into the breadcrumbs. Put the coated pieces on a plate and set aside for 5 minutes.

In a large skillet, heat the olive oil and melt half the butter. Fry the fillets for 3 minutes on each side. Drain the fillets on paper towels, then transfer them to the baking dish.

Cut each tomato in half lengthwise. Arrange the tomato halves, the mushrooms, scallions and parsley on and around the fish. Bake for 15 minutes.

While the fish is baking, melt the remaining butter in a saucepan over low heat. Blend in the flour. Add the beef broth a little at a time, stirring constantly, then add the tomato paste, oregano and salt and pepper to taste. Mix well.

Pour the sauce over the fish and cook for 10 minutes more.

Sautéed Pickerel

serves 4

4 8-ounce pickerel fillets
6 tablespoons lemon juice
⅔ cup yellow cornmeal
3 tablespoons grated sharp cheddar cheese
1 teaspoon crushed fennel seeds
salt to taste
black pepper to taste
3 tablespoons olive oil
3 tablespoons butter
1 teaspoon finely chopped parsley
2 lemons, quartered

Wash and dry the fillets. Put them into a large shallow bowl and pour the lemon juice over them. Set aside for 10 minutes.

In a shallow bowl, combine the cornmeal, grated cheese, fennel and salt and pepper to taste.

In a large skillet melt the butter and heat the olive oil over low heat.

Dip the fillets into the cornmeal mixture and coat them thoroughly. Put the fillets into the skillet and increase the heat to medium. Cook the fillets for 6 minutes per side.

Drain the fillets on paper towels. Put them on a serving platter, sprinkle the parsley over them, garnish with the lemon quarters and serve.

Deep-Fried Pike

serves 4

4 8-ounce pike fillets
1 cup vegetable oil
4 tablespoons yellow cornmeal
4 tablespoons cracker meal
4 tablespoons grated Parmesan cheese
salt to taste
black pepper to taste
1 egg
1 lemon, quartered

Wash and dry the fillets and set aside. Heat the oil in a large skillet.

In a large shallow bowl, combine the cornmeal, cracker meal, Parmesan cheese, and salt and pepper to taste.

In another shallow bowl beat the egg.

Dip the fillets in the egg and then roll them in the cornmeal mixture.

Fry the fillets over a medium-high heat for 3 minutes per side. Carefully remove them from the skillet and drain them on paper towels. Arrange them on a serving platter, garnish with the lemon quarters and serve.

BAKED PIKE IN DILL SAUCE

serves 4

1 3-pound pike, cleaned
salt to taste
1 egg
1 tablespoon water
4 tablespoons unflavored breadcrumbs
2 bacon slices, halved
2 cups light cream
yolk of 1 hard-cooked egg
½ cup vegetable oil
1½ teaspoons cider vinegar
½ teaspoon Worcestershire sauce
½ teaspoon dry mustard
½ teaspoon sugar
black pepper to taste
¼ cup heavy cream
1½ teaspoons dried dill

Wash and dry the pike. Rub the cavity with salt. Set the fish aside. Preheat the oven to 425°F. Lightly butter a baking dish large enough to hold the fish.

In a small bowl, combine the egg and water and beat lightly. Spread the breadcrumbs on a plate. Brush the outside of the fish with the egg mixture, then roll the fish in the breadcrumbs.

Cut 4 slashes in one side of the fish and stuff a piece of bacon into each one.

Put the fish into the baking dish. Bake for 40 minutes, basting with the light cream every 5 minutes.

In a small mixing bowl, chop the egg yolk. Beat in the vegetable oil, vinegar, Worcestershire sauce, mustard, dill and sugar and salt and pepper to taste. In another bowl whip the heavy cream until it is thick and holds its shape. Fold the whipped cream into the egg yolk mixture and blend thoroughly. Cover the bowl and refrigerate until the fish is cooked.

Transfer the cooked fish to a serving platter and pour the creamy dill over it. Serve immediately.

BAKED STUFFED PIKE

serves 6

1 4-pound pike, cleaned and scaled,
without backbone, but with head and tail
left intact
6 tablespoons melted butter
1 cup finely chopped onions
1 cup finely chopped mushrooms
1 cup seasoned breadcrumbs
¼ cup grated Parmesan cheese
¼ cup milk
6 anchovies, ground to a paste
1 tablespoon capers
2 tablespoons finely chopped parsley
½ cup sour cream
1 teaspoon black pepper
3 tablespoons lemon juice

Prepare the stuffing first. In a medium-sized skillet, brown the onions in the butter. Cook for 2 to 3 minutes. Stir in the mushrooms and cook for 5 minutes longer.

In a large mixing bowl, combine the breadcrumbs, milk, anchovies, capers, parsley and Parmesan cheese. Mix thoroughly. Set the stuffing aside.

Preheat the oven to 425°F. Rinse the fish inside and out, and pat completely dry. Fill the cavity of the fish with the stuffing. Pour the butter, mushrooms and onions over the fish. Bake the fish 45 to 50 minutes, basting with the pan juices every 5 to 7 minutes.

While the fish is cooking, combine the sour cream, salt, pepper and lemon juice together in a small bowl. Chill.

Remove the fish from the oven. Remove the stuffing from the cavity of the fish and place it in a large mixing bowl. Add half the fish drippings and half the onions and mushrooms from the baking pan. Mix well. Place the stuffing back in the fish. Reduce the oven temperature to 250°F. Return the fish to the oven for 5 minutes.

Pour the remaining fish drippings, along with the remaining mushrooms and onions from baking pan into a small saucepan. Add the chilled sour cream mixture and cook over low heat, stirring frequently until heated through. Do not allow the sauce to boil.

Arrange the fish on a serving platter. Pour some of the sauce over the fish and serve. Serve the remainder of the fish sauce in a sauceboat on the side.

POMPANO À LA MAÎTRE d'HÔTEL

serves 4

1 4-pound pompano or
2 2-pound pompanos
1 tablespoon olive oil
1 tablespoon butter
2 tablespoons lemon juice
1 lemon, sliced
salt to taste
black pepper to taste
parsley sprigs for garnish

MAÎTRE d'HÔTEL SAUCE:
1 tablespoon butter
1 tablespoon flour
1 tablespoon lemon juice
1 tablespoon chopped parsley
2 cups fish stock, chicken broth or water
1 egg yolk, beaten

Preheat the broiler.

Clean the fish. If the fish are large, split them down the back; if they are small, broil them whole.

Season the fish with salt, pepper and olive oil.

Put the fish in a broiler pan and broil until well browned, about 10 to 12 minutes per side. Turn the fish once.

When done, remove the fish to a heated serving platter and dot with the butter. Sprinkle them with the lemon juice.

To make the maître d'hôtel sauce, place the butter and flour in a saucepan. Heat and stir until well blended. Do not burn. Continue mixing over low heat and add the fish stock, chicken broth or water. Stir well. Add the lemon juice and chopped parsley. Bring the sauce to a boil and cook for about 15 minutes, or until the sauce is reduced by about half. Remove the sauce from the heat and stir in the beaten egg yolk. Mix until well blended. Serve with the broiled fish.

NEW ORLEANS POMPANO EN PAPILLOTE

serves 4

8 pompano fillets
1½ teaspoons butter
1½ teaspoons flour
½ cup white wine
salt to taste
black pepper to taste
8 large shrimp, cooked and chopped
½ cup crabmeat, cooked and flaked

Preheat the oven to 450°F.

Cut the parchment paper or heavy aluminum foil into squares big enough to fold around 2 fish fillets. Place 2 fillets on each piece of paper or foil.

In a saucepan, melt the butter. Stir in the flour. Slowly add the white wine and cook over low heat, stirring constantly, until the mixture is smooth and thick. Season to taste with the salt and pepper.

Spoon the sauce over the fish. Top with the chopped shrimp and crabmeat. Fold the parchment paper or foil over the fish to form a leakproof package.

Put the package on a baking sheet and bake for 15 minutes. If parchment paper is used, it will puff and brown. Serve immediately in the paper or foil package.

STUFFED POMPANO

serves 4

4 small whole pompanos
1 pound cooked shrimp, peeled and deveined
1 egg, well beaten
½ teaspoon salt
¼ teaspoon black pepper
⅛ teaspoon cayenne pepper
3 tablespoons sherry
1 cup light cream

Preheat the oven to 350°F.

Clean and wash the fish. Split the fish, leaving the heads and tails intact.

Place the fish in a greased, shallow baking dish. The dish should be large enough to hold all the fish in one layer.

Chop the shrimp finely. In a small bowl, combine the shrimp, egg, salt, black pepper, cayenne pepper, sherry and ½ cup of the light cream.

Stuff the cavities of the fish with the shrimp mixture. Pour the remaining cream over the fish and bake for 40 minutes. Baste occasionally. Serve the fish hot with the pan juices.

DEEP-FRIED PORGY

serves 4

3 pounds porgy or butterfish fillets,
unskinned
2 teaspoons salt
½ teaspoon black pepper
1 cup yellow cornmeal
lard or oil for deep frying

Wash and dry the fillets. Score them on the fleshy side with a sharp knife, making approximately 3 small slashes per fillet.

Season the fillets well with salt and pepper on both sides. Dip them into the cornmeal. Make sure the fillets are coated evenly. Gently shake off the excess corn-meal.

In a large deep skillet heat a ½-inch layer of oil or lard. When it is very hot, add the fish. Fry for 4 minutes on the first side. Turn the fillets carefully and fry for 3 to 4 minutes longer or until they are golden brown. Drain the fillets well on paper towels and serve hot.

PORGY WITH PICKLED LEMON

serves 6

4 lemons
4 tablespoons coarse salt
1 cup olive oil
1 3-pound porgy, cleaned
1 teaspoon ground coriander
1 tablespoon paprika
¼ teaspoon cayenne pepper

One day before cooking the fish, trim the lemons and slice them into thin rounds. Arrange the slices on a dish and sprinkle them with 2 tablespoons of the salt and 2 tablespoons of the olive oil. Cover the dish with plastic wrap and let stand at room temperature for 8 hours. Turn the lemon slices over and sprinkle them with the remaining salt and 2 tablespoons of the olive oil. Cover the dish and let stand at room temperature for 8 hours or overnight.

To cook the fish, grease a baking dish. Preheat the broiler. Arrange half the lemon slices in the bottom of the baking dish. Place the fish on top of the slices. Cover the fish with the remaining lemon slices.

Combine the coriander, paprika and cayenne pepper with the remaining olive oil in a small bowl. Sprinkle the mixture over the fish.

Broil the fish, basting often with the pan juices, for 20 minutes.

142

BAKED REDFISH

serves 4

1 4-pound redfish
3 to 4 tablespoons butter
salt to taste
cayenne pepper to taste
6 shrimps, cooked and coarsely chopped
¼ cup chopped capers
lemon wedges for garnish

Preheat the oven to 400°F.

Clean and wash the fish. Pat dry.

Place 2 tablespoons of the butter, cut up into small pieces, inside the fish. Dot the outside of the fish with the remaining butter. Season the fish to taste with salt and cayenne pepper.

Place the fish in a well-buttered shallow baking dish. Cover it closely with a piece of well-buttered brown paper or aluminum foil cut to fit. Bake for 40 minutes or until the fish flakes easily with a fork.

Five minutes before the fish is ready, remove it from the oven. Sprinkle the capers and shrimp around the fish. Return to the oven for 5 minutes.

Serve surrounded with the shrimp and capers and garnished with lemon wedges.

SMOKED REDFISH

serves 4

1 4-pound redfish
2 garlic cloves, crushed
salt to taste
black pepper to taste
grated rind of 1 lemon
½ cup lemon juice
¼ pound melted butter
2 tablespoons Worcestershire sauce
½ teaspoon Tabasco sauce
1 teaspoon chopped parsley

Clean and wash the fish. Pat it dry. Rub the fish with the garlic, salt, black pepper, and lemon rind.

In a small bowl combine the lemon juice, butter, Worcestershire sauce, Tabasco sauce and parsley. Mix well.

Cover the head and tail of the fish with pieces of aluminum foil.

Place the fish on an oiled grill over low coals. Cover the grill and smoke the fish for about 1 hour or until the fish flakes easily. Do not overcook. Baste the fish with the lemon sauce every 15 minutes.

Cool before serving.

BLACKENED REDFISH

serves 8

8 8-ounce skinned redfish or any other firm
white fish fillets
2 cups butter
¼ cup lemon juice
1 tablespoon dried thyme
2 teaspoons black pepper
1½ teaspoons cayenne pepper
1 teaspoon salt

Remove any small bones from the fish fillets, using tweezers if necessary. Put the fillets into the refrigerator and leave them until they are very well chilled. Do not remove the fillets until needed—they must be very cold.

In a large skillet, melt the butter over low heat. Add the lemon juice, thyme, pepper, cayenne pepper and salt. Stir well and cook for 10 minutes. Pour the mixture into a large shallow dish or bowl and cool.

Heat a large, cast-iron skillet over high heat until it is very hot. Do not grease the skillet.

Remove the fish fillets from the refrigerator and dip them into the cooled butter mixture. In batches, put the fillets into the skillet. The fish will turn black and cook almost instantly. Turn and quickly cook on the other side. There will be a lot of smoke in the kitchen. Remove the fillets from the skillet and keep warm on a plate. Cook the remaining fillets as above.

After all the fish has been cooked, add the remaining butter mixture to the skillet. Cook over high heat, stirring to loosen the brown bits on the sides and bottom of the skillet, until the butter is dark brown.

Spoon the browned butter over the fish and serve immediately.

BACON-BAKED ROCKFISH

serves 4

1 3-pound rockfish
salt to taste
black pepper to taste
flour
6 thick bacon strips
1 large onion, diced
½ cup chopped scallion
3 tablespoons brandy
1 cup water

Preheat the oven to 350°F.

Make three ½-inch-deep cuts in each side of the fish. Sprinkle the fish with salt, pepper and flour on both sides. Wrap the bacon strips around the fish.

Put the fish in a shallow baking dish. Sprinkle the onions and scallions on top of the fish. Pour the water and brandy into the baking dish and cover. Bake for 20 minutes, then remove the cover and continue to bake until the fish is well-browned. Serve with Worcestershire sauce.

BACON-BAKED SALMON

serves 6

1 whole salmon, about 4 pounds
8 slices white bread, moist and crumbled
4 tablespoons butter, melted
1 small onion, finely chopped
3 tablespoons chopped parsley
1 teaspoon oregano
salt to taste
black pepper to taste
1 teaspoon paprika
½ pound sliced bacon

Clean, wash and dry the salmon.

In a mixing bowl, combine the crumbled bread, butter, onion, chopped parsley, oregano and salt and pepper to taste. Mix well.

Stuff the cavity of the fish with the mixture. Fasten the fish closed with toothpicks.

Preheat the oven to 350°F.

Wrap slices of bacon around the salmon until the entire fish is covered with the bacon. Sprinkle the paprika over the bacon.

Put the salmon into a shallow baking dish. Bake for 1 hour.

When the fish is done, carefully transfer it to a serving platter. Remove the toothpicks and serve.

BAKED SALMON IN CREAM SAUCE

serves 4

1 3-pound salmon, cleaned
3 tablespoons grated Parmesan cheese
4 tablespoons flour
salt to taste
black pepper to taste
4 tablespoons butter
1 cup canned tomato purée
1 small onion, finely chopped
2 garlic cloves, finely chopped
1 tablespoon Worcestershire sauce
2 tablespoons water
½ cup light cream

Rinse and dry the salmon. In a shallow bowl combine the Parmesan cheese, 3 tablespoons flour, and salt and pepper to taste. Dredge the salmon in the mixture, coating it well. Shake off any excess.

Preheat the oven to 400°F.

Melt the butter in a large, shallow, flameproof baking dish over low heat. Put the fish into the dish and bake for 8 minutes. Turn the fish and bake for 7 minutes on the other side.

Remove the dish from the oven. Add the tomato purée, onion, garlic and Worcestershire to the pan juices and stir gently. Return the dish to the oven and bake for 30 minutes more, basting the salmon every 5 minutes with the pan juices.

In a small bowl mix the remaining 1 tablespoon flour with the water and set aside.

When the fish is done, carefully transfer it to a serving platter and set aside in a warm place.

Pour the pan juices into a saucepan and add the cream and the water and flour mixture. Cook over low heat, stirring frequently, for 5 minutes, or until the sauce thickens. Pour the sauce over the fish and serve.

BARBECUED SALMON

serves 6 to 8

1 5- to 6-pound salmon, cleaned
salt to taste
black pepper to taste
2 tablespoons butter, softened and cut into
pieces
½ medium-sized onion, thinly sliced
½ lemon, sliced
2 parsley sprigs
vegetable oil
lemon wedges

Sprinkle the salmon inside and out with the salt and pepper. Dot with the butter. Arrange overlapping slices of onion, lemon and parsley in the cavity. Brush the fish with oil.

Wrap the salmon in heavy aluminum foil; seal the edges with double folds. Place the package on a grill over medium-hot coals. Carefully turn the package every 10 minutes. Test the salmon for doneness after 45 minutes. The fish is done when it flakes easily when tested with a fork at the thickest part.

To serve, transfer the salmon to a serving platter and fold back the foil. Cut between the bones and meat with a spatula; lift off each serving. Serve with lemon wedges.

BASKET-GRILLED SALMON

serves 6 to 8

1 5- to 6-pound salmon, cleaned
lemon juice
1 teaspoon salt
½ teaspoon black pepper
¾ cup coarsely chopped green pepper
¾ cup coarsely chopped celery
¾ cup coarsely chopped onion
¼ cup chopped parsley
⅛ teaspoon dried thyme
⅛ teaspoon dried marjoram
¼ cup olive oil
1 cup water

Brush the salmon inside and out with the lemon juice.

In a bowl combine the salt, pepper, green pepper, celery, onion, parsley, thyme, and marjoram. Mix well. Stuff the cavity of the fish with the mixture. Close the cavity with skewers or sew it closed with heavy thread.

Place the fish on a clean piece of chicken wire and shape it around the fish to form a basket. Place the basket on a grill over medium-hot coals. Turn and baste often with a mixture of the olive oil and 1 cup water. The salmon will take about 1½ hours to cook.

Carefully remove the fish from the basket. Most of the skin will stick to the basket. Place the salmon on a platter and serve.

BROILED SALMON STEAKS

serves 4

½ pound butter
½ cup lemon juice
½ cup brandy
4 8-ounce salmon steaks
1 tablespoon finely chopped parsley
½ teaspoon oregano
salt to taste
black pepper to taste
1 teaspoon paprika

First make clarified butter. Melt the butter in a small saucepan over low heat. When the butter has melted, remove the pan from the heat and cool slightly. With a large spoon, skim the clear butter from the top into a small bowl. Discard the milky solids.

Preheat the broiler.

In a small saucepan combine the clarified butter, lemon juice and brandy. Cook over low heat until the butter starts to turn brown. Remove the saucepan from the heat.

Brush both sides of each steak with the butter sauce. Arrange the steaks in the broiler pan. Put the pan under the broiler 6 inches from the flame and cook for 5 minutes. Remove from the broiler, turn the steaks and brush with the remaining butter sauce. Sprinkle with the parsley, oregano, paprika and salt and pepper to taste. Broil for 5 minutes more and serve.

BROILED LEMON-BUTTERED
SALMON STEAKS

serves 4

4 tablespoons butter
¼ teaspoon grated lemon rind
3 tablespoons lemon juice
salt to taste
black pepper to taste
4 8-ounce salmon steaks
1 lemon, quartered

In a small saucepan over very low heat, combine the butter, lemon rind, lemon juice and salt and pepper to taste. Remove the pan from the heat and set aside.

Preheat the broiler. Line the broiler pan with aluminum foil. Arrange the salmon steaks on the foil. Brush them with the butter mixture.

Broil the steaks for 6 minutes, basting every 2 minutes. Turn the steaks and broil for 6 minutes more, basting every 2 minutes.

Transfer the salmon steaks to a serving platter, garnish with the lemon quarters and serve.

COLD POACHED SALMON STEAKS

serves 6

4 cups salted water
5 black peppercorns
1 tablespoon lemon juice
1 tablespoon lime juice
6 5-ounce salmon steaks
2 large cucumbers, finely grated
½ cup sour cream
¼ cup mayonnaise
1 tablespoon finely chopped parsley
1 tablespoon finely chopped onion
2 teaspoons red wine vinegar
salt to taste
black pepper to taste

In a large pot combine the salted water, peppercorns, lemon juice and lime juice. Bring to a boil. Put three salmon steaks into the pot, reduce the heat and simmer for 10 minutes. Remove the steaks with a slotted spoon, pat them dry with paper towels and arrange on a serving platter. Repeat the same procedure with the remaining salmon steaks. When the salmon is cool, cover the platter with plastic wrap and refrigerate.

To make the sauce, in a mixing bowl combine the cucumber, sour cream, mayonnaise, parsley, onion, vinegar and salt and pepper to taste. Mix well. Refrigerate for 2 hours before serving.

SALMON CAKES

serves 8

3 pounds drained canned salmon
1 teaspoon salt
black pepper to taste
1 cup chopped onion
½ pound butter, softened
½ cup flour
½ cup heavy cream
¾ cup vegetable oil

Chop the salmon very finely in a mixing bowl. Add the salt and pepper. Add the onions, cream, butter and flour and mix until smooth. Shape the mixture into balls or cakes.

Heat the oil in a large heavy skillet. Add the salmon cakes and fry until golden brown on all sides.

CRABMEAT-STUFFED SALMON

serves 8

1 5- to 6-pound salmon, cleaned
4 tablespoons butter
3 celery stalks, chopped
1 medium-sized onion, chopped
1 small sweet red pepper, chopped
salt to taste
½ teaspoon dried oregano
black pepper to taste
½ pound cooked crabmeat
2 cups garlic-flavored croutons
2 tablespoons olive oil

Clean, wash and dry the salmon and set aside. Preheat the oven to 350°F.

Melt the butter in a medium-sized saucepan. Add the celery, onion, and red pepper. Cook over low heat, stirring frequently, until the vegetables are soft.

While the vegetables are cooking, in a large mixing bowl combine the crabmeat, croutons, oregano and salt and pepper to taste.

When the vegetables are cooked, add them to the crabmeat mixture and mix thoroughly.

Fill the cavity of the salmon with the mixture and skewer closed with wooden toothpicks.

Put the fish into a shallow baking dish and brush each side with the olive oil.

Bake for 1½ hours, basting every 15 minutes.

When the fish is cooked transfer it to a serving platter, remove the toothpicks and serve.

Cut strips
½ c buttr / parsley
2TB Lemon juice

GRILLED STUFFED SALMON

serves 6

1 5-pound salmon, cleaned
¼ cup lemon juice
1 small green pepper, chopped
1 small sweet red pepper, chopped
3 celery stalks, chopped
1 small red onion, chopped
1 tomato, chopped
¼ cup chopped parsley
1 teaspoon oregano
salt to taste
black pepper to taste
¼ cup olive oil
1 teaspoon paprika

Rub the inside cavity of the salmon with the lemon juice. Set aside.

In a mixing bowl, combine the green pepper, red pepper, celery, red onion, tomato, parsley, oregano and salt and pepper to taste. Mix well. Stuff the cavity of the fish with the mixture. Sew the fish closed. Rub the outside of the fish with the olive oil.

Put the fish on a large sheet of heavy aluminum foil, and sprinkle half the paprika over it. Turn the fish over and sprinkle the other side with the remaining paprika. Wrap the fish tightly in the foil.

Cook the fish over hot coals for 1½ hours, turning it every 15 minutes.

Carefully remove the foil. Most of the skin will come off too. With a sharp knife remove any skin that does not come off and scrape off any darkened meat. Serve immediately.

RUM-POACHED SALMON WITH VINAIGRETTE

serves 6

1 large salmon, cleaned
½ cup light rum
1¾ cups chicken broth
1 onion, sliced
2 bay leaves
leaves from 1 celery head, chopped
2 lemons, sliced
1½ cups olive oil
⅓ cup white wine vinegar
⅓ cup dark rum
1 teaspoon sugar
1 teaspoon paprika
¼ cup chopped fresh coriander
salt to taste
black pepper to taste
4 hard-cooked eggs, finely chopped
1 cucumber, peeled and thinly sliced

Preheat the oven to 375°F.

Line a large, shallow baking dish with a large sheet of heavy aluminum foil. Put the fish into the dish. Pour the light rum and chicken broth over the fish. Cover the fish with the onion slices, bay leaves, celery leaves and lemon slices. Place a second large sheet of aluminum foil over the top of the fish and crimp the two pieces of foil together. Bake the fish for 40 minutes.

While the fish bakes, make the vinaigrette sauce. In a blender or food processor combine the olive oil, vinegar, dark rum, sugar, paprika, coriander and salt and pepper to taste. Blend until the sauce thickens. Pour the sauce into a mixing bowl. Mix in the chopped eggs. Cover the bowl and refrigerate.

When the fish is done, remove it from the oven and set aside. After 30 minutes remove the top piece of foil, carefully lift the fish out of the baking dish, and transfer it to a serving platter. Discard the cooking juices. Using a sharp knife, remove the skin from both sides of the fish. Scrape away all the dark meat.

Cover the fish with plastic wrap and refrigerate for 2 hours.

Serve the salmon garnished with the cucumber slices. Stir the vinaigrette sauce and spoon some over each serving.

SALMON WITH SCALLOPS FILLING
AND LETTUCE SAUCE

serves 6

½ pound chilled fresh scallops
1 egg white
½ teaspoon lemon juice
salt to taste
⅛ teaspoon cayenne pepper
⅛ teaspoon nutmeg
½ cup very cold heavy cream
6 6- to 8-ounce fresh salmon fillets
1 cup dry white wine
½ cup water
1 shallot, finely chopped
1 bay leaf
3 whole black peppercorns
¼ teaspoon dried tarragon
2 tablespoons butter
1 head soft lettuce
1 cup heavy cream
black pepper to taste

Put the scallops, egg white, lemon juice, salt, cayenne pepper and nutmeg into the container of a food processor or blender. Purée until smooth and well blended.

Pour the purée into a mixing bowl set into a larger mixing bowl filled with ice. Stir in the ½ cup very cold cream, a little at a time. Stir well after each addition; do not add more cream until the previous addition is absorbed. Cover the mixture and refrigerate for 2 hours.

Trim the lettuce and cut it into julienne strips.

Spread the salmon fillets on a working surface. Spread the scallops mixture over the fillets, leaving a 1-inch border all around. Starting at the narrow end of the fillet, roll the fillets up and fasten in place with wooden toothpicks.

In a skillet large enough to hold the salmon rolls in one layer, combine the wine, water, shallot, bay leaf, peppercorns and tarragon. Add the salmon rolls and cook over medium heat until the mixture just simmers. Cover the skillet and cook over very low heat until the filling is just set when tested with a fork, about 10 minutes.

While the salmon cooks, melt the butter in another skillet. Add the julienned lettuce, cover, and cook over low heat until just wilted, about 5 minutes. Stir occasionally. Put the lettuce into the container of a food processor or blender and process until smooth. Set aside.

Remove the salmon rolls from the skillet and put them on a plate. Set aside.

Strain the salmon cooking liquid through a fine sieve and return the liquid to the skillet. Discard any solids remaining in the sieve. Bring the liquid to a boil over medium heat. Continue to boil until the liquid is reduced to ¼ cup. Add the cream and continue to boil until the sauce is thickened. Add the lettuce purée and stir well. Season with salt and pepper.

Slice the salmon rolls into ½-inch rounds. Remove the toothpicks. Distribute the sauce evenly among six individual serving plates. Put the salmon rounds on top of the sauce and serve immediately.

Salmon with Lime and Walnut Oil

serves 6

rind of 1 lime, cut into strips
7 tablespoons chilled sweet butter
4 8-ounce salmon steaks
2 tablespoons lime juice
3 tablespoons walnut oil
salt to taste
black pepper to taste
1 teaspoon finely chopped mint

Preheat the oven to the lowest setting.

In a small saucepan, bring ½ cup of water to a boil. Add the lime rind and boil for 1 minute. Remove the rind from the water with a slotted spoon and drain on a paper towel.

Melt 2 tablespoons of the butter in a large skillet. Put the salmon steaks into the skillet and cook them over medium-high heat until each side is lightly browned, about 4 minutes per side. When the salmon is cooked, transfer the steaks to four serving dishes and keep warm in the oven.

Add to the skillet the lime juice, lime rind, remaining butter and the walnut oil. Cook over low heat until the mixture is hot and has thickened. Season to taste with salt and pepper.

Spoon sauce over each salmon steak, sprinkle with mint and serve.

Broiled Shad

serves 4

4 8-ounce shad fillets, with skin
5 tablespoons butter
½ teaspoon oregano
3 tablespoons lemon juice
1 teaspoon finely chopped parsley
½ teaspoon paprika
salt to taste
black pepper to taste

Wash and dry the shad fillets. Put the fillets skin-side down, on the greased rack of the broiler pan. Set aside. Preheat the broiler.

In a small saucepan, melt the butter. Stir in lemon juice, oregano, parsley, and salt and pepper to taste. Brush the fillets with the sauce and sprinkle them with the paprika.

Broil the fillets for 8 minutes, basting every 2 minutes with the sauce. Turn the fillets and cook for 6 more minutes, basting every 2 minutes.

Transfer the fillets to a serving platter and pour the remaining sauce over them. Serve immediately.

STUFFED SEA TROUT

serves 6

1 5- to 6-pound sea trout, cleaned
¼ cup diced salt pork
1 shallot, finely chopped
1 pound fresh shrimp, shelled,
deveined and chopped
½ cup sliced mushrooms
¾ cup unflavored breadcrumbs
1 tablespoon chopped parsley
¼ teaspoon dried thyme
salt to taste
black pepper to taste
¼ cup lemon juice

Wipe the fish clean and dry gently. Rub the fish cavity with some salt.

Heat a skillet and add the salt pork. Cook until the pieces are crisp. Remove the pork and reserve.

Add the shallot to the drippings and sauté over medium heat until tender. Add the mushrooms and shrimp to the skillet, increase the heat and cook quickly, stirring frequently for 5 minutes, or until the shrimp are pink and firm.

Add the breadcrumbs, parsley, thyme, salt, pepper and pork pieces. Stir all ingredients together.

Preheat the oven to 400°F. Stuff the cavity of the sea trout with the mixture. Pour half the lemon juice over the stuffing.

Place the fish on a buttered baking dish Close the cavity, using thread or skewers. Brush some melted butter over the skin and dust with salt and pepper. Sprinkle the remaining lemon juice over the fish.

Bake for 40 minutes or until the fish is white, firm to the touch and flakes easily.

BAKED STUFFED SHAD

serves 6

1 large shad, at least 4 pounds, with roe
3 tablespoons lemon juice
2 cups water
4 scallions, finely chopped
¼ cup vegetable oil
2 eggs, beaten
1 cup unflavored breadcrumbs
½ cup water
½ teaspoon dried basil
½ cup lemon juice
2 tablespoons Worcestershire sauce
1 dash Angostura bitters

Remove the roe from the fish. Put the water into a pot and bring it to a boil. Add the 3 tablespoons of lemon juice. Gently add the roe and cook until it is firm, about 3 to 5 minutes. Remove the membrane from the roe.

Heat the vegetable oil in a skillet. Add the chopped scallions and sauté until tender. Add the roe, eggs and breadcrumbs. Stir all the ingredients together. Add the water, a little at a time, moistening the stuffing until it is the way you like it. Fold in the basil and season with salt and pepper to taste.

Preheat the oven to 325°F.

Stuff the shad with the roe stuffing and close the cavity with wooden toothpicks or skewers. Place the shad in a moderately deep baking dish, and add enough cold water to fill the dish to a depth of 1 inch. Pour the Worcestershire sauce and bitters over the fish.

Bake for 40 minutes, basting every 5 minutes with the pan juices.

Fettuccini with Shad Roe

serves 4

1 pound shad roe
3 tablespoons butter
3 tablespoons plus 2 teaspoons olive oil
2 garlic cloves, finely chopped
2 ripe tomatoes, peeled, seeded and chopped
¾ pound fettuccini
salt to taste
black pepper to taste
4 tablespoons heavy cream
2 tablespoons finely chopped parsley

Wash the roe. Poach them in a small saucepan of boiling water for 4 to 5 minutes, or until firm. Drain well and remove the membranes. Set the roe aside.

In a large skillet, melt the butter and blend in the 3 tablespoons of olive oil. Add the garlic and tomatoes and cook over medium heat for 8 minutes, stirring frequently. Add the roe to the skillet and continue to cook over medium heat until the roe begins to flake. Using a wooden spoon, break the roe into pieces. Reduce the heat to very low and continue to cook the roe, stirring occasionally.

While the roe is cooking, bring 2 quarts of salted water to a boil. Cook the fettuccini until it is *al dente*. Drain well. Transfer the fettuccini to a serving dish and toss with the 2 teaspoons of olive oil.

Season the roe mixture with salt and pepper to taste. Add the cream and the parsley and mix thoroughly. Pour the roe mixture over the fettuccini and serve.

Planked Shad

serves 4 to 6

3 to 4 1-pound shad
melted butter
salt to taste
black pepper to taste
¼ cup butter
1 tablespoon lemon juice

Preheat the broiler.

Clean and split the shad. Place the fish skin-side down on an oiled and pre-heated wooden plank. Brush the fish with the melted butter and sprinkle with salt and pepper to taste.

Broil the fish for 15 to 20 minutes, or until they flake easily. Do not turn the fish. Place the fish on a serving platter.

In a mixing bowl, cream the ¼ cup butter until it is softened. Add the lemon juice slowly, creaming until it is entirely blended into the butter. Spread the mixture over the cooked fish and serve at once.

If a plank is not available, use a broiler-proof platter.

SHAD ROE WITH MUSTARD SAUCE

serves 4

4 8-ounce shad roe
5 tablespoons butter
1 teaspoon paprika
1 teaspoon dry mustard
8 tablespoons heavy cream
1 teaspoon lemon juice
salt to taste
black pepper to taste

Preheat the broiler.

Bring 1 cup of water to a boil in a large skillet. Put the roe into the water. Reduce the heat to low and simmer the roe for 5 minutes. Remove the roe from the water, drain them well, and put them on the greased rack of the broiler pan. Dot the roe with 4 tablespoons of the butter and sprinkle with half the paprika. Broil for 3 minutes. Turn the roe, sprinkle the rest of the paprika over them and broil for 3 more minutes.

While the roe are cooking, in a small saucepan melt the remaining butter. Mix in the mustard. Add the cream and simmer, stirring frequently, over medium-low heat for 10 minutes. Remove the pan from the heat and stir in the lemon juice and salt and pepper to taste.

When the roe are cooked, transfer them to a serving platter, pour the sauce over them and serve.

PAN-FRIED SMELTS

serves 4

16 smelts, cleaned
1 teaspoon salt
½ teaspoon black pepper
½ cup yellow cornmeal
½ cup flour
½ cup butter
3 tablespoons bacon drippings

Clean the fish but leave the heads intact. Wash and pat dry. Rub the fish with the salt and pepper.

In a large bowl combine the flour and cornmeal. Roll the fish, one at a time, in the mixture. Coat them well and shake off any excess.

In a large skillet, heat the butter together with the bacon drippings. When the fat is very hot, add the smelts, three at a time. Fry, turning once, until the fish are golden brown, about 3 minutes per side.

Carefully remove the fish from the skillet and drain them on paper towels. Serve hot.

ORIENTAL BAKED SHAD

serves 4

2 1-pound shad fillets
¼ cup soy sauce
3 tablespoons sherry
2 teaspoons sugar
3 thin slices ginger root, crushed
3 scallions, sliced
½ cup dried Chinese black mushrooms
½ cup canned sliced bamboo shoots

In a shallow baking dish combine the soy sauce, sherry, sugar, ginger, and scallions. Mix well. Add the shad fillets and turn to coat them evenly. Cover the dish and marinate in the refrigerator 4 to 5 hours or overnight.

In a small bowl soak the dried mushrooms in enough boiling water to cover until they are soft, about 20 minutes. Drain the mushrooms. Discard the stems and slice the caps.

Remove the shad from the refrigerator. Remove the ginger from the marinade. Bake the fish in the marinade for 10 minutes.

Scatter the mushrooms and bamboo shoots over the shad. Bake 5 minutes longer or until the fish flakes easily.

SAUTÉED SMELTS

serves 4

16 smelts, cleaned
beer
½ cup flour
¼ cup finely ground almonds
2 teaspoons salt
½ teaspoon black pepper
¼ pound butter
lemon wedges

Clean the smelts but leave the heads intact. Wash and dry the fish. Place them in a large bowl and add enough beer to cover them completely. Refrigerate for 2 hours.

Remove the fish from the beer and pat dry.

In a bowl combine the flour, ground almonds, salt, and pepper. Roll the smelts in the mixture until they are lightly coated.

Melt the butter in a deep skillet. When hot, open the fish and add them to the skillet, slit-side down. Fry until crisp. Turn the fish and brown the skin sides. This will take about 5 to 8 minutes depending on the size of the fish.

Fry as many fish as will fit into the skillet comfortably at one time. Add more butter if necessary.

Remove the fish from the skillet. Drain them on paper towels and serve hot with lemon wedges.

BAKED RED SNAPPER

serves 6

1 4-pound red snapper, cleaned
4 tablespoons butter
1 teaspoon cayenne pepper
6 shrimp, cooked and chopped
4 tablespoons capers, chopped
1 tablespoon lemon juice
1 tablespoon chopped parsley
1 teaspoon salt
2 lemons, quartered

Wash and dry the red snapper. Preheat the oven to 400°F. Lightly butter a shallow baking dish large enough to hold the fish.

In a medium-sized mixing bowl, combine 2 tablespoons of the butter, cut in small pieces, with the cayenne pepper, shrimp, capers, lemon juice, parsley and salt to taste. Mix carefully but thoroughly. Stuff the fish with the mixture. Close the cavity with wooden toothpicks. Rub the outside of the fish with the remaining butter.

Put the fish into the baking dish and cover with aluminum foil. Bake for 45 minutes.

Carefully transfer the fish to a platter, remove the toothpicks, garnish with the lemon wedges and serve.

GULF-STYLE RED SNAPPER

serves 4

4 8-ounce red snapper fillets
salt to taste
black pepper to taste
1 teaspoon oregano
2 tablespoons butter, softened
4 carrots, chopped
1 celery stalk, chopped
2 tablespoons chopped parsley
6 uncooked shrimp, peeled and chopped
1 cup dry vermouth
1 bay leaf

Wash and dry the red snapper fillets. Rub them with the salt, pepper and oregano. Put the fillets into a buttered casserole dish. Preheat the oven to 400°F.

In a large mixing bowl, combine the butter, carrots, celery, parsley, shrimp, dry vermouth and bay leaf. Mix thoroughly. Pour the sauce over the fish.

Cover the dish and bake the fish for 30 minutes, or until the fish flakes with the touch of a fork. Serve hot from the casserole dish.

HAWAIIAN RED SNAPPER

serves 4 to 6

1 4- to 5-pound whole red snapper, cleaned
coarse salt
meat of 1 fresh coconut, broken into small
pieces
1 cup water
2 tablespoons sherry
1 orange, peeled and sectioned
1 fresh pineapple, cut into chunks
1 papaya, sliced

Season the fish well, inside and out, with coarse salt. Place the fish in a shallow buttered baking dish.

In an electric blender or food processor, combine the coconut meat and water. Blend at high speed for 30 seconds. Strain through a sieve into a bowl. Press with the back of a spoon to extract all the liquid. Let the liquid stand for 1 hour or until the coconut cream has risen to the top. Skim off the cream and pour over the fish. (Canned coconut milk may be used instead, but the results are not as good.)

Preheat the oven to 350°F.

Bake the fish for 20 minutes. Pour the sherry into the pan and bake for 25 minutes longer or until the fish flakes easily. About 5 minutes before the fish is done, add the orange, pineapple and papaya pieces to the baking dish.

LEMON-LIME RED SNAPPER

serves 4

4 scallions, chopped
¼ cup lime juice
2 teaspoons grated lemon rind
salt to taste
¼ teaspoon nutmeg
¼ teaspoon cinnamon
4 8-ounce red snapper fillets, with skin

In a mixing bowl combine the scallions, lime juice, grated lemon rind and salt to taste. Pour the mixture into a shallow baking dish large enough to hold all the fillets in one layer.

Rinse and dry the fillets. Put the fillets skin-side down into the baking dish, then turn them over. Allow the fish to stand in the marinade, skin-side up, for 30 minutes at room temperature.

Preheat the oven to 400°F.

Turn the fillets skin-side down and sprinkle them with the nutmeg and cinnamon. Cover the dish and bake for 15 minutes, or until the fish flakes easily with a fork. Baste every 3 minutes with the pan juices. Serve hot from the baking dish.

POACHED RED SNAPPER

serves 6

1 large red snapper, cleaned
¼ cup red wine vinegar
1 cup white wine
2 teaspoons sugar
1 teaspoon salt
½ cup olive oil
2 garlic cloves, minced
2½ cups water

Clean and fillet the fish. Reserve the head and bones.

In a small pot, combine the reserved fish trimmings with the vinegar, olive oil, wine, water, sugar, salt and garlic. Cover and simmer over low heat for 30 minutes.

Strain the fish stock mixture through a fine sieve. Discard any solids that remain in the sieve.

Preheat the oven to 425°F.

Place the red snapper fillets in a large baking pan. Pour the fish stock mixture over the fillets. Bake for 30 minutes. Pour off the cooking liquid and serve in a gravy boat on the side. Serve hot.

RED HOT SNAPPER

serves 4

4 8-ounce red snapper fillets
2 tablespoons olive oil
1 garlic clove, finely chopped
1 large onion, chopped
½ cup of pimento-stuffed green olives, sliced
½ small sweet red pepper, chopped
1 teaspoon ground cumin
1 teaspoon chili powder
1 dried hot red chili, finely chopped
6 tablespoons lemon juice
6 tablespoons orange juice
salt to taste
black pepper to taste

Wash and dry the red snapper fillets. Put the fillets into a lightly buttered baking dish. Preheat the oven to 375°F.

In a large skillet over medium-low heat, heat the olive oil. Add the garlic and chopped onion. Cook, stirring constantly until the onion is soft. Add the sliced olives, sweet red pepper, cumin, chili powder, chili pepper and mix well. Add the lemon juice, orange juice and salt and pepper to taste and stir until well blended. Simmer for 5 minutes.

Pour the sauce over the fish. Bake, uncovered, for 20 minutes. Carefully transfer the fillets to a serving platter. Pour the sauce over them and serve.

RED SNAPPER À LA CHAMPAGNE

serves 4

4 8-ounce red snapper fillets
8 tablespoons butter
4 tablespoons lemon juice
1 lemon, thinly sliced
4 garlic cloves, finely chopped
1 teaspoon oregano
1 teaspoon black pepper
½ cup sweet champagne
1 tablespoon paprika

Wash and dry the red snapper fillets.

In a large skillet put 4 tablespoons of the butter in slices. Sprinkle the lemon juice over the butter, then sprinkle with the chopped garlic. Arrange the fillets in the skillet. Slice the remaining butter and put the slices on the fish. Sprinkle the fish with the oregano and pepper. Arrange the lemon slices over the fish. Cook, uncovered, over medium heat for 20 minutes.

Pour the champagne into the skillet. Sprinkle the fillets with the paprika. Cook for 10 minutes more.

Transfer the fillets to a serving platter. Pour the sauce over them and serve.

ROASTED RED SNAPPER WITH FRESH MINT

serves 4

1 3-pound red snapper, cleaned
salt to taste
black pepper to taste
15 fresh mint sprigs
3 tablespoons olive oil
1 teaspoon paprika
½ cup Clarified Butter
3 tablespoons lemon juice

Preheat the oven to 400°F.

Season the cavity of the fish with salt and pepper. Stuff the cavity with 7 of the mint sprigs. Close the cavity with wooden toothpicks. Rub the outside of the fish with the olive oil, salt and pepper. Put the fish on a rack in a baking pan. Sprinkle the paprika over the fish. Bake for 45 minutes.

While the fish roasts, chop the remaining mint sprigs. Put the clarified butter in a small saucepan over low heat. Add the chopped mint and lemon juice and mix well. Simmer for 2 minutes. Strain the sauce through a cheesecloth, discarding the bits of mint that remain in the cloth.

Carefully transfer the fish to a serving platter. Remove the toothpicks. Pour the minted butter sauce over the fish and serve.

RED SNAPPER WITH GRAPEFRUIT

serves 4

4 8-ounce red snapper fillets
5 tablespoons vegetable oil
1 teaspoon paprika
1 teaspoon black pepper
4 tablespoons flour
1 carrot, cut into strips
½ sweet red pepper, cut into strips
½ green pepper, cut into strips
1 onion, sliced and broken into rings
2 garlic cloves, finely chopped
1 tablespoon slivered ginger root
1 cup orange juice
2 tablespoons white wine
1 small grapefruit, divided into segments,
each segment cut in half

Wash and dry the red snapper fillets. Rub each fillet with ½ tablespoon of the vegetable oil.

In a large, shallow bowl, combine the paprika, pepper and flour. Dredge each fillet in the flour mixture. Shake off any excess flour.

In a large skillet over medium heat, heat the remaining 3 tablespoons of oil. When the oil bubbles, put the fillets into the skillet. Cook them for 5 minutes. Carefully turn them and cook for 5 minutes more. Remove the fillets from the skillet and drain them on paper towels.

Carefully transfer the fillets to a lightly buttered casserole dish. Set aside. Preheat the oven to 325°F.

Return the skillet with the oil in it to low heat. Add the red and green peppers, carrots, onion, garlic, ginger root, orange juice and white wine. Simmer for 15 minutes.

Pour the contents of the skillet over the fish. Add the grapefruit. Cover the casserole dish and bake for 15 minutes. Serve hot.

SMOKED RED SNAPPER

serves 6

4 pounds red snapper fillets
2 garlic cloves, finely chopped
grated rind of 1 lemon
salt to taste
black pepper to taste
¾ cup lemon juice
8 tablespoons butter
2 tablespoons Worcestershire sauce
½ teaspoon Tabasco sauce
1 tablespoon finely chopped parsley
1 teaspoon liquid smoke

Wash and dry the red snapper fillets. In a small bowl, combine the garlic, grated lemon rind and salt and pepper to taste. Rub the fillets with the mixture.

In a large skillet, melt the butter over low heat. Stir in the lemon juice, Worcestershire sauce, Tabasco sauce, liquid smoke and chopped parsley. Mix well.

Put the fillets into the skillet and cook over low heat for 1 hour, basting the fish with the sauce every 15 minutes. Use a loose-fitting cover over the skillet.

Cool to room temperature before serving.

Baked Fillets of Sole

serves 4

½ cup finely chopped mushrooms
2 shallots, finely chopped
1 teaspoon chopped chives
1 tablespoon chopped parsley
salt to taste
black pepper to taste
½ cup unflavored breadcrumbs
4 8-ounce sole fillets
½ cup shredded Swiss cheese
½ cup white wine
½ cup chicken broth

Preheat the oven to 350°F. Butter a shallow baking dish.

In a mixing bowl combine the mushrooms, shallots, chives, parsley, and salt and black pepper to taste. Sprinkle the bottom of the baking dish with half of the mushroom mixture. Sprinkle half the breadcrumbs over the mushroom mixture. Arrange the fillets on top of the breadcrumbs.

Top the sole fillets with the remaining mushroom mixture. Sprinkle the mushroom mixture with the remaining breadcrumbs. Top with the shredded Swiss cheese. Add the wine and chicken stock and bake for 20 to 25 minutes. Serve from the baking dish.

Sautéed Sole

serves 4

4 tablespoons flour
4 tablespoons cracker meal
salt to taste
black pepper to taste
3 tablespoons butter
3 tablespoons olive oil
4 8-ounce sole fillets
8 thin lemon slices
1 tablespoon lemon juice
⅓ cup hazel nuts
⅓ cup pine nuts
⅔ cup raisins

Turn oven on to the lowest setting.

In a large shallow bowl, combine the flour, cracker meal and salt and pepper to taste. Set aside.

In a large skillet, melt the butter and heat the olive oil over low heat.

While the butter mixture is heating, rinse the fillets and leave them damp. Roll the fillets in the flour mixture. Put them into the skillet and cook them for 3 minutes on each side.

Drain the fillets on paper towels, then transfer them to a serving platter. Put two slices of lemon on each fillet, then put the platter into the oven.

Add the lemon juice, hazelnuts and pine nuts to the skillet and cook, stirring frequently, for 3 minutes. Add the raisins and cook for 3 more minutes. Spoon the sauce over the fillets and serve.

Poached Sole

serves 4

4 6- to 8-ounce fillets of sole or flounder
1 tablespoon butter, cut into pieces
¼ cup finely chopped shallots
¼ teaspoon dried rosemary
½ teaspoon salt
¼ teaspoon black pepper
½ cup dry white wine
1 cup water
½ cup heavy cream
2 egg yolks

Preheat the oven to 350°F.

Generously butter a shallow baking dish large enough to hold the fillets in one layer. Sprinkle the shallots over the bottom of the pan.

Season the fillets on both sides with the rosemary, salt, and pepper. Arrange the fillets in the baking dish. Pour in the wine and water and dot the fillets with the butter.

Cover the dish with buttered waxed paper. Bake for 10 minutes or until the fillets flake easily. Remove the dish from the oven and transfer the fillets to a serving platter. Keep warm.

Strain the pan juices through a sieve into a saucepan. Quickly bring the liquid to a boil. Cook, uncovered, until the liquid is reduced to approximately 1 cup. Stir in the cream and cook over high heat, stirring constantly, until the mixture begins to thicken. Reduce the heat to very low.

In a small bowl beat the egg yolks. Pour ½ cup of the cream mixture into the egg yolks and whisk to blend. Slowly pour the yolk mixture back into the remaining cream mixture. Whisk constantly. Cook over very low heat for 2 to 3 minutes or until the sauce thickens. Be very careful not to let the sauce approach the boiling point or it may curdle. Remove the sauce from the heat and pour it over the fish fillets. Serve immediately.

POACHED SOLE WITH TOMATOES

serves 6

2 cups dry vermouth
2 large onions, sliced
4 parsley sprigs
1 bay leaf
2 tablespoons fresh basil leaves or
1 teaspoon dried basil
1 tablespoon black pepper
1 cup chopped celery
1 quart water
½ teaspoon dried thyme
1 teaspoon salt
1 cup cherry tomatoes
4 pounds sole or flounder fillets
4 egg yolks, beaten
1 cup heavy cream

To make the poaching liquid, combine the vermouth, onions, parsley, bay leaf, basil, pepper, celery, water, thyme and salt in a large pot. Simmer over low heat for 30 minutes.

Arrange the fillets on a large square of cheesecloth. Top with the cherry tomatoes and wrap the cheesecloth closed.

Strain the broth into a fish poacher or large covered skillet. Add the cheesecloth with the fish and tomatoes and simmer gently over low heat for 10 minutes.

Remove the fish and tomatoes from the poacher. Remove them from the cheesecloth and arrange them on a serving platter. Keep warm.

Whisk the egg yolks and cream into the broth remaining in the poacher. Cook over medium heat, stirring constantly, for 5 minutes or until the sauce thickens. Do not let the sauce boil.

Serve the fish topped wih the sauce and garnished with lemon slices.

167

SOLE WITH GREEN SAUCE

serves 4

4 8-ounce sole *or* flounder fillets
¾ cup fish stock
½ cup white wine *or* dry vermouth
2 bay leaves
6 whole black peppercorns
2 sprigs fresh dill

GREEN SAUCE:
½ cup finely chopped fresh parsley
½ cup finely chopped fresh dill
1 finely chopped garlic clove
finely chopped white part of
1 hard-cooked egg
¼ teaspoon dry mustard
2 tablespoons lemon juice *or*
wine vinegar
¼ teaspoon black pepper
½ cup vegetable *or* olive oil

Roll up the fillets and put them, seam-side down, into a large skillet. Add the fish stock, white wine, bay leaves, peppercorns and dill. Cover the skillet and simmer over medium heat until fish flakes easily with a fork, about 10 to 12 minutes. Turn off the heat, uncover the skillet and leave the fish in the skillet.

To make the green sauce, in a small bowl combine the parsley, dill, garlic, egg white, mustard, lemon juice or vinegar and black pepper. Mix well. Slowly blend in the oil to make a thick sauce.

Remove the fillets from the skillet with a slotted spoon. Place one fillet on each serving plate and top with the green sauce.

SOLE IN ORANGE SAUCE

serves 4

1 tablespoon butter
1 onion, finely chopped
1 tablespoon grated orange rind
½ cup orange juice
4 8-ounce sole fillets
2 tablespoons butter, melted
1 tablespoon chopped coriander
½ teaspoon salt
½ teaspoon black pepper
1 teaspoon tarragon vinegar

Preheat the broiler.

Melt 1 tablespoon of the butter in a saucepan. Add the onion and cook over medium heat for 5 minutes. Add the orange rind and orange juice. Stir well and bring the mixture to a boil. Remove the saucepan from the heat and set aside.

Arrange the fillets on a greased broiler pan. Brush them with the melted butter and sprinkle them with the coriander, salt and pepper. Broil the fillets until they are lightly browned, about 10 minutes. Do not turn the fillets.

Return the orange sauce to the heat and add the vinegar. Cook until the sauce is hot but hot boiling.

Arrange the fillets on a serving platter. Pour the orange sauce over the fillets and serve at once.

STUFFED SOLE IN CREOLE SAUCE

serves 6

7 tablespoons butter
4 tablespoons finely chopped onion
4 tablespoons finely chopped celery
2 tablespoons finely chopped sweet red pepper
2 tablespoons flour
½ cup light cream
½ cup fine unflavored breadcrumbs
½ teaspoon oregano
1 cup cooked crabmeat, flaked
1 cup cooked shrimp, chopped
4 tablespoons chopped parsley
2 teaspoons Worcestershire sauce
1 teaspoon Tabasco sauce
salt to taste
black pepper to taste
6 8-ounce sole fillets

CREOLE SAUCE:
2 tablespoons butter
4 cups canned tomatoes
2 garlic cloves, finely chopped
1 bay leaf
¼ teaspoon cayenne pepper
salt to taste
black pepper to taste
1 tablespoon flour

Preheat the oven to 350°F. In a large skillet melt 4 tablespoons of butter. Add to the butter the onion, celery and red pepper. Cook over low heat, stirring frequently, until the vegetables are tender, about 5 minutes. Carefully stir in the flour and continue stirring until smooth. Add the cream and continue over low heat, stirring constantly, until the mixture has thickened. Remove the skillet from the heat and add the breadcrumbs, oregano, crabmeat, shrimp, parsley, Worcestershire sauce, Tabasco sauce and salt and pepper to taste. Mix well.

Lay the sole fillets out on a working surface. Spoon one-sixth of the mixture on each fillet. Roll up the fillet and secure with a wooden toothpick. Melt the remaining butter in a small saucepan. Brush the stuffed sole with the melted butter. Put them into a baking dish and bake them for 20 minutes.

While the fish is cooking, prepare the Creole sauce. In a medium-sized saucepan melt half the butter. Add the tomatoes, garlic, bay leaf, cayenne pepper and salt and pepper to taste. Cook over medium heat for 20 minutes.

In a small saucepan, melt the remaining butter. Stir in the flour. Continue to cook over low heat, stirring constantly until flour turns light brown. Add the flour and butter mixture to the tomato mixture and stir until blended.

Reduce the oven temperature to 300°F. Remove the stuffed sole fillets from the oven. Pour the Creole sauce over the fillets. Bake for 30 minutes more. Serve hot.

BAKED SWORDFISH PARMESAN

serves 6

6 8-ounce swordfish steaks
4 tablespoons olive oil
½ teaspoon paprika
salt to taste
black pepper to taste
4 tablespoons cornmeal
4 tablespoon grated Parmesan cheese
½ cup flour
2 lemons, quartered

Wash and dry the swordfish steaks and set aside. Preheat the oven to 350°F.

Pour the olive oil into the broiler pan and blend in the paprika and salt and pepper to taste. On a plate combine the flour, cornmeal and Parmesan cheese.

Dip the steaks into the olive oil mixture, then roll them in the flour mixture. Pour the remaining olive oil from the pan, but leave enough to coat the bottom.

Arrange the steaks on the broiler pan and put into the oven for 5 minutes.

Preheat the broiler if it is separate from the oven.

Remove the pan from the oven and put it under the broiler. Broil for 15 minutes or until the crust on the fish is golden. Serve immediately, garnished with the lemon quarters.

BROILED SWORDFISH WITH SOY SAUCE BUTTER

serves 4

4 8-ounce swordfish steaks
salt to taste
black pepper to taste
4 tablespoons butter, softened
2 teaspoons soy sauce
1 teaspoon lemon juice
1 teaspoon paprika
1 lemon, quartered
parsley sprigs

Wash and dry the swordfish steaks. Season them on both sides with salt and pepper to taste. Put the steaks in a shallow, buttered baking dish. Preheat the broiler. (If the broiler is gas, be sure the baking dish is flameproof.)

In a small mixing bowl, combine the butter, soy sauce and lemon juice. Spread the mixture on the steaks.

Broil the fish for 8 minutes, turning the steaks once.

Transfer the fish to a serving platter, garnish with the lemon quarters and parsley sprigs and serve.

COATED SWORDFISH STEAKS

serves 4 to 6

2 pounds swordfish steaks
3 tablespoons olive oil
¼ teaspoon paprika
½ teaspoon salt
12 teaspoons cornmeal
4 teaspoons flour

Preheat the oven to 350°F.

Wipe but do not wash the fish. Pour the olive oil into a shallow, flameproof baking dish and blend in the paprika and salt.

Place the swordfish steaks in the dish, one at a time, and turn to coat both sides with the oil mixture. Place the fish in a shallow dish and sprinkle with the cornmeal and flour.

Return the fish to the baking dish and bake for 5 minutes. Remove the dish from the oven and place it under the broiler until the coating is golden brown, about 15 to 20 minutes. Do not turn the steaks as they broil.

MARINATED SWORDFISH STEAKS

serves 4

4 8-ounce swordfish steaks
½ cup olive oil
3 tablespoons soy sauce
2 tablespoons dry sherry
2 tablespoons lemon juice
1½ teaspoons finely chopped ginger root
1 teaspoon grated orange rind
salt to taste
black pepper to taste

Wash and dry the swordfish steaks and set aside.

In a mixing bowl, combine the olive oil, soy sauce, sherry, lemon juice, ginger, orange rind and salt and pepper to taste. Mix thoroughly.

Put the steaks into a baking dish in a single layer. Pour the marinade over them. Cover the dish and refrigerate for 4 hours.

Preheat the broiler. Put the steaks on the rack of the broiler pan and place under the broiler. Put the baking dish with the marinade into the oven to warm.

Broil the steaks for 6 minutes on each side, brushing with the marinade every 2 minutes.

Transfer the steaks to a serving platter. Pour the remaining marinade over them and serve.

SWORDFISH WITH APPLES

serves 4

4 8-ounce swordfish steaks
3 tablespoons butter
5 tablespoons brown sugar
2 large apples, peeled, cored and finely
chopped
½ teaspoon grated nutmeg
¼ teaspoon cinnamon

Wash and dry the swordfish steaks and set aside.

In a large skillet, melt the butter. When it is completely melted, add the brown sugar and mix well. Add the chopped apples, nutmeg and cinnamon and cook over low heat, stirring constantly, for 2 minutes.

With a slotted spoon move the apple mixture to one side of the skillet. Put the steaks into the skillet one at a time, covering each steak with one-fourth of the mixture. Cover the skillet and cook over low heat for 10 minutes, or until the fish flakes when touched with a fork.

SWORDFISH WITH PEAS

serves 4

4 8-ounce swordfish steaks
½ cup olive oil
1 garlic clove, crushed
salt to taste
black pepper to taste
1 cup thick tomato juice
1 cup shelled fresh peas or thawed
frozen peas
1 teaspoon finely chopped parsley

Heat the oil in a large skillet over medium heat. Add the garlic and the swordfish steaks. Brown the steaks on one side. Turn the steaks and sprinkle them with salt and pepper. Remove the garlic and add the tomato juice. Bring the liquid to a boil. Reduce the heat and simmer for 15 to 20 minutes, or until the fish flakes easily.

Remove the fish from the skillet and set aside in a warm place.

Add the peas to the skillet and cook until they are tender, about 3 to 5 minutes. Return the fish to the skillet and cook until the steaks are heated through, about 1 minute.

Arrange the steaks on a serving platter. Pour the peas and tomato sauce over the steaks and garnish with the chopped parsley. Serve hot.

BROILED TILE FISH WITH PARSLEY BUTTER

serves 4

4 8-ounce tile fish steaks
salt to taste
black pepper to taste
1 tablespoon butter, softened
2 tablespoons finely chopped parsley
1 teaspoon lemon juice

Preheat the broiler.

In a small bowl blend the butter with the parsley and lemon juice. Mix well.

Sprinkle the tile fish steaks on both sides with salt and pepper to taste. Spread the top sides of the steaks with the parsley butter.

Arrange the steaks in a broiling pan. broil for 8 to 10 minutes. Do not turn the steaks. Serve hot.

TILE FISH IN MUSTARD CREAM SAUCE

serves 6

6 8-ounce tile fish steaks
1 cup white wine
1 teaspoon salt
1 teaspoon cayenne pepper
4 tablespoons butter
2 tablespoons olive oil
3 tablespoons Dijon-style mustard
3 tablespoons lemon juice
6 tablespoons light cream
½ teaspoon paprika

Wash and dry the tile fish steaks. Sprinkle them with the salt and cayenne pepper.

Melt the butter in a large skillet. Blend in the olive oil. Over medium heat, brown the steaks lightly on each side, then carefully pour in the wine. Partially cover the skillet, reduce the heat and simmer the steaks for 10 minutes.

While the steaks are simmering, in a small saucepan combine the mustard, lemon juice, cream and paprika. Cook over low heat, stirring constantly.

Carefully transfer the fish steaks to a serving platter, pour the sauce over them and serve.

BAKED TROUT

serves 4

4 8-ounce trout, cleaned
2 tablespoons plus 1 teaspoon butter
1 tablespoon water
3 tablespoons lemon juice
salt to taste
black pepper to taste
½ teaspoon oregano
2 tablespoons chopped chives
1½ teaspoons flour
1 cup heavy cream
½ cup garlic-flavored breadcrumbs

Rinse and dry the trout. Preheat the oven to 375°F.

Use 1 teaspoon of the butter to grease a baking dish large enough to hold all the fish in one layer. Put the fish into the dish and add the water, lemon juice, oregano, chives and salt and pepper to taste. Bake the fish for 10 minutes.

In a small saucepan melt 1 tablespoon of the butter over low heat. Add the flour and stir until well blended. Slowly stir in the cream. Cook, stirring constantly, until the sauce thickens.

Remove the fish from the oven and pour the sauce over them. Sprinkle the fish with the breadcrumbs. Melt the remaining butter and drizzle it over the top. Return the fish to the oven and bake for 15 minutes more. Serve immediately.

BROILED TROUT WITH SESAME SAUCE

serves 6

6 8-ounce trout
4 tablespoons butter, melted
4 tablespoons sesame seeds
3 tablespoons lemon juice
1 teaspoon finely chopped parsley
salt to taste
black pepper to taste

Preheat the broiler. Clean, wash and dry the trout. Cover the broiler with heavy aluminum foil. Grease the foil. Put the fish in the pan and set aside.

In a small saucepan, melt the butter over low heat. Remove the pan from the heat and mix in the sesame seeds, lemon juice, parsley and salt and pepper to taste.

Brush the fish with half of the sesame sauce. Put the pan in the broiler 4 inches below the heat. Cook for 6 minutes. Remove the pan from the broiler. Turn the fish carefully and brush the other side with the remaining sauce. Cook for 5 more minutes, or until the fish flakes with the touch of a fork. Transfer to a serving platter and serve immediately.

BUTTER-STUFFED TROUT

serves 4

1 4-pound trout, cleaned
2 tablespoons dry sherry
¾ cup butter
1 scallion, chopped
2 tablespoons chopped parsley
½ cup finely chopped mushrooms
1 garlic clove, crushed
1 teaspoon salt
black pepper to taste
1 cup dry white wine
1 cup heavy cream
2 egg yolks
¼ cup brandy, warmed

Rinse the fish and pat it dry. Brush the inside of the fish with the sherry. Chill the fish for 2 hours.

Preheat the oven to 375°F.

In a small bowl cream the butter and scallion together. Add the parsley, mushrooms, garlic, and 1 teaspoon salt. Mix until well combined.

Remove the fish from the refrigerator and place it in a baking pan. Spread the remaining mixture on the outside of the fish. Pour the wine over the fish and bake for 45 minutes. Baste frequently.

Remove the fish from the refrigerator and place it in a baking pan. Spread the mixture on the outside of the fish. Pour the wine over the fish and bake for 45 minutes. Baste frequently.

In a small saucepan combine the cream and egg yolks. Slowly beat the hot liquid into the egg mixture. Cook over low heat for 2 to 3 minutes, stirring constantly. Season with salt and pepper to taste.

Pour the heated brandy over the fish. Carefully light the brandy and baste the fish with the spirit until the flame dies out. Pour the cream sauce over the fish and serve immediately.

PAN-FRIED TROUT

serves 4

4 8-ounce trout
2 teaspoons salt
1 teaspoon black pepper
½ teaspoon oregano
½ cup flour
½ cup yellow cornmeal
3 tablespoons butter
6 tablespoons vegetable oil
1 lemon, quartered

Clean the fish, leaving the heads and tails intact. Mix together the salt, pepper and oregano. Rub the cavity of each fish with the mixture.

In a large, shallow bowl, combine the flour and the cornmeal. Set aside.

Melt the butter and heat the vegetable oil in a large skillet until the mixture is very hot.

Roll each fish in the flour mixture until completely coated. Shake off any excess flour and carefully put it into the skillet. Cook the fish for 5 minutes on each side. Carefully remove the fish, drain them on paper towels, then transfer to a serving platter. Garnish with the quartered lemon and serve.

POACHED TROUT WITH SCALLIONS

serves 4

4 small whole trout, cleaned
1 cup water
⅛ teaspoon salt
¾ cup chopped scallions
1 cup dry white wine
1 tablespoon butter
3 tablespoons flour
2 cups milk
1 teaspoon salt
½ teaspoon black pepper
⅛ teaspoon cayenne pepper
1 egg yolk, beaten

In a large saucepan combine the water, ⅛ teaspoon salt, and wine. Bring to a boil. Add the fish and lower the heat slightly. Cover the saucepan and poach the fish for 4 minutes.

Melt the butter in a skillet. Add the scallions and sauté for 2 to 3 minutes. Add the flour. Stir well and cook for 5 minutes longer. Add the milk, salt, pepper, and cayenne pepper. Stir until well blended.

Remove the skillet from the heat and stir in the egg yolk. Do not return the skillet to the heat.

Remove the trout from the poaching liquid and place them on a platter. Pour the sauce over the fish and serve.

PARMESAN FRIED TROUT

serves 4

4 8-ounce trout
salt to taste
black pepper to taste
½ cup flour
4 tablespoons cornmeal
4 tablespoons unflavored
breadcrumbs
4 tablespoons grated Parmesan cheese
2 eggs
1 cup olive oil
8 tablespoons butter
¼ cup lime juice
2 tablespoons finely chopped chives
1 teaspoon paprika

Clean the fish, leaving the heads and tails intact. Rub the inside and outside of each fish with salt and pepper. Set aside.

Put the flour into a shallow bowl. In another shallow bowl combine the cornmeal, breadcrumbs and Parmesan cheese. In a third bowl, beat the eggs. Dredge each fish in the flour, then dip it in the egg. Next, roll each fish in the cornmeal mixture, coating it evenly.

In a large skillet, heat the olive oil over medium heat. When the oil starts to bubble, carefully put the fish into the skillet. Cook for 5 minutes on each side.

While the fish are cooking, melt the butter in another skillet. Remove the skillet from the heat and stir in the lime juice, chives and paprika.

When the fish are cooked, drain them on paper towels, arrange them on a serving platter, pour the sauce over them and serve.

TROUT WITH ALMONDS AND PINE NUTS

serves 4

4 8-ounce trout
3 tablespoons olive oil
1 teaspoon oregano
½ teaspoon salt
1 teaspoon black pepper
1 teaspoon paprika
6 tablespoons butter
3 tablespoons lemon juice
2 tablespoons dry sherry
2 tablespoons finely chopped parsley
4 tablespoons sliced almonds
4 tablespoons pine nuts

Clean the trout and rub them with the olive oil. Combine the oregano, salt, pepper and paprika. Put the fish on a platter and rub the inside and outside of each one with the oregano mixture. Set aside.

In a large skillet melt 4 tablespoons of the butter. Add the lemon juice, sherry and parsley and mix well. Add the almonds and pine nuts and cook over low heat until they start to turn golden.

With a large spoon, push the nuts to one side of the skillet. Add the remaining butter. When it has melted, put the fish into the skillet, covering each one with some of the nuts. Partly cover the skillet and cook the fish over low heat for 15 minutes on each side, or until they flake with the touch of a fork. Transfer the fish to a serving platter and serve.

TROUT IN RED WINE

serves 6

1 cup dry red wine
½ cup olive oil
½ cup cold water
½ cup finely chopped onions
1 teaspoon dried mint
½ teaspoon dried rosemary
1 teaspoon dried thyme
1 bay leaf, crumbled
½ teaspoon black pepper
½ teaspoon salt
6 trout, cleaned
3 egg yolks, beaten

In a large baking dish, combine all the ingredients except the trout and egg yolks. Mix well. Add the trout and marinate at room temperature for 40 minutes.

Preheat the oven to 350°F.

Stir the beaten egg yolks into the marinade. Bake, covered, for 25 minutes. Serve hot.

TROUT WITH SEAFOOD SAUCE

serves 6

2 onions, diced
6 8-ounce trout fillets
salt to taste
black pepper to taste
paprika
½ cup lemon juice
6 tablespoons butter
2 tablespoons flour
9 large cooked shrimp, shelled, deveined
and chopped
4 large black olives, chopped
6 large white mushrooms, coarsely
chopped
1 dozen small oysters, shelled
½ cup dry white wine
grated Cheddar cheese

Preheat the oven to 350°F.

Grease a baking dish with some butter, and spread the onion on the bottom. Lay the trout fillets side by side on top of the onions. Season them with salt and pepper and a dusting of paprika. Spoon ¼ cup of the lemon juice over each fillet. Bake the fillets for 25 minutes.

While the fillets are baking, prepare the sauce. Melt the butter in a skillet over low heat. Slowly blend in the flour. Slowly stir in the remaining lemon juice, then add the shrimp, olives, mushrooms, oysters and wine. Simmer the sauce in the skillet until the shrimp and oysters are opaque and the mushrooms are soft and tender, about 8 to 12 minutes.

When fillets have cooked for 25 minutes, remove the baking dish from the oven. With a spatula, remove four of the fillets. Arrange the remaining fillets in the center of the dish so that they overlap slightly. Spoon some of the seafood sauce over the two fillets. Use the spatula to lay two more fillets on top, being careful not to break the fillets. Spoon on more sauce, and repeat a with last two fillets and the remainder of the sauce.

Sprinkle the fish with the grated cheese and dust with a little paprika for color. Return the dish to the oven and bake for another 10 to 12 minutes, or until the cheese has melted and the sauce is piping hot. Serve in the baking dish.

BAKED TUNA STEAKS

serves 6

6 fresh tuna steaks
salt to taste
black pepper to taste
½ teaspoon grated nutmeg
1½ cups clam juice
4 tablespoons butter
½ teaspoon oregano
½ teaspoon white pepper
4 teaspoons tomato paste
3 tablespoons lemon juice

Wash and dry the fillets and put them into a large buttered baking dish. Preheat the oven to 350°F.

Sprinkle the fish with ¼ teaspoon of salt, ¼ teaspoon of black pepper and the nutmeg. Pour the clam juice over the fish. Cover the dish with aluminum foil. Bake the fish for 30 minutes.

Carefully transfer the fish to a serving platter and return it to the oven, but turn the oven off.

Pour the juice from the baking dish into a saucepan. Add the butter, oregano, white pepper, tomato paste and the lemon juice. Season to taste with salt and black pepper. Cook over medium heat, stirring constantly, until the sauce is hot and well-blended.

Remove the platter from the oven, pour the sauce over the fish and serve.

TUNA IN LIME MARINADE

serves 6

6 8-ounce fresh tuna steaks
¾ cup lime juice
2 garlic cloves, finely chopped
6 tablespoons olive oil
1½ teaspoons finely chopped fresh ginger
1 teaspoon slivered lime rind
1 teaspoon finely chopped parsley
salt to taste
black pepper to taste

Wash the tuna steaks, dry with paper towels and set aside.

In a large shallow bowl combine the lime juice, garlic, olive oil, ginger, lime rind, parsley and salt and pepper to taste. Put the tuna steaks in the bowl and turn them several times to coat them well. Cover the bowl and refrigerate for 4 hours.

Preheat the broiler. Put the tuna steaks on the rack in the broiler pan. Broil for 6 minutes on each side, basting every 2 minutes with the marinade. Put the rest of the marinade in a saucepan and cook over low heat. When the tuna is cooked, transfer the steaks to a serving platter, pour the hot marinade over them and serve.

ORIENTAL TUNA

serves 4

1½ pounds fresh tuna fillets, skin removed
6 tablespoons soy sauce
2 tablespoons olive oil
½ cup slivered almonds
2 ¼-inch slices ginger root
2 leeks, white part only, chopped
½ cup sliced canned bamboo shoots, drained
8 canned straw mushrooms, drained
8 tablespoons dry sherry
½ sweet red pepper, chopped
½ green pepper, chopped

Wash and dry the tuna fillets and cut them into strips 2 inches long and ¼ inch wide. Put the tuna pieces on a plate, sprinkle with 2 tablespoons of the soy sauce and set aside.

In a large skillet, heat 1 tablespoon of the olive oil. Add the fish and cook over high heat, stirring constantly, for 3 minutes. Transfer the fish and the juices to a plate and set aside.

Add the remaining 1 tablespoon olive oil to the skillet. Add the almonds and ginger root and cook, stirring constantly, for 2 minutes. Add the sherry, remaining soy sauce, leeks, mushrooms, bamboo shoots, red pepper and green pepper and simmer over low heat, stirring frequently, for 8 minutes, or until the vegetables are soft.

Return the fish to the skillet and cook over low heat, stirring frequently, for 5 minutes. Serve.

TUNA WITH SNOW PEAS AND MUSHROOMS

serves 6

2 pounds fresh tuna fillets, skin removed
salt to taste
black pepper to taste
½ teaspoon cayenne pepper
3 tablespoons lemon juice
4 tablespoons butter
¼ cup water
1 white onion, halved and thinly sliced
6 ounces snow peas
8 ounces canned straw mushrooms, drained
4 white radishes, thinly sliced
1 tablespoon finely chopped parsley
¼ cup olive oil

Wash and dry the tuna fillets. Cut them into 1-inch cubes. Season to taste with salt and pepper and set aside.

Combine the butter and the water in a large skillet and bring to a simmer. Add the onion, snow peas, mushrooms and radishes. Cook, stirring constantly, until the snow peas are tender but still crisp. Remove the skillet from the heat and stir in the parsley, lemon juice and cayenne pepper. Cover to keep warm.

In another skillet, heat the olive oil. Add the tuna cubes and cook, over medium-high heat, for 3 minutes, stirring carefully and constantly with a slotted spoon.

Transfer the vegetables to a serving dish. Add the tuna. Toss gently and serve.

BROILED WEAKFISH WITH DRAWN BUTTER SAUCE

serves 4 to 6

6 8-ounce weakfish fillets
2 tablespoons tarragon vinegar
2 tablespoons olive oil
¼ teaspoon black pepper
½ teaspoon salt
1 lemon, quartered

DRAWN BUTTER SAUCE:
3 tablespoons flour
3 tablespoons melted butter
¼ teaspoon salt
¼ teaspoon black pepper
1½ cups hot water
3 tablespoons butter, cut into small pieces
1 teaspoon lemon juice

Preheat the broiler.

Wash and dry the fillets. Rub them with the vinegar.

In a small bowl combine the olive oil, salt, and pepper. Roll the fillets in the oil mixture.

Place the fillets in a greased broiler pan and broil slowly, turning frequently and basting with the olive oil mixture, until the fish flakes easily with a fork.

To make the drawn butter sauce, combine the butter, melted butter, salt, and pepper in a medium-sized saucepan. Slowly stir in the hot water and bring to a boil over moderate heat. Cook for 5 minutes.

Lower the heat and add the pieces of cut-up butter alternately with the lemon juice. Stir well until the butter is melted. Serve the sauce hot over the fish. Garnish with the lemon quarters.

WHITEFISH WITH LEMON BUTTER SAUCE

serves 4

1 3-pound whitefish, cleaned
3 tablespoons lemon juice
1 teaspoon paprika
¼ pound butter, melted
½ teaspoon salt
½ teaspoon black pepper
2 lemons, quartered

Remove the head and tail from the whitefish. Split the fish down the back and remove the backbone. Preheat the broiler.

Put the fish in a shallow flameproof baking dish or on a broiler pan covered with aluminum foil, skin-side down. In a small saucepan combine the lemon juice, butter, paprika and salt and pepper to taste. Cook over low heat until the sauce is hot. Brush the fish generously with the sauce.

Broil the fish for 30 minutes, basting with the sauce every 5 minutes. When the fish flakes easily with a fork, remove it from the broiler and carefully transfer it to a serving platter. Pour the remaining sauce over the fish. Serve garnished with the lemon quarters.

WHITEFISH WITH WALNUT SAUCE

serves 4

4 8-ounce whitefish fillets
1 teaspoon salt
2 carrots, thinly sliced
1 leek, thinly sliced
2 onions, chopped
4 tablespoons celery leaves
1 teaspoon finely chopped parsley
4 garlic cloves, finely chopped
1 cup finely chopped walnuts
2 tablespoons flour
1 garlic clove, crushed
1 teaspoon sugar
½ teaspoon black pepper

Wash and dry the fillets and rub with the salt. Set aside.

Put the carrots, leek, onions, celery leaves, parsley and chopped garlic into a large pot with enough water to cover. Bring the liquid to a boil, reduce the heat, and simmer for 30 minutes.

Cut each fillet into 3 or 4 pieces and add them to the pot. Cook for 10 more minutes. Remove the pot from the heat and set aside to cool.

Grind the walnuts very finely and put them into a bowl with the flour and crushed garlic. Mix well. Add enough cold water to make a thick paste. Add the pepper, sugar, and 2 tablespoons of liquid from the fish mixture. Transfer the sauce to a saucepan. Cook over medium heat, stirring frequently, for 20 minutes, or until the sauce is creamy, but not too thick.

Use a slotted spoon to transfer the fish and vegetables from the pot to a serving platter. Spoon the sauce over the fish and serve.

WHITING WITH MUSHROOMS

serves 4

4 8-ounce whiting, cleaned
½ cup milk
¼ cup flour
9 tablespoons butter
1 onion, finely chopped
½ pound mushrooms, coarsely chopped
salt to taste
black pepper to taste
⅛ teaspoon nutmeg
3 tablespoons lemon juice
1 tablespoon chopped parsley

Dip the fish into the milk and then dredge them in the flour.

Melt 3 tablespoons of the butter in a heavy skillet. Add the fish and sauté on one side until browned. Turn the fish and sauté until the other sides are browned. Remove the fish from the skillet and arrange them on a serving dish. Set aside in a warm place.

Heat 3 more tablespoons of the butter in the skillet. Add the onions and sauté until they are transparent, about 3 minutes. Add the mushrooms and sauté for 4 minutes. Add the salt, pepper and nutmeg and sauté for 1 minute longer. Pour the mushroom mixture over the fish.

Heat the remaining butter in the skillet over high heat until it begins to turn brown. Add the lemon juice and parsley. Pour the butter sauce over the fish and serve.

Molluscs

Abalone Steak

serves 4

4 abalone steaks
2 eggs
½ teaspoon salt
¼ teaspoon black pepper
1½ cups unflavored breadcrumbs
6 tablespoons butter
1 lemon, thinly sliced

Lay the abalone steaks flat on a hard surface. With a kitchen mallet or the flat side of a cleaver, pound the steaks until they are about ⅓-inch thick.

In a small bowl beat the eggs. Add the salt and pepper and stir well. Dip each abalone steak into the eggs and then roll it in the breadcrumbs.

In a large skillet, melt 4 tablespoons of the butter over moderate heat. Add the abalone steaks and sauté until lightly browned on one side, about 2 to 3 minutes. Turn and brown on the other side. Do not overcook or the steaks will be very tough.

Remove the steaks to a serving platter. Melt the remaining butter in the skillet and pour it over the steaks. Serve with lemon slices.

Clam Fritters

serves 4

2 cups finely chopped clams
2 egg whites
2 egg yolks
1 cup fine unflavored breadcrumbs
1 tablespoon finely chopped chives
salt to taste
black pepper to taste
⅓ cup milk
½ cup olive oil

Beat the egg whites in a bowl until they are stiff.

In a mixing bowl beat the egg yolks until they are thick. Add the clams, breadcrumbs, chives, salt and pepper. Mix well. Stir in the milk. Fold in the egg whites.

Heat the olive oil in a heavy deep skillet over medium heat. Carefully drop the clam batter by teaspoons into the oil. Do not crowd the skillet. Cook, turning once, until the fritters are browned on both sides, about 5 minutes.

Drain the fritters on paper towels. Transfer to a serving platter and serve hot with lemon wedges.

CLAM OMELET

serves 4

2 tablespoons melted butter
6 eggs, separated
6 tablespoons butter
1 cup milk
½ teaspoon salt
¼ teaspoon black pepper
1 cup chopped clams

Melt the butter in an omelet pan over low heat.

Meanwhile, beat the egg yolks in a bowl until blended. Add the milk, stir well, and add the salt, pepper and clams. Stir and add the 2 tablespoons melted butter.

In a separate bowl, beat the egg whites until they are stiff but not dry. Fold the whites into the egg yolk mixture.

Pour the egg mixture into the omelet pan (the butter should all be melted by now). With a spatula, lift the omelet as it sets so that the butter reaches every part. When the omelet is golden brown, fold it and serve very hot.

CLAM OMELET WITH MUNSTER CHEESE

serves 4

6 eggs
1 cup milk
1 cup chopped cooked clams
3 scallions, chopped
¼ cup chopped mushrooms
½ teaspoon cayenne pepper
salt to taste
black pepper to taste
6 tablespoons butter
½ pound grated Munster cheese

In a large mixing bowl beat the eggs. Add the milk, clams, scallions, mushrooms, cayenne pepper and salt and pepper to taste. Mix well.

In each of two identically sized skillets, melt 3 tablespoons of the butter over low heat. When the butter is very hot, pour half the egg mixture into each skillet. Cover the skillets loosely and cook over medium heat for 5 minutes. Use a spatula occasionally to loosen the egg from the bottoms of the skillets.

Sprinkle the cheese over the top of the eggs in one of the skillets. Using two spatulas, quickly but carefully transfer the omelet without the cheese onto the top of the omelet with the cheese. Cut the omelet into 4 wedges and serve.

STEAMED CLAMS

serves 6

2 cups water
1 small onion, sliced
100 clams, in the shell
1 cup butter
3 tablespoons lemon juice
1 teaspoon oregano
½ teaspoon paprika
salt to taste
black pepper to taste

In a large pot, bring the water to a boil. Add the onion. Return to a boil.

Scrub the clams thoroughly and put them into the boiling water. Cook until all the shells open. Discard any clams that do not open.

Transfer 2 tablespoons of the cooking liquid to a saucepan. Add the butter and cook over low heat until it melts. Blend in the lemon juice, oregano, paprika and salt and pepper to taste.

While the sauce is heating, drain the clams and arrange them on a serving platter. Pour the sauce into small bowls for dipping and serve.

STEAMED SOFT-SHELL CLAMS

serves 6

100 soft-shell clams
1 cup melted butter
1 small onion, sliced
1 tablespoon lemon juice

Scrub the clams thoroughly. Place them in a large pot with 1 cup cold water and the sliced onion. Cover the pot tightly and bring to a boil, stirring once or twice. Do not let the clams come to a frothy boil. After 5 to 8 minutes, all the clams should be opened. Discard any clams that do not open. Remove them from the pot and save the broth.

Strain the broth through a piece of cheesecloth and serve the clams.

Melt the butter and mix in the lemon juice. Serve with the clams for dipping.

FRIED CLAM CAKES

serves 6

2 tablespoons butter
½ shallot, finely minced
1¼ cups soft, unflavored breadcrumbs
2 eggs, beaten
2 cups chopped cooked clams
½ cup chopped celery
1 tablespoon lemon juice
2 tablespoons chopped parsley
½ teaspoon salt
white pepper to taste
½ cup heavy cream
1 egg
peanut *or* vegetable oil

Melt the butter in a saucepan. Add the shallot and sauté until tender.

Add ½ cup of the breadcrumbs, the clams, celery, lemon juice, parsley, salt and a dusting of white pepper. Cook over medium heat, stirring constantly, for 5 minutes.

Slowly fold the cream into the clam mixture, stirring with a wooden spoon until evenly blended.

Pour the clam mixture into a bowl, cover and chill for two hours.

In a shallow bowl, beat the egg thoroughly with a little water until it froths.

Spread the remaining breadcrumbs on a large plate.

Remove the clam mixture from the refrigerator, and shape into flat, 2-inch round cakes.

Dip each cake in the breadcrumbs, covering it completely. Then dip each cake in the beaten egg, and then coat again with another layer of breadcrumbs.

After each cake is prepared, set it on paper towels to dry. Allow the cakes to dry for at least 10 minutes.

Coat a skillet with a thin layer of peanut or vegetable oil, and fry the cakes, a few at a time, over moderate heat, until they are crisp and golden brown.

SUMMER CLAMBAKE

serves 18 to 20

18 lobsters (or 1 for each person), at least
1 pound each
36 ears corn, with the husks and silk
removed (save the husks)
18 baking potatoes in their skins, scrubbed
6 frying chickens, quartered
9 quarts steamer clams
4 pounds butter
salt and pepper shakers

Here's a feast that's perfect for an ocean or lakefront beach party! You'll need some special equipment before you start: a steel trash can with lid, enough wood for a large fire that will burn for at least an hour, a sand-dug fire pit, 18 large pieces of cheesecloth at least a yard square, a ball of twine, and a strong standing grill.

First, build a large hot fire in the pit. Then get at least two people to help you prepare the food.

Lay about ½ quart of the clams in the center of each cheesecloth square. Next build layers of lobster, corn, potatoes, and chicken on top of the clams, putting a thin layer of corn husks between each layer of food. When all the food has been piled in mounds on the cloth, draw in the corners of the cheesecloth and tie them tightly with twine so that they form closed sacks.

Take the corn husks (or seaweed if you're near the ocean) and put them in a thick layer in the bottom of the trash can. Add enough sea water or clear lake water to cover the layer of husks or seaweed.

Lay the food sacks in the trash can on top of the husks or seaweed and cover the can. Place the grill over the center of the fire, and carefully put the can on the grill. Place a heavy rock on the lid to secure it tightly.

Keep the fire hot and roaring for 1 hour while the food bakes. Check every 20 minutes or so to see if the food is becoming scorched. If it is, then the water is evaporating too quickly. Add small amounts of water to keep the can full of steam.

If the fire gets too high or a bit out of hand, douse it with water a little around the edges.

After the food has baked for a full hour, put out plenty of butter, salt and pepper and serve everyone with as much as they can eat.

MUSSELS IN BEER

serves 4

1½ cups beer
2 garlic cloves, finely chopped
½ teaspoon crushed hot red pepper flakes
1 bay leaf
2 parsley sprigs
5 pounds mussels
8 tablespoons butter
1 teaspoon Dijon-style mustard
1 teaspoon lemon juice
1 teaspoon soy sauce
1 tablespoon finely chopped parsley
salt to taste
black pepper to taste

Combine the beer, garlic, red pepper, bay leaf and parsley sprigs in a large pot. Bring to a boil.

Scrub and debeard the mussels. Put them into the beer mixture and cook until the shells open. Discard any mussels that do not open.

Melt the butter in a saucepan. Blend in the mustard, lemon juice, soy sauce, chopped parsley and salt and pepper to taste. Whisk to blend well and cook over low heat until the sauce is hot. Transfer the sauce to a serving bowl.

Drain the mussels. Divide the mussels into four soup bowls and serve with the sauce.

FRIED MUSSELS PARMESAN

serves 4

48 mussels, about 4 pounds, scrubbed and debearded
2 eggs
2 tablespoons cold water
4 tablespoons unflavored breadcrumbs
1 teaspoon garlic powder
4 tablespoons grated Parmesan cheese
1 cup olive oil

Put the mussels into a steamer basket and steam them over boiling water until the shells open, about 6 minutes. Discard any mussels that do not open.

Remove the mussels from the shells and discard the shells. Dry the mussels on paper towels.

In a small bowl beat the eggs and cold water together. On a plate mix together the breadcrumbs, garlic powder and Parmesan cheese.

Dip the mussels into the egg mixture and then roll them in the breadcrumb mixture.

Heat the olive oil in a skillet over medium heat until it is very hot. Add the mussels and fry them until they are golden brown. Drain on paper towels and serve hot.

COLD MUSSELS IN SPICY SAUCE

serves 4

5 pounds mussels, scrubbed, cleaned and
debearded
¾ cup dry white wine
½ cup olive oil
2 onions, very finely chopped
4 garlic cloves, very finely chopped
2 teaspoons ground cumin
2 pounds ripe tomatoes, peeled, seeded
and finely chopped
2 35-ounce cans Italian plum tomatoes,
drained and finely chopped
4 4-inch hot green chili peppers, seeded
and finely chopped
¼ cup finely chopped whole scallions
¼ cup finely chopped fresh coriander
leaves

Put the wine into a large heavy pot and add the mussels. Cover the pot and steam over high heat until the mussels open, about 5 to 8 minutes. Shake the pot occasionally. Discard any mussels that do not open.

Using a slotted spoon, transfer the mussels to a large, shallow baking dish. Reserve the liquid. Remove the top shells from the mussels and discard them. Loosen the mussels in the lower shells, but leave them in the shells. Loosely cover the dish with damp paper towels and plastic wrap. Refrigerate for 4 hours or overnight.

Strain the reserved cooking liquid into a bowl through a sieve lined with a double thickness of damp cheesecloth. Set aside.

Heat the olive oil in a skillet. When hot, add the onions and cook over moderate heat until softened, about 5 minutes. Add the garlic and cook, stirring constantly, until softened, about 2 to 3 minutes longer. Sprinkle the cumin over the onions and garlic and cook, stirring often, over low heat for 1 minute. Add the fresh and canned tomatoes and ¾ cup of the cooking liquid. Bring the mixture to a boil. Reduce the heat and simmer, stirring constantly, until the sauce has thickened slightly, about 10 minutes.

Add the chili peppers, scallions, salt and pepper. Stir well. Remove the skillet from the heat and let the sauce cool. Add the chopped coriander and stir well.

Remove the mussels from the refrigerator and arrange on four individual serving plates. Spoon the sauce into four individual small bowls and serve with the mussels for dipping.

FRIED MUSSELS

serves 4

48 mussels, about 4 pounds
2 eggs, beaten
½ cup unflavored breadcrumbs
1 cup olive oil
watercress for garnish
lemon slices for garnish

Scrub, rinse, and debeard the mussels.

Steam the mussels in a large pot until they open. Discard any mussels that do not open. Shell the mussels and reserve some of their liquid. Chill.

Dry the mussels thoroughly on paper towels. In a small bowl beat the eggs with 2 tablespoons of the cold mussel liquid. Dip the mussels in the egg mixture and roll in the breadcrumbs.

In a deep skillet heat the olive oil to 375°F. Add the mussels and fry until they are golden brown. Drain on paper towels. Serve hot, garnished with watercress and lemon slices.

MARINATED MUSSELS

serves 4

48 mussels about 4 pounds
½ cup water
1 onion, diced
1 teaspoon oregano
½ cup white wine
2 tablespoons dry sherry
3 tablespoons lemon juice
½ teaspoon cayenne pepper
½ teaspoon paprika
salt to taste
black pepper to taste
4 tablespoons olive oil
4 tablespoons butter
2 tablespoons finely chopped parsley

Scrub and debeard the mussels. Put them into a steamer basket and cook over boiling water until the shells open. Discard any mussels that do not open. Drain, remove the mussels from the shells and discard the shells. Set the mussels aside.

In a large glass or ceramic (not metal) bowl, combine the water, onion, oregano, white wine, sherry, lemon juice, cayenne pepper, paprika and salt and pepper to taste. Mix well. Stir in the olive oil. Mix well again and add the mussels to the bowl. Stir to make sure that all the mussels are covered by the marinade. Cover the bowl and refrigerate for 1 hour.

In a large skillet, melt the butter. With a slotted spoon, add the mussels to the skillet and stir. Add the marinade. Cook over medium heat, constantly basting the mussels with the marinade.

When the mussels are cooked, after about 8 minutes, transfer them from the skillet, using a slotted spoon, to a serving bowl. Sprinkle with the parsley and serve.

MUSSELS RAVIGOTE

serves 4 to 6

1 cup dry vermouth
2 parsley sprigs
3 shallots, quartered
1 small onion, quartered
1 garlic clove, crushed
1 teaspoon salt
1 tablespoon black pepper
80 fresh mussels, scrubbed and debearded

SAUCE:
4 shallots, minced
1 teaspoon dried tarragon
¼ teaspoon dried chervil
2 tablespoons red wine vinegar
2 tablespoons balsamic vinegar
¼ cup dry vermouth
1¼ cups mayonnaise
1 tablespoon drained capers
1 tablespoon minced fresh chives or
1 teaspoon dried chives
1 tablespoon black pepper
1 teaspoon salt
2 teaspoons Dijon-style mustard

Put the vermouth, parsley, shallots, onion, garlic, salt and pepper into a large saucepan. Stir well and add the mussels. Cover and steam until the mussels have opened, about 5 to 10 minutes. Discard any unopened mussels. Drain well. Fully open the cooked mussels, discarding the empty half shell. Do not remove the mussels from their shells.

Put the shallots, tarragon, chervil, red wine vinegar, balsamic vinegar and vermouth in a small saucepan. Cook over high heat until most of the liquid is gone.

Put the shallot mixture into the container of a food processor or blender. Add the mayonnaise, capers, chives, salt, pepper and mustard. Blend until the sauce is well mixed.

Refrigerate the mussels and sauce until ready to serve, but no longer than 24 hours.

HANGTOWN FRY

serves 4

12 oysters, shelled
flour
salt to taste
black pepper to taste
9 eggs
fine unflavored breadcrumbs
3 tablespoons butter

Drain the oysters thoroughly on paper towels.
Beat 1 egg in a small bowl.
Place the breadcrumbs in another small bowl.

Combine the flour, salt, and pepper in a bowl. Dip each oyster into the flour mixture, then into the egg, and then into the breadcrumbs to coat well.

Heat the butter in a large skillet. Add the oysters and fry until golden brown on both sides, about 3 minutes.

Beat the remaining 8 eggs with salt and pepper to taste. Pour the eggs over the oysters in the skillet. Cook until the eggs are firm on the bottom. Turn the eggs with a large spatula and continue to cook on the other side for 1 to 2 minutes. Remove from the skillet and serve.

Mussels in Rice

serves 6

48 mussels, about 4 pounds
7 tablespoons butter
2 tablespoons beef marrow
2 medium-sized onions, chopped
6 ounces uncooked rice
2 tablespoons lemon juice
½ cup white wine
½ teaspoon oregano
salt to taste
black pepper to taste
½ cup freshly grated Parmesan cheese

Scrub and debeard the mussels. Put them into a large pot with 1 cup of water. Steam the mussels until they open. Discard any mussels that do not open. Remove the mussels from the shells. Discard the shells. Set the mussels aside. Reserve the cooking liquid.

In a large skillet, melt 3 tablespoons of the butter. Blend in the beef marrow. Add the onions and cook over medium heat, stirring constantly until they are lightly browned. Add the rice and the reserved liquid. Mix well. Cover and cook the rice over low heat for 15 minutes.

Add the wine, lemon juice, oregano and salt and pepper to taste. Mix thoroughly. Continue to cook for 15 minutes, stirring occasionally.

Add the mussels to the rice and simmer for 10 more minutes. Melt the remaining butter.

Transfer the rice and mussels to a serving bowl. Sprinkle with Parmesan cheese and melted butter and serve.

Baked Oysters

serves 4

24 large oysters
3 tablespoons butter
1 tablespoon lemon juice
½ teaspoon ground oregano
¼ teaspoon cayenne pepper
salt to taste
black pepper to taste
2 teaspoons chopped chives

Preheat the oven to 375°F.

Scrub, rinse and dry the oysters. Put them into a baking pan. Bake the oysters for 3 minutes, or until they open.

While the oysters are baking, in a saucepan melt the butter. Blend in the lemon juice, oregano, cayenne pepper and salt and pepper to taste. Remove the saucepan from the heat and stir in the chives.

When the oysters open, remove them from the oven. Remove and discard the upper shells. Baste each oyster generously with the butter mixture. Bake the oysters for 3 more minutes. Serve hot.

SCALLOPED OYSTERS

serves 6

1 cup crushed corn flakes
1 cup unflavored breadcrumbs
salt to taste
black pepper to taste
2 tablespoons sherry
2 tablespoons light cream
8 tablespoons butter, melted
1 garlic clove, finely chopped
1½ pounds shucked oysters with liquid

Preheat the oven to 400°F. Butter a 2-quart baking dish.

In a large mixing bowl, combine the corn flakes and the breadcrumbs. Add salt and pepper to taste and stir in the sherry, cream, butter and garlic.

Drain the oysters and reserve the liquid.

Put a layer of the breadcrumb mixture on the bottom of the baking dish. Cover the crumbs with a layer of the oysters. Continue to make layers (not more than two layers of oysters) until you have used all the ingredients. The top layer should be the crumb mixture. Carefully pour the oyster liquid over the top. Bake for 20 minutes. Serve hot.

SCRAMBLED OYSTERS

serves 6

36 oysters
salt to taste
black pepper to taste
7 eggs, beaten
4 tablespoons light cream
½ cup unseasoned croutons
1 tablespoon butter
parsley sprigs

Shell and chop the oysters. Season them with salt and pepper.

Beat the eggs in a mixing bowl. Stir in the cream and add the croutons. Mix until the croutons are coated with the egg mixture.

Melt the butter in a skillet over moderate heat. Add the egg mixture. When the eggs begin to get firm, stir in the oysters. Cook for 30 seconds and stir well again. Serve garnished with the parsley sprigs.

STEAMED OYSTERS

serves 4

48 fresh oysters
8 tablespoons butter
2 tablespoons lemon juice
½ teaspoon cayenne pepper
salt to taste
black pepper to taste

Fill a large skillet halfway with water. Bring to a boil. Scrub, rinse and dry the oysters. Put the oysters into a steamer basket. Put the steamer basket on top of the skillet. Steam the oysters for 15 minutes, or until the shells open.

Melt the butter in a small saucepan. Blend in the lemon juice, cayenne pepper and the salt and pepper to taste. Heat the mixture over low heat, stirring consta...

Put the oysters on a large servi... Serve with the butter sauce on the ... dipping.

FETTUCCINI WITH SCALLOPS

serves 6

2 pounds scallops
½ pound carrots, julienned
⅓ cup plus 2 teaspoons olive oil
½ cup dry vermouth
½ teaspoon cayenne pepper
1 teaspoon finely chopped fresh thyme *or*
¼ teaspoon dried thyme
1 teaspoon oregano
2 garlic cloves, finely chopped
salt
2 large onions, thinly sliced
¼ cup lemon juice
4 tablespoons finely chopped parsley
2 tablespoons finely chopped chives
black pepper to taste
¾ pound fettuccini

Wash the scallops, dry them and cut each one in half. Set aside.

In a large skillet, combine the carrots, ⅓ cup of olive oil, vermouth, cayenne pepper, thyme, oregano, garlic and salt to taste. Bring to a simmer, cover the skillet and cook for 5 minutes. Add the onions and continue to simmer until the carrots and onions are tender, but still crisp. Transfer to a large glass bowl.

Add the scallops, lemon juice, parsley, chives and black pepper to taste to the mixture and mix thoroughly. Cover the bowl with aluminum foil and set aside. The scallops will "cook" in the mixture.

Bring 2 quarts of salted water to a boil and cook the fettuccini until it is *al dente*. Drain the fettuccini in a colander, rinse with cold water and drain well.

Transfer the fettuccini to a serving dish and toss with the remaining 2 teaspoons of olive oil. Pour the scallop mixture over the fettuccini and toss gently but well. Serve at room temperature.

FRIED SCALLOPS

serves 4

2 pounds bay scallops
4 tablespoons flour
4 tablespoons unflavored breadcrumbs
½ teaspoon cayenne pepper
4 tablespoons grated Romano cheese
1 tablespoon finely chopped parsley
1 egg
¼ cup milk
1 cup olive oil

Wash the scallops and put them on a clean kitchen towel to dry.

In a large shallow bowl combine the flour, breadcrumbs, cayenne pepper, Romano cheese and parsley. In another bowl, beat the egg and the milk together. Heat the olive oil in a large skillet to 375°F.

Dip the scallops into the egg mixture and then roll them in the flour mixture. Put the scallops into the oil and cook for 4 minutes, using tongs to turn them. Transfer the scallops to paper towels to drain. Serve immediately.

SAUTÉED SCALLOPS

serves 4

2 pounds bay scallops
4 tablespoons flour
4 tablespoons cracker meal
salt to taste
black pepper to taste
6 tablespoons butter
½ cup dry vermouth
3 tablespoons chopped chives

Wash and dry the scallops. Turn the oven to the lowest setting and put a serving platter into the oven to warm.

In a shallow bowl combine the flour, cracker meal and salt and pepper to taste. Add the scallops and roll them to coat all sides. Shake off any excess flour.

In a large skillet, melt the butter over low heat. Add the scallops to the skillet and cook over medium heat for 5 minutes, stirring gently and constantly. Transfer the scallops to the platter in the oven.

Add the vermouth to the skillet and bring to a boil. Stir and scrape loose the brown bits left in the skillet. Pour the sauce over the scallops, sprinkle with the chives and serve.

Scallops in Butter and Brandy Sauce

serves 4

2 pounds sea scallops
1 teaspoon salt
1 cup butter
4 tablespoons brandy
1 tablespoon chopped parsley

Wash the scallops and put them into a saucepan with the salt and enough water to cover. Bring the water to a simmer and gently cook the scallops for 3 minutes. Drain well in a colander.

While the scallops are draining, melt the butter in a large skillet over medium-high heat. Add the scallops. Cook, stirring gently, until the butter turns light brown.

In a small saucepan, heat the brandy until it sizzles. Carefully ignite the brandy and pour it over the scallops. When the flame dies out, transfer the scallops to a serving bowl, sprinkle with parsley and serve.

Scallops with Orange Sauce

serves 6

2 pounds bay or sea scallops
½ cup orange juice
2 teaspoons Worcestershire sauce
4 tablespoons light cream
3 egg yolks
½ cup dry white wine
½ teaspoon black pepper
4 tablespoons flour
½ teaspoon cayenne pepper
6 tablespoons butter

Sprinkle the scallops with 2 tablespoons of the orange juice.

Combine the cream, egg yolks, Worcestershire sauce, wine and remaining orange juice in the top half of a double boiler. Cook the sauce in the double boiler over boiling water, stirring constantly, until it thickens. Remove the sauce from the heat and set aside in a warm place.

Put the flour in a bowl and season it with the black pepper. Lightly dredge the scallops in the flour. Shake off any excess.

Melt 3 tablespoons of the butter in a skillet over medium heat. Add the scallops and sauté until they are golden, about 10 minutes. Drain the scallops on paper towels.

Reheat the sauce in the double boiler. Gradually stir in the remaining butter and the cayenne pepper.

Serve the scallops with the sauce on the side.

CRUSTACEANS

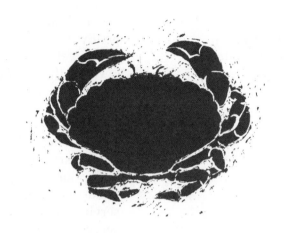

BOILED CRABS

serves 4

4 medium-sized whole crabs
salt to taste
8 tablespoons butter
1 tablespoon olive oil
1 tablespoon lemon juice
1 teaspoon oregano
½ teaspoon black pepper
2 garlic cloves, finely chopped

In a large pot, bring 8 quarts of water to a boil over high heat. While waiting for the water to boil, take a small sharp knife and insert the blade under the back of the top shell of one crab. Pry off the shell and remove the spongy parts underneath. Repeat with the other crabs. Wash them all thoroughly.

Add salt to the boiling water, then add the crabs. When the water returns to a boil, reduce the heat and simmer the crabs for 15 minutes.

While the crabs are cooking, in a small saucepan melt the butter. Add the olive oil, lemon juice, oregano, black pepper and garlic. Continue to stir until thoroughly mixed. Remove the saucepan from the heat.

When the crabs are ready, drain them and crack the claws and legs. Put the crabs on a serving platter. Divide the butter mixture into four small bowls and serve immediately.

BOILED DUNGENESS CRABS

serves 4

4 Dungeness crabs
8 quarts boiling water
½ cup salt
½ cup melted butter

Prepare the crabs by inserting the blade of a small knife under the back of the top shell. Pry the shell off. Remove the spongy parts under the shell and wash the body thoroughly.

Add the salt to the water. Place the crabs in the water and quickly return the water to the boiling point. Reduce the heat and simmer the crabs for 15 minutes. Drain.

Crack the claws and legs. Serve the crabs hot with melted butter.

CRAB LEGS CREOLE

serves 4

12 large crab legs
salt to taste
black pepper to taste
2 cups milk
4 tablespoons flour
8 tablespoons butter
2 garlic cloves, finely chopped
1 teaspoon oregano
2 tablespoons finely chopped parsley
1 teaspoon paprika
2 lemons, quartered

Shell the crab legs and remove the cartilage from the meat. Wash the legs and dry them thoroughly. Set aside.

In a large shallow bowl combine ¼ teaspoon salt, ¼ teaspoon pepper and the milk. Put the flour in another large, shallow bowl. Put the crab legs into the milk and soak them for 30 minutes.

A few minutes before the crab legs have finished soaking, in a small saucepan melt the butter. Add the garlic and oregano and mix well. Remove the pan from the heat and set aside.

Take the crab legs, one by one, from the milk and pat them lightly with the flour. Put the crab legs on a rack in the broiler pan. Turn on the broiler. Brush each leg with some of the butter mixture. Broil the crab legs for 15 minutes. Turn the legs carefully and broil the other side for 7 minutes.

Carefully transfer the crab legs to a serving platter. Pour the remaining butter mixture over them and sprinkle with parsley and paprika. Garnish with lemon quarters and serve.

FRIED CRAB LEGS

serves 6

18 crab legs
2 eggs
2 tablespoons milk
4 tablespoons flour
4 tablespoons cracker meal
4 tablespoons grated Parmesan cheese
12 tablespoons butter
2 garlic cloves, finely chopped
1 tablespoon lemon juice
1 teaspoon oregano

Shell the crab legs and remove the cartilage from the meat. Wash thoroughly. Put the crabmeat on a clean kitchen towel to dry.

In a small mixing bowl, beat the eggs. Add the milk and mix well.

In a large, shallow bowl, combine the flour, cracker meal and Parmesan cheese. Dip the crab legs first in the egg mixture, then dredge them in the flour mixture. Shake off any excess flour.

In a large skillet, over low heat, melt half the butter. Put the crab legs into the skillet, increase the heat to medium, and fry until they are browned and crisp on the edges. Turn and fry the other side.

While the crab legs are cooking, in a small saucepan melt the remaining butter. Add the garlic, lemon juice and oregano.

Drain the crab legs on paper towels. Transfer them to a serving platter and serve immediately with the butter mixture in a dish on the side for dipping.

CRAB CAKES

serves 6

2 pounds crab legs
4 tablespoons butter
2 medium-sized onions, finely chopped
1 cup soft unflavored breadcrumbs
3 eggs, beaten
1 teaspoon dry mustard
1 teaspoon Worcestershire sauce
salt
2 tablespoons light cream
½ cup flour
1 cup olive oil
3 lemons, quartered

In a large pot bring 2 quarts of water to a boil over high heat. Add the crab legs. When the water returns to a boil, reduce the heat. Simmer the legs for 15 minutes. Drain the crab legs, shell them, and remove the cartilage. Flake the meat into a large bowl.

In a large skillet, melt the butter. Add the onions and cook over low heat until they are soft but not brown. Pour the contents of the skillet over the crab meat. Add the breadcrumbs and mix thoroughly.

In a small bowl beat the eggs. Add the mustard, Worcestershire sauce and salt to taste. Mix well and add to the crab mixture. Then add the cream and mix thoroughly.

Shape the crab mixture into 12 cakes. Put the flour on a plate. Dredge the cakes in the flour.

Heat the olive oil in a large skillet. When the oil is hot, add the cakes. Fry until they are golden brown, about 3 minutes. Carefully turn the crab cakes and cook the other sides. Serve with the lemon quarters.

FRIED SOFT-SHELL CRABS

serves 6

12 soft-shell crabs
2 eggs, beaten
½ cup flour
½ teaspoon salt
¼ teaspoon pepper
½ cup butter

Rinse the crabs in cold water and dry them thoroughly.

In a small bowl, beat the eggs. In another bowl, combine the flour, salt and pepper. Dip the crabs in the eggs and then dredge them in the flour mixture. Shake off the excess flour.

Heat the butter in a skillet over low heat. Place in the skillet as many crabs as will lie flat at one time. Fry the crabs until they are browned and crisp on the edges. Turn and fry until the other side is browned. Serve very hot with butter.

BROILED SOFT-SHELL CRABS

serves 6

12 soft-shell crabs
½ pound butter
9 tablespoons lemon juice
⅛ teaspoon cayene pepper
salt to taste
black pepper to taste
½ cup flour

CREAM SAUCE:
1½ tablespoons butter
1 teaspoon flour
1 cup fish stock or water
salt to taste
black pepper to taste
2 egg yolks, beaten
¼ cup cream
1 tablespoon lemon juice

Preheat the broiler.

Wash the crabs in cold water and dry well.

In a small saucepan melt the butter. Add the lemon juice and cayenne pepper.

Sprinkle the crabs with salt and pepper. Dip them in the melted butter and then dredge them in the flour, shaking off the excess.

Arrange the crabs on a broiler rack and place it 4 inches from the heat for 8 minutes, turning the crabs frequently.

To make the cream sauce, melt the butter in the top of a double boiler over hot but not boiling water. Blend in the flour; stir in the fish stock or water. Simmer for 10 minutes and season with salt and pepper. Remove the sauce from the heat. Add the egg yolks and the cream. Return to the heat and cook, stirring constantly, for 3 minutes. Do not let the sauce boil. Add the lemon juice and serve immediately over the crabs.

SAUTÉED SOFT-SHELL CRABS

serves 6

12 soft-shell crabs
flour
2 tablespoons ground ginger
butter
salt to taste
black pepper to taste

Rinse the crabs thoroughly and drain well. Fill a small plastic or paper bag one-quarter full with flour. Add the ginger and mix. Put the crabs in the bag, one at a time, and shake until they are well coated with flour.

Melt enough butter in a skillet to fill it to a depth of ½ inch. Heat the butter until it bubbles. Add as many crabs to the skillet as will fit without the crabs touching each other. Dust the tops of the crabs with salt and pepper and fry until the crabs are golden brown on the bottom. Turn the crabs over, dust again with salt and pepper, and fry until golden brown on the other side. Fry all the crabs in this manner, adding more butter as needed.

Serve the crabs hot, with the butter and drippings spooned over them. Garnish with lemon slices.

SOFT-SHELL CRABS À LA CREOLE

serves 6

12 soft-shell crabs
2 cups milk
4 tablespoons flour
½ cup melted butter
salt to taste
black pepper to taste
2 lemons, quartered
parsley sprigs

Clean the crabs and rinse them well in cold water. Dry with a clean towel and season generously with salt and pepper.

Season the milk with salt and pepper. Place the crabs in the milk and soak them for 30 minutes.

Remove the crabs from the milk and pat them lightly with the flour. Shake off any excess. Brush each crab with melted butter.

Preheat the broiler.

Place the crabs on a rack set in a broiler pan. Broil until the crabs are a delicate brown, about 15 minutes. Turn the crabs over after about 7 minutes.

Serve on a platter garnished with lemon quarters and parsley. Pour a little melted butter and chopped parsley over the crabs. Serve hot.

SAUTÉED CRAB WITH PROSCIUTTO

serves 4

2 pounds crab legs
5 tablespoons sweet butter
6 tablespoons finely chopped shallots
1 teaspoon oregano
1 tablespoon lemon juice
4 teaspoons finely chopped parsley
1 teaspoon black pepper
16 thin slices prosciutto
1 lemon, quartered
watercress sprigs

In a large pot, bring 2 quarts of water to the boil. Add the crab legs. When the water returns to a boil reduce the heat. Simmer the legs for 10 minutes.

Drain the crab legs, shell them and remove the cartilage from the meat. Rinse and dry the meat on paper towels. Break up the meat and put it into a medium-sized bowl.

In a large skillet, over medium heat, melt the butter. Add the shallots. Cook, stirring constantly, for 2 minutes. Add the crabmeat and mix well. Add the lemon juice and oregano. Continue stirring until the crabmeat is hot.

Remove the skillet from the heat and stir in the parsley and black pepper. Mix well.

Arrange four slices of prosciutto on each of four warmed serving plates. Top with equal portions of the crab mixture. Garnish each plate with a lemon wedge and watercress sprigs, and serve.

BOILED CRAWFISH

serves 6

50 crawfish (crayfish)
1 garlic clove, chopped
1 teaspoon whole allspice
6 whole cloves
2 quarts white wine
3 tablespoons salt
1 teaspoon cayenne pepper
3 bay leaves
1 teaspoon Tabasco sauce

Wash and drain the crawfish. Set aside. Put the garlic, allspice and cloves on a small square of cheesecloth and tie closed with a piece of string to make a little pouch.

Bring 4 quarts of water to a boil in a very large pot. Add the herb pouch and continue to boil for 5 minutes.

Add the wine, salt, cayenne pepper, bay leaves, Tabasco sauce and the crawfish and bring the liquid back to a boil. Cook for 20 minutes or until the crawfish are bright red.

Remove the pot from the heat and let the crawfish cool in the liquid for 30 minutes. Drain the crawfish and serve with hot sauce.

CRAWFISH CREOLE

serves 6

2 bay leaves
¼ teaspoon whole cloves
12 black peppercorns
1 parsley sprig
1 cinnamon stick
2 cups milk
2 tablespoons butter
2 tablespoons flour
1 teaspoon cayenne pepper
1 teaspoon Tabasco sauce
1 teaspoon nutmeg
salt to taste
3 tomatoes, seeded and finely chopped
36 crawfish, shelled and diced
12 mushrooms, finely chopped

Put the bay leaves, cloves, peppercorns, parsley and cinnamon stick on a square of cheesecloth. Tie the square closed to make an herb bouquet. Set aside.

In a medium-sized saucepan, bring the milk to a boil over medium heat. While the milk heats, melt the butter in a large saucepan. Add the flour and cook, stirring often, for 3 minutes. When the milk boils, gradually stir it into the butter mixture. Stir in the cayenne pepper, Tabasco sauce, nutmeg and salt to taste. Add the herb bouquet and cook over medium heat for 15 minutes.

Remove the herb bouquet and add the tomatoes, crawfish meat and mushrooms. Cook over medium heat for 5 minutes, stiring often. Serve hot.

ORIENTAL LOBSTER

serves 4

½ cup peanut oil
2 garlic cloves, finely chopped
1 teaspoon Chinese black bean paste
½ pound ground pork
2 pounds cooked lobster, cut in chunks
1½ cups chicken broth
4 slices fresh ginger root
1 teaspoon sesame oil
1 teaspoon soy sauce
4 scallions, chopped
1 teaspoon cornstarch dissolved in
1 tablespoon water
2 eggs, beaten

Heat the oil in a wok or large skillet over high heat. Add the garlic and the black bean paste and cook, stirring constantly, for 30 seconds. Add the pork and stir fry for 30 seconds.

Add the lobster and stir fry for 30 seconds more.

Add the chicken broth, ginger, sesame oil, soy sauce, scallions and cornstarch mixture and cook, stirring frequently, for 4 more minutes. When the sauce begins to thicken pour in the eggs and stir once. Remove from the heat and serve.

BOILED CRAYFISH

serves 4 to 6

2 pounds live crayfish
2 quarts boiling water
2 tablespoons salt
1 tablespoon caraway seeds
1 teaspoon chopped fresh dill *or*
½ teaspoon dried dill

In a large pot, bring the water to a boil. Add the salt, caraway seeds and dill. Boil for 1 minute.

Drop the live crayfish into the boiling water. Cook for *exactly* 5 minutes.

Drain the crayfish well, chill them for 1 hour, and serve.

BROILED LOBSTER

serves 4

4 8-ounce lobster tails
½ pound butter
2 tablespoons unflavored breadcrumbs
2 tablespoons grated Romano cheese
1 teaspoon paprika
1 teaspoon oregano
1 tablespoon lemon juice
2 garlic cloves, finely chopped
1 tablespoon finely chopped parsley
1 lemon, quartered

Split the lobster shells and remove the tail meat intact. Put the tails on their backs on a rack in a broiler pan.

In a small saucepan, melt the butter over very low heat. As the butter begins to melt, brush each tail with about 1 tablespoon. Sprinkle ½ tablespoon of breadcrumbs, ½ tablespoon of cheese and ¼ teaspoon of paprika over each tail. Set the broiler pan aside and preheat the broiler.

To the butter in the saucepan add the oregano, lemon juice, garlic and parsley. Stir thoroughly. Remove the pan from the heat. Keep warm.

Put the lobster tails under the broiler. Broil the lobster for 10 minutes. Remove the pan from the broiler. Baste the lobster with the butter mixture. Turn the tails over and baste the other side. Broil for 8 minutes more.

Transfer the tails to a serving platter and garnish with the lemon quarters. Pour the remaining butter sauce into 4 small bowls for dipping. Serve immediately.

BOILED LOBSTER TAILS

serves 4

4 tablespoons salt
6 black peppercorns
1 bay leaf
4 8-ounce lobster tails
8 tablespoons butter
1 garlic clove, finely chopped
½ teaspoon oregano
1 teaspoon lemon juice
1 lemon, quartered

In a large pot, combine 4 quarts of water with the salt, peppercorns and bay leaf. Bring to a boil.

While waiting for the water to boil, remove the lobster meat from the shells. Wash and dry the meat.

Put the lobster into the boiling water. Cover the pot and bring the water back to a boil. Reduce the heat and simmer for 10 minutes.

In the top of a double boiler, over hot water, melt the butter. Stir in the garlic, oregano and lemon juice.

Carefully remove the lobster from the water and drain in a colander. Divide the butter mixture into 4 small bowls for dipping. Put the lobster on a serving platter, garnish with the lemon quarters and serve.

LOBSTER MARINARA

serves 4

¼ cup olive oil
2 garlic cloves, finely chopped
2 tablespoons finely chopped parsley
4 cups canned tomatoes
½ green pepper, finely chopped
1 large onion, finely chopped
¼ cup white wine
¼ teaspoon cayenne pepper
3 tablespoons lemon juice
salt to taste
4 8-ounce lobster tails

Heat the olive oil in a large skillet over medium heat. Add the garlic, parsley, tomatoes, green pepper, onion, white wine, cayenne pepper, lemon juice and salt to taste. Simmer gently for 1 hour.

Fifteen minutes before the sauce is ready, preheat the oven to 450°F. Remove the lobster meat from the shells. Put the lobster meat into a steamer basket and steam over boiling water for 5 minutes.

Put the lobster tails into a baking dish and pour the tomato sauce over them. Cover the dish and bake for 20 minutes. Serve immediately with pasta.

LOBSTER NEWBURG

serves 4

4 8-ounce lobster tails
8 tablespoons butter
½ teaspoon oregano
¼ teaspoon grated lemon rind
1 garlic clove, finely chopped
¼ cup dry sherry
¼ cup heavy cream
salt to taste
¼ teaspoon cayenne pepper
3 tablespoons flour

In a large pot, bring 4 quarts of water to a boil over high heat.

Remove the lobster meat from the shells. Drop the meat into the pot. When the water returns to a boil, lower the heat and simmer the lobster for 10 minutes. Drain the lobster meat well and cut it into chunks.

In a large skillet over low heat, melt the butter. Mix in the oregano, grated lemon rind and garlic. Add the lobster meat and cook, stirring constantly, for 2 minutes. Add the sherry and remove the skillet from the heat.

Using a slotted spoon, remove the lobster meat from the skillet, allowing as much butter as possible to drip back into the pan. Put the lobster into a bowl and set aside.

Pour the butter from the skillet into the top of a double boiler over hot, not boiling, water. Stir in the cream and the flour. Stir until the sauce thickens and is smooth. Add salt to taste, the cayenne pepper and lobster and continue to cook for 15 minutes, stirring constantly. Do not let the sauce boil.

Pour the mixture into a serving bowl, cover and let stand for 30 minutes before serving. Alternatively, refrigerate for 24 hours, then reheat and serve.

OYSTER-STUFFED LOBSTERS

serves 4

2 medium-sized onions, chopped
1 celery stalk with leaves, chopped
4 tablespoons butter
4 mushrooms, sliced
2 cups shelled oysters, with liquid
4 cups unflavored breadcrumbs
2 tablespoons chopped parsley
1 teaspoon salt
black pepper to taste
½ teaspoon dried thyme
4 1-pound lobsters

Melt the butter in a shallow skillet. Add the onion and celery and sauté until they are tender. Add the mushrooms and cook 2 to 3 minutes until they are a glazed, golden brown.

Strain the oysters and save their liquid. Chop the oysters finely and add them to the skillet. Sauté while stirring until the pieces begin to curl and become tender.

Add the breadcrumbs, parsley, salt, pepper and thyme. Stir all the ingredients together with a wooden spoon. While stirring, slowly add the reserved oyster liquid until the stuffing is moist and clings together.

With a large, heavy knife, split the lobsters and remove the entrails and roe. Crack the claw shells with a nutcracker.

Place the lobsters split-side up on a foil-covered broiling rack. Stuff the cavities with the oyster stuffing. Fold the foil over the lobsters and broil for 15 minutes. Unfold the foil and broil again for 3 to 5 minutes.

Serve with melted butter and lemon wedges.

Baja Shrimp

serves 4

1¼ pounds shrimp, peeled and
deveined
12 small dried hot red peppers
1 cup cider vinegar
1 cup water
1 teaspoon salt
½ teaspoon dried oregano
1 medium-sized onion, sliced
½ cup olive oil
boiling water

Split the peppers lengthwise and remove the seeds and vein. Place the peppers on a piece of aluminum foil and place under the broiler for 5 seconds.

Combine the cider vinegar and the water. Soak the peppers in the mixture for 2 hours.

Place the peppers and their liquid in the container of a blender or food processor. Add the salt, oregano, onion and oil. Blend the mixture for 2 minutes or until well mixed.

Cook the shrimp in a large pot of boiling water for 5 minutes. Drain well and place in a large bowl. Add the blended pepper mixture to the shrimp and marinate in the refrigerator overnight.

Remove the shrimp from the marinade and serve cold with hot rice.

BATTER SHRIMP

serves 4

1 pound shrimp, uncooked and shelled
1½ tablespoons olive oil
¼ teaspoon salt
¼ teaspoon black pepper
2 tablespoons lemon juice
1 cup olive oil

BATTER:
1 cup flour
¼ teaspoon salt
1 egg, beaten
¾ cup warm water
1½ tablespoons olive oil

In a small bowl beat together 1½ tablespoons of the olive oil with the salt, pepper and lemon juice. Place the shrimp in a bowl and pour the olive oil mixture over them. Let stand for 30 minutes.

To make the batter, mix the flour and salt in a bowl. In a separate bowl, combine the beaten egg, olive oil and warm water. Add the egg mixture gradually to the flour, beating until smooth.

Thread the shrimp onto small skewers or long toothpicks and dip them into the batter. In a deep skillet, heat the olive oil to 375°F. Fry the shrimp until they are golden brown. Drain on paper towels.

BROILED SHRIMP IN GARLIC SAUCE

serves 6

2½ pounds large shrimp
4 garlic cloves, finely chopped
½ onion, finely chopped
4 tablespoons chopped parsley
8 tablespoons butter
1 teaspoon oregano
salt to taste
black pepper to taste
1 teaspoon paprika

Shell the shrimp, but leave the tails on. Remove the veins. With a sharp knife, butterfly the shrimps down the back. Wash the shrimp thoroughly. Flatten them on paper towels and pat dry with more paper towels. Set aside. Preheat the broiler.

In a saucepan, combine the garlic, onion, parsley and butter. Cook over low heat, stirring constantly. As the butter melts add the oregano and salt and pepper to taste.

Keep the butter mixture over very low heat. Dip each shrimp into the mixture. Then put it on a large shallow broiler pan. The shrimp should fit in a single layer. Sprinkle the shrimp with the paprika. Broil for 7 minutes, or until the shrimp are sizzling.

Transfer the shrimp to a serving platter. Pour the remaining butter sauce over them and serve.

BROILED MARINATED SHRIMP

serves 6

2 garlic cloves, crushed
2 tablespoons red wine vinegar
½ cup olive oil
2 teaspoons ground cumin
2 teaspoons chili powder
½ teaspoon black pepper
3 teaspoons dried basil
2 pounds medium-sized shrimp,
shelled and deveined

In a small bowl combine the garlic and vinegar. Set aside.

In a large mixing bowl, combine the olive oil, cumin, chili powder, black pepper and basil. Add the shrimp and mix well. Add the garlic and vinegar mixture and mix well again. Cover the bowl and refrigerate for 3 hours.

Preheat the broiler. Remove the shrimp from the marinade and put them in a broiler pan. Brush the shrimp with the marinade. Broil for 10 minutes, brushing the shrimp with the marinade every 2 minutes.

Transfer the shrimp to a serving platter. Pour the remaining marinade over them and serve.

CURRIED SHRIMP AND SCALLOPS WITH SPINACH

serves 4

½ cup butter
4 tablespoons finely chopped onion
2 sweet red peppers, cut into rings
4 teaspoons finely chopped garlic
8 mushrooms, thinly sliced
4 tablespoons finely chopped scallions
4 teaspoons curry powder
¼ teaspoon cayenne pepper
12 large shrimp, cleaned, shelled and
deveined
12 large sea scallops
2 cups dry white wine
20 fresh spinach leaves, well rinsed
salt to taste
black pepper to taste

Melt the butter in a skillet over medium-low heat. Add the onion, red peppers, and garlic. Cook, stirring constantly, until the onion is soft, about 5 minutes.

Add the mushrooms, scallions, curry powder, cayenne pepper, shrimp and scallops. Stir until the shellfish are coated with the curry powder. Stir in the wine and cook over medium-high heat until the shrimp and scallops are barely cooked, about 3 minutes. Add the spinach and cover the skillet. Cook until the spinach is wilted, about 1 minute. Season with salt and pepper, transfer to a serving platter, and serve at once.

FRIED SHRIMP ROMANO

serves 4

4 tablespoons olive oil
salt to taste
2 tablespoons lemon juice
2 pounds large shrimp
½ cup flour
4 tablespoons cracker meal
4 tablespoons grated Romano cheese
black pepper to taste
1 egg
½ cup warm water
1 cup warm water

In a large mixing bowl, combine 3 tablespoons of the olive oil, salt and the lemon juice. Set aside.

Shell the shrimp and remove the veins. Add the shrimp to the marinade in the mixing bowl. Mix well. Set aside for 30 minutes.

While the shrimp are marinating, in a small bowl combine the flour, cracker meal and the grated cheese.

In another bowl, combine salt, pepper, 1 tablespoon of olive oil, the egg and the warm water. Beat until well mixed.

In a large skillet, heat the corn oil to 375°F. While the oil is heating, gradually add the flour mixture to the egg mixture, beating constantly until smooth.

Remove the shrimp from the marinade with a slotted wooden spoon. Skewer each shrimp on a wooden toothpick. Dip each shrimp into the batter, then put it into the hot oil. Cook until the shrimp are golden brown. Drain them on paper towels, transfer them to a serving platter and serve.

LOUISIANA SHRIMP

serves 6

2 pounds shrimp
4 tablespoons butter
1 cup unflavored breadcrumbs
2 garlic cloves, finely chopped
½ teaspoon Tabasco sauce
salt to taste
¾ cup dry vermouth
¼ teaspoon black pepper
¼ teaspoon cayenne pepper

In a large pot, bring 3 quarts of water to a boil over high heat. Add the shrimp. When the water returns to a boil, reduce the heat and simmer the shrimp for 5 minutes.

Drain the shrimp, shell them and remove the veins. Put the shrimp on paper towels to dry.

Preheat the oven to 350°F. Grease a 15-inch baking dish with butter.

In a medium-sized saucepan, melt the butter over low heat. Remove the pan from the heat and mix in the breadcrumbs, garlic, Tabasco sauce and salt to taste. Mix well and return the pan to extremely low heat.

Quickly arrange the shrimp in the baking pan. Pour over them the vermouth and then the butter mixture. Sprinkle with black pepper and cayenne pepper. Bake for 20 minutes. Serve hot.

PICKLED SHRIMP

serves 6 to 8

2 pounds uncooked shrimp, in the shell
¼ cup mixed pickling spices
1 cup vegetable oil
¾ cup white vinegar
1 teaspoon salt
¼ teaspoon black pepper
2 teaspoons celery seeds
1 teaspoon Tabasco sauce
1 large onion, chopped

In a saucepan combine the unshelled shrimp and pickling spices. Add enough cold fresh water to cover the shrimp completely. Cover the saucepan tightly and bring the liquid to a boil. Reduce the heat and simmer for 3 to 5 minutes. Remove the saucepan from the heat and allow the shrimp to cool in the liquid. When the shrimp are completely cool, shell them.

In a small bowl, combine the vegetable oil, vinegar, salt, pepper, celery seeds and Tabasco sauce. Mix well.

Arrange alternate layers of shrimp and chopped onions in a bowl. Add the oil-vinegar mixture, cover and chill 8 hours or overnight.

SHRIMP CREOLE

serves 8

2 cups water
3 garlic cloves, finely chopped
4 whole cloves
1 teaspoon cinnamon
3 cups canned whole tomatoes
2 tablespoons finely chopped parsley
4 bay leaves
1 teaspoon oregano
2 teaspoons hot red pepper flakes
1 teaspoon black pepper
½ teaspoon cayenne pepper
½ teaspoon Tabasco sauce
1 tablespoon salt
1 sweet red pepper, coarsely chopped
1 large head celery, with leaves, coarsely chopped
3 pounds medium-sized shrimp, shelled and deveined

In a large pot combine the water, garlic, cloves, cinnamon, tomatoes, parsley, bay leaves, oregano, red pepper flakes, black pepper, cayenne pepper, Tabasco sauce and salt. Bring the mixture to a boil over high heat.

Add the sweet red pepper and celery. When the liquid returns to the boil, reduce the heat to medium and simmer for 20 minutes.

Add the shrimp to the pot and raise the heat. Simmer for 10 minutes. Remove the pot from the heat and let cool for 20 to 30 minutes. Serve at room temperature.

SHRIMP CURRY

serves 6

2 medium-sized onions, finely chopped
½ green pepper, finely chopped
2 garlic cloves, finely chopped
3 tablespoons butter
2 cups sour cream
2 teaspoons lemon juice
½ teaspoon grated lemon rind
3 teaspoons curry powder
½ teaspoon chili powder
1 teaspoon black pepper
1½ pounds cooked shrimp, shelled and deveined

Melt the butter in a saucepan. Add the onions, pepper and garlic and sauté for 3 minutes. Add the sour cream, lemon juice, lemon rind, curry powder, chili powder and pepper. Stir well. Add the shrimp and cook, stirring constantly, until the shrimp are thoroughly hot. Do not let the sour cream boil. Serve immediately with rice.

SHRIMP JALAPEÑO

serves 4

24 large shrimp
½ cup cornstarch
½ teaspoon salt
5 tablespoons butter
2 tablespoons olive oil
⅓ cup dry sherry
4 jalapeño peppers, seeded and thinly
sliced

Remove the shells and the veins from the shrimp. Wash them and pat dry on paper towels.

On a plate, combine the cornstarch and salt. Roll the shrimp in the cornstarch until they are completely covered. Shake off any excess cornstarch. Put the shrimp on a platter and set aside.

In a medium-sized skillet, melt the butter and heat the olive oil over medium heat. Add the shrimp and cook only until they begin to turn pink.

Push the shrimp to one side and add the sherry and the jalapeño peppers. Heat briefly. Carefully ignite the sherry, using a long match, and shake the skillet back and forth until the flame dies out.

Transfer the shrimp to a serving platter, pour the sauce from the skillet over them and serve.

SHRIMP MEXICANO

serves 4

12 small hot chili peppers
1 cup cider vinegar
1 cup water
1½ pounds medium-sized shrimp
1 tablespoon lemon juice
1 teaspoon salt
1 teaspoon oregano
1 medium-sized onion, thinly sliced
½ cup olive oil

Preheat the broiler.

Remove the stems from the peppers and slice them down their length. Remove the seeds and veins. Wash the peppers and dry them. Put them on a piece of aluminum foil on the broiler pan. Put them under the broiler for 10 seconds. Set aside for 2 hours.

About 30 minutes before the peppers are ready, shell the shrimp and remove the veins.

In a large pot, bring 3 quarts of water to a boil over high heat. Add the shrimp to the pot. When the water returns to the boil, reduce the heat and simmer the shrimp for 3 minutes. Drain the shrimp well, then put them into a large bowl.

Pour the peppers and the soaking liquid into a blender or food processor. Add the lemon juice, salt, oregano, onion and olive oil. Blend for about 2 minutes. Pour the mixture over the shrimp, cover the bowl and refrigerate overnight.

Remove the shrimp from the marinade with a slotted spoon. Serve over hot rice.

SHRIMP ON TAP

serves 4

3 cups beer
2 garlic cloves, chopped
1 teaspoon celery seeds
2 tablespoons finely chopped parsley
1 teaspoon Tabasco sauce
3 tablespoons lemon juice
salt to taste
2 pounds medium-sized shrimp, shelled and deveined
8 tablespoons butter

In a large saucepan combine the beer, garlic, celery seed, parsley, Tabasco sauce, lemon juice and salt to taste. Over medium-high heat bring the beer to a boil.

When the beer is at full boil, add the shrimp. When it returns to the boil, reduce the heat and simmer the shrimp for 5 minutes.

In a small saucepan, melt the butter over low heat. Set aside in a warm place.

Drain the shrimp and transfer them to a serving bowl. Pour the melted butter into four small bowls for dipping. Serve immediately.

SHRIMP PASTA WITH MOZZARELLA

serves 6

2 pounds cooked shrimp, shelled and deveined
3 egg whites
1 cup heavy cream
3 tablespoons lemon juice
¼ cup light rum
salt to taste
4 scallions, finely chopped
1 teaspoon paprika
36 large pasta shells
1½ pounds shredded mozzarella cheese
2 tablespoons chopped chives

Put the shrimp and egg whites into the container of a blender or food processor. Blend until a smooth paste is formed.

Empty the shrimp paste into a mixing bowl. Add the cream, lemon juice, rum and salt to taste. Mix thoroughly. Add the scallions and blend well. Cover the bowl and refrigerate for 2 hours.

About 30 minutes before the shrimp paste is thoroughly chilled, cook the pasta shells in a large pot of boiling water until they are tender. Do not overcook the shells. Drain the shells well.

Preheat the oven to 350°F.

Grease a baking dish large enough to hold all the shells in a single layer. With a teaspoon, fill each pasta shell with some of the shrimp mixture. Arrange the shells in the baking dish. Sprinkle the shredded mozzarella cheese over the shells. Sprinkle the cheese with the paprika.

Bake until the cheese is melted and golden, about 20 minutes. Sprinkle the shells with chopped chives and serve hot.

SHRIMP WITH BLACKEYED PEAS

serves 6

¾ cup vegetable oil
½ cup finely chopped onion
2 garlic cloves, chopped
½ pound shrimp, shelled, deveined and cut into thirds
1 cup diced ham
½ cup tomato sauce
1 small hot red pepper, seeded and finely chopped
2 cups cooked blackeyed peas

Heat the oil in a large saucepan. Add the onion and garlic and sauté until the onion is transparent, about 4 minutes. Add the shrimp and cook for 8 minutes. Add the ham and tomato sauce, reduce the heat and simmer for 10 minutes. Add the hot red pepper, reduce the heat to very low and simmer for 5 minutes longer. Add the blackeyed peas and cook until the peas are heated through, about 5 minutes.

SHRIMP WITH SUN-DRIED TOMATOES AND GOAT CHEESE

serves 4

¼ pound sun-dried tomatoes packed in olive oil
2 teaspoons finely chopped garlic
3 tablespoons olive oil
3 tablespoons rinsed and drained capers
½ teaspoon dried oregano
1½ pounds large shrimp, cleaned, peeled and deveined
2 cups crumbled goat cheese

Preheat the oven to 450°F.

Chop the sun-dried tomatoes finely and reserve the olive oil. There should be about ½ cup of the tomatoes.

Put the tomatoes, reserved olive oil, garlic, 3 tablespoons olive oil, capers, oregano and shrimp into a large mixing bowl. Mix well.

Fill four individual ramekins or small individual soufflé dishes with the shrimp mixture. Sprinkle the goat cheese evenly over each dish.

Bake until the cheese is melted, about 10 to 12 minutes. Serve immediately.

SHRIMP WITH ZUCCHINI

serves 4

1 pound medium-sized shrimp, shelled
and deveined
3 tablespoons olive oil
1 tablespoon lemon juice
1 small green pepper, diced
1 small sweet red pepper, diced
2 garlic cloves, finely chopped
1 large onion, coarsely chopped
2 large tomatoes, seeded and coarsely
chopped
2 small zucchini, thinly sliced
salt to taste
black pepper to taste

Heat the olive oil in a large skillet. Add the lemon juice and mix well. Add the green pepper and red pepper and cook, stirring constantly, over medium heat for 3 minutes. Add the garlic and onion and cook, stirring constantly, for 3 minutes longer. Add the zucchini and tomatoes and salt and pepper to taste. Stir well, cover the skillet and simmer for 5 minutes.

Add the shrimp to the vegetables in the skillet and stir well. Cover the skillet and simmer for 5 minutes longer. Transfer the mixture to a serving bowl and serve at once.

WEST COAST SHRIMP

serves 4

24 jumbo shrimp
12 tablespoons butter
8 tablespoons olive oil
2 teaspoons salt
4 garlic cloves, finely chopped
3 tablespoons finely chopped parsley
1 teaspoon oregano
1 teaspoon paprika
4 tablespoons white wine

With a sharp knife, split each shrimp three-quarters of the way down the back, but do not remove the shell. Wash the shrimp well and pat dry with paper towels. Put six shrimp in each of 4 ovenproof serving dishes, with the cut side spread open and the tails sticking up.

Preheat oven to 400°F.

In a large mixing bowl, combine the melted butter, olive oil, salt, garlic, parsley, oregano and white wine. Mix thoroughly. Spoon equal amounts of the sauce over each of the shrimp dishes. Sprinkle with paprika.

Place the dishes in the oven for 8 minutes. Serve immediately.

Page numbers in *italic* refer to the illustrations

Abalone Steak, 184
Almonds: Almond Sauce, 33
  Halibut Steaks with Almond Sauce, 129
  Poached Fish with Almonds, 98
  Trout with Pine Nuts and, 178
Anchovies: Anchovied Mushrooms, 9
  Fried Mozzarella with Anchovy Sauce, 16
Andalusian Mussel Salad, 64
Anisette: Bass with Anisette Pepper Sauce, 103
Appetizers, 8–32
Apples, Swordfish with, 172
Apricots: Apricot Sauce, 33
  Broiled Halibut Steaks with Apricot Sauce, *110*, 130
Artichokes: Artichokes with Sardines, 8
  Scallop and Artichoke Soup, 46
Aspic, Bass in, 102
Avocado: Avocado Shrimp Boats, 65
  Clam Guacamole, 19
  Fish with Avocado Mayonnaise, 94

Bacon: Bacon-Baked Rockfish, 145
  Bacon-Baked Salmon, 145
Baja Shrimp, 210
Basket-grilled Salmon, 147
Bass: Baked Bass with Vermouth Sauce, 102
  Bass Baked with Fennel, 104
  Bass in Aspic, 102
  Bass Stuffed with Shrimp and Chestnuts, 114
  Bass with Anisette Pepper Sauce, 103
  Bass with Goat Cheese and Walnut Topping, 113
  Bass with Goat Cheese (Chèvre) Topping, 115
  Grilled Bass with Herbs, 103
  Stuffed Bass with Raisin Sauce, 116
Batter Shrimp, 211
Beans: Bean and Tuna Salad, 65
  Shrimp and Three-Bean Salad, 77, *82*
Beer: Mussels in Beer, 189
  Shrimp on Tap, *111*, 217
Blackened Redfish, 144
Blackeyed peas, Shrimp with, 218
Blowfish: Broiled Blowfish, 117
  Broiled Blowfish with Maître d'Hôtel Sauce, 117
Bluefish: Baked Bluefish, 118
  Baked Bluefish with Sardines, 118
  Broiled Bluefish with Spicy Sauce, 119
  Marinated Bluefish, 19
  Marinated Bluefish with Horseradish, 119
Brandy: Scallops in Butter and Brandy Sauce, 197
Breaded Perch, 136
Brochettes *see* Kabobs
Broiled Fish Steaks with Green Peppercorns, 92

Butter: Butter and Brandy Sauce, 197
  Butter Garlic Sauce, 33
  Butter-stuffed Trout, 175
  Clarified Butter, 34
  Drawn Butter Sauce, 182
  Green Peppercorn Butter, 35
  Lemon Butter Sauce, 36
  Parsley, 173
  Salmon Dill Butter, 36
  Soy Sauce, 170
Butterfish, Deep-fried Parmesan, 120

Canapés: Caviar, 10
  Smoked Salmon, 23
Capers: Crab Salad with Hot Caper Dressing, 66
Casseroles and stews, 48–63
Catfish: Catfish Fry, 120
  Oven-fried Sherry Catfish, 121
  Southern-fried Catfish, 121
Cauliflower: Shrimp and Cauliflower Salad, 76
Caviar: Caviar Canapés, 10
  Caviar Italiano, 60
  Pasta with Ricotta and Caviar, 122
  Tarama Salad, 89
Ceviche, Scallops, 73
Champagne, Red Snapper à la, 163
Cheese: Baked Shrimp Parmesan, 9
  Bass with Goat Cheese and Walnut Topping, 113
  Bass with Goat Cheese (Chèvre) Topping, 115
  Clam Omelet with Munster Cheese, 185
  Deep-fried Parmesan Butterfish, 120
  Fried Mozzarella with Anchovy Sauce, 16
  Fried Mussels Parmesan, 189
  Parmesan Fried Trout, 177
  Shrimp Pasta with Mozzarella, 217
  Shrimp with Sun-dried Tomatoes and Goat Cheese, 218
Cheese, soft: Clam Dip, 21
  Crab Dip, 12
  Seafood Mousse, 24
  Pasta with Ricotta and Caviar, 122
Chestnuts, Bass Stuffed with Shrimp and, 114
Chicken: Summer Clambake, 188
Chickpeas, Fresh Tuna Salad with, 90
Chili peppers: Shrimp Mexicano, 216
Cider: Flounder with Cider Sauce, *84*, 124
Clams: Clam and Pasta Salad, 66
  Clam Dip, 21
  Clam Fritters, 184
  Clam Guacamole, 19
  Clam Omelet, 185
  Clam Omelet with Munster Cheese, 185
  Clam Sauce for Pasta, 34
  Clams Casino, 22
  Deviled Clams, 11
  Flounder with Shrimp and Clam Sauce, 126
  Fried Clam Cakes, 187
  Grilled Cherrystone Clams, 16
  Manhattan Clam Chowder, 43

New England Clam Chowder, 44, *81*
  Portuguese Clams, 20
  Steamed Clams, 186
  Steamed Soft-shell Clams, 186
  Stuffed Clams, 28, *83*
  Summer Clambake, 188
Cocktail Sauce, 35
Cod: Barbecued Cod, 122
  Broiled Cod in Lemon Butter Sauce, *107*, 123
  Codfish Pie, 61
  Codfish Chowder, 39
  Mint Cod Salad, 67
Colonial Fish Pot, 57
Corn: Corn and Shrimp Chowder, 40
  Shrimp and Corn Soufflé, 59
  Summer Clambake, 188
Crab: Boiled Crabs, 198
  Boiled Dungeness Crabs, 199
  Broiled Soft-shell Crabs, 202
  Crab Cakes, 201
  Crab Casserole, 56, *88*
  Crab Legs Creole, 199
  Crab Soufflés, 13
  Crab Stew, 49
  Fried Crab Legs, 200
  Fried Soft-shell Crabs, 201
  Sautéed Crab with Prosciutto, 204
  Sautéed Soft-shell Crabs, 203
  Soft-shell Crabs à la Creole, 203
Crabmeat: Crab and Fruit Salad, 67
  Crab Bisque, 39
  Crab Cocktail, 25
  Crab Dip, 12
  Crab Puffs, 12
  Crab Salad with Hot Caper Dressing, 66
  Crabmeat Spread, 12
  Crabmeat-stuffed Salmon, 150
  Deviled Eggs with Crabmeat, 11
  Haddock Stuffed with Crabmeat, 128
  She-Crab Soup, 47
  Stuffed Haddock, 128
Cranberries: Lobster Salad with, 69
  Mackerel Stuffed with, *107*, 134
Crawfish: Boiled Crawfish, 204
  Crawfish Creole, 205
  Creole Salpicon, 48
Crayfish, Boiled, 206
Cream Sauce, 202
Creamy Mussel Soup, 45
Creole Salpicon, 48
Crèpes, Tuna, 30
Croquettes: Fish, 15
  Shrimp, 25
Cucumber, Fish Soup with Onions, Tomatoes and, 42
Curry: Curried Shellfish with Spinach, 60
  Curried Shrimp and Scallops with Spinach, 212
  Shrimp Curry, 215

Deep Sea Chowder, 41
Deviled Clams, 11
Deviled Eggs with Crabmeat, 11
Dill: Baked Pike in Dill Sauce, 138
  Dill Sauce, 35
  Salmon Dill Butter, 36

Dips: Clam, 21
  Crab, 12
Down-East Haddock Chowder, 41
Drawn Butter Sauce, 182

Eel, Fried, 123
Eggs: Clam Omelet, 185
  Clam Omelet with Munster Cheese,
    185
  Deviled Eggs with Crabmeat, 11
  Fish and Eggs, 95
  Scrambled Oysters, 194
  Shrimp and Egg Bake, 63
Escabèche, 14, 94
  with Lime, 13

Fancy Tuna Salad, 89
Fennel, Bass Baked with, 104
Fettucini: with Scallops, 195
  with Shad Roe, 157
Fish and Eggs, 95
Fish and Potato Hash, 57
Fish in Parchment, 96
Fish with Avocado Mayonnaise, 94
Fish Croquettes, 15
Fish Soup with Onions, Cucumbers
  and Tomatoes, 42
Fisherman's Stew with Rouille, 50
Fishkabobs, 14, *105*
Flounders: Flounder with Cider Sauce,
  84, 124
  Flounder with Garlic and Tomatoes,
    124
  Flounder with Grapes, 125
  Flounder in Mustard Sauce, 125
  Flounder with Shrimp and Clam
    Sauce, 126
  Poached Flounder with Saffron, 127
  Spiced Flounder, 126
  Spicy Fish Appetizer, 27
Fritters: Clam, 184
  Shrimp, 27
Fruit and Mussel Salad, 70

Garlic: Broiled Shrimp in Garlic Sauce,
    211
  Butter Garlic Sauce, 33
  Flounder with Garlic and Tomatoes,
    124
Ginger, Marinated Squid with, 79
Glazed Whole Baked Fish, 97
Grapefruit: Red Snapper with, 164
  Shellfish Salad with, 75
Grapes, Flounder with, 125
Green Peppercorns: Broiled Fish
    Steaks with, 92
  Green Peppercorn Butter, 35
Green Sauce, 168
Grilled Fish with Fresh Fruits, 95
Guacamole, Clam, 19
Gulf-style Red Snapper, 160

Haddock: Down-East Haddock
    Chowder, 41
  Haddock Diane, 127
  Haddock Pudding, 62
  Haddock Stuffed with Crabmeat, 128
  Stuffed Haddock, 128
Halibut: Baked Halibut, 129

Barbecued Halibut, *112*, 132
Broiled Halibut Steaks with Apricot
    Sauce, *110*, 130
Escabèche with Lime, 13
Halibut Soup, 42
Halibut Steaks with Almond Sauce,
    129
Halibut Steaks with Red and Green
    Topping, 131
Pecan Halibut Steaks, 132
Ham: Sautéed Crab with Prosciutto,
    204
Hangtown Fry, 192
Hawaiian Red Snapper, 161
Herrings: Broiled Herring Bits, 10
  Herring Salad, 68
  Salt Herring Salad, 68
Horseradish: Horseradish Cream, 36
  Marinated Bluefish with, 119

Island Shrimp Balls, 17
Italian Fish Stew, 51

Jalapeño, Shrimp, 216
Jellied Fish, 17

Kabobs: Fishkabobs, 14, *105*
  Scallop Brochettes, 23
Kortlax, 18

Lemon: Broiled Cod in Lemon Butter
    Sauce, *107*, 123
  Broiled Lemon-buttered Salmon
    Steaks, 148
  Lemon Butter Sauce, 36
  Lemon Fried Fish, 97
  Lemon-Lime Red Snapper, 161
  Porgy with Pickled Lemon, 142
  Whitefish with Lemon Butter Sauce,
    182
Lettuce: Salmon with Scallops Filling
    and Lettuce Sauce, 153
  Stuffed Fillets Baked in, 100
Lime: Escabèche with Lime, 13
  Lemon-Lime Red Snapper, 161
  Lime-Grilled Fish Steaks, 98
  Salmon with Lime and Walnut Oil,
    86, 154
  Scallops Ceviche, 73
  Seviche, 26
  Tuna in Lime Marinade, 180
Linguini: Caviar Italiano, 60
  Pasta with Ricotta and Caviar, 122
Lobster: Boiled Lobster Tails, 207
  Broiled Lobster, 206
  Lobster Bisque, 43
  Lobster Marinara, 207
  Lobster Newburg, 208
  Lobster Salad, 69, *85*
  Lobster Salad with Cranberries, 69
  Oriental Lobster, 205
  Oyster-stuffed Lobsters, 209
  Summer Clambake, 188
Louisiana Shrimp, 214

Mackerel: Broiled Mackerel, 133
  Broiled Spiced Mackerel, 133
  Mackerel Stuffed with Cranberries,
    107, 134

Pickled Mackerel, 22
Maître d'Hôtel Sauce, 117, 140
Manhattan Clam Chowder, 43
Mardi Gras Seafood Gumbo, 52
Mayonnaise: Avocado, 94
  Tartar Sauce, 37
Melon, Shrimp Salad with, 76
Mint: Mint Cod Salad, 67
  Roasted Red Snapper with, 163
Monkfish: Monkfish Catalan, 134
  Monkfish in Cream Sauce, 135
Mousse, Seafood, 24
Mushrooms: Anchovied Mushrooms, 9
  Haddock Diane, 127
  Tuna with Snow Peas and, 181
  Whiting with Mushrooms, 183
Mussels: Andalusian Mussel Salad, 64
  Cold Mussels in Spicy Sauce, 190
  Creamy Mussel Soup, 45
  Fried Mussels, 191
  Fried Mussels Parmesan, 189
  Fruit and Mussel Salad, 70
  Marinated Mussel Salad, 71
  Marinated Mussels, 191
  Mussel Soup, 44
  Mussels in Beer, 189
  Mussels in Rice, 193
  Mussels Ravigote, 192
  Pickled Mussels, 20
Mustard: Flounder in Mustard Sauce,
    125
  Shad Roe with Mustard Sauce, 158
  Tile Fish in Mustard Cream Sauce,
    173

New England Clam Chowder, 44, *81*
New Orleans Pompano en Papillote,
    141

Okra: Mardi Gras Seafood Gumbo, 52
Omelets: Clam Omelet, 185
  Clam Omelet with Munster Cheese,
    185
Onions, Fish Soup with Cucumbers,
    Tomatoes and, 42
Orange: Crab and Fruit Salad, 67
  Scallops with Orange Sauce, 197
  Sole in Orange Sauce, 168
Oriental Baked Shad, 159
Oriental Lobster, 205
Oriental Tuna, 181
Oysters: Baked Oysters, *106*, 193
  Hangtown Fry, 192
  Oyster Casserole, 58
  Oyster Soup, 45
  Oyster Stew, 52
  Oyster Stew with Sesame Seeds, 53
  Oyster-stuffed Lobsters, 209
  Scalloped Oysters, 194
  Scrambled Oysters, 194
  Steamed Oysters, 195

Papaya, Seafood Salad in, 74
Parmesan Fried Trout, 177
Parsley: Green Sauce, 168
  Parsley Butter, 173
Pasta: Clam and Pasta Salad, 66
  Clam Sauce for Pasta, 34
  Pasta with Ricotta and Caviar, 122

Seafood Pasta Salad, 75
  Shrimp Pasta with Mozzarella, 217
Pâté, Tuna Spinach, 32
Peaches: Stuffed Fillets Baked in
  Lettuce Leaves, 100
Pears: Fruit and Mussel Salad, 70
Peas, Swordfish with, 172
Pecan Halibut Steaks, 132
Peppercorns see Green Peppercorns
Peppers: Bass with Anisette Pepper
    Sauce, 103
  Fisherman's Stew with Rouille, 50
  Shrimp Gumbo, 55
Perch: Baked Perch, 135
  Breaded Perch, 136
Pickerel: Pickerel Stew, 55
  Sautéed Pickerel, 137
Pie, Codfish, 61
Pike: Baked Pike in Dill Sauce, 138
  Baked Stuffed Pike, 139
  Deep-fried Pike, 137
Pine nuts, Trout with Almonds and,
  178
Pineapple: Grilled Fish with Fresh
    Fruits, 95
  Planked Shad, 157
Poached Fish with Almonds, 98
Pompano: New Orleans Pompano en
    Papillote, 141
  Pompano à la Maître 'Hôtel, 140
  Stuffed Pompano, 141
Porgy: Deep-fried Porgy, 142
  Porgy with Pickled Lemon, 142
Pork: Stuffed Giant Shrimp, 29
Portuguese Clams, 20
Potato: Fish and Potato Hash, 57
Prosciutto, Sautéed Crab with, 204

Raisins: Stuffed Bass with Raisin
    Sauce, 116
Red Hot Snapper, 162
Red Snapper: Baked Red Snapper, 160
  Gulf-style Red Snapper, 160
  Hawaiian Red Snapper, 161
  Lemon-Lime Red Snapper, 161
  Poached Red Snapper, 162
  Red Hot Snapper, 162
  Red Snapper à la Champagne, 163
  Red Snapper with Grapefruit, 164
  Roasted Red Snapper with Fresh
    Mint, 163
  Smoked Red Snapper, 164
Redfish: Baked Redfish, 143
  Blackened Redfish, 144
  Smoked Redfish, 143
Rice: Mussels in Rice, 193
  Shrimp and Rice Soup, 47
Roast Whole Fish, 99
Rockfish, Bacon-Baked, 145
Roe see Caviar; Shad roe
Rouille, Fisherman's Stew with, 50
Rum-poached Salmon with
    Vinaigrette, 152
Saffron, Poached Flounder with, 127
Salads, 64–91
Salmon: Bacon-Baked Salmon, 145
  Baked Salmon in Cream Sauce, 146
  Barbecued Salmon, 147
  Basket-grilled Salmon, 147

Broiled Lemon-buttered Salmon
    Steaks, 148
  Broiled Salmon Steaks, 148
  Cold Poached Salmon Steaks, 149
  Crabmeat-stuffed Salmon, 150
  Grilled Stuffed Salmon, 151
  Kortlax, 18
  Pickled Salmon, 21
  Rum-poached Salmon with
    Vinaigrette, 152
  Salmon Cakes, 149
  Salmon Salad, 72
  Salmon Salad with Vinaigrette, 72
  Salmon with Lime and Walnut Oil,
    86, 154
  Salmon with Scallops Filling and
    Lettuce Sauce, 153
  Sweet and Sour Salmon, 63
  see also Smoked salmon
Salt Herring Salad, 68
Sardines: Artichokes with, 8
  Baked Bluefish with, 118
  Stuffed Sardines, 31
Sauces: Almond, 33, 129
  Anisette Pepper, 103
  Apricot, 33, 130
  Butter and Brandy, 197
  Butter Garlic, 33
  Cider, 124
  Clam Sauce for Pasta, 34
  Cocktail, 35
  Cream, 135, 146, 202
  Creole, 93, 169
  Dill, 35, 138
  Drawn Butter, 182
  Garlic, 211
  Green, 168
  Lemon Butter, 36, 182
  Lettuce, 153
  Maître d'Hôtel, 117, 140
  Mustard, 125, 158
  Mustard Cream, 173
  Orange, 168, 197
  Raisin, 116
  Seafood, 179
  Sesame, 174
  Shrimp and Clam, 126
  Southern-style Tartar, 37
  Spicy, 119, 190
  Tartar, 37
  Tomato and Onion, 134
  Vermouth, 102
  Walnut, 183
Saucy Creole Fish, 93
Scallions, Poached Trout with, 176
Scalloped Oysters, 194
Scalloped Tuna, 62
Scallops: Curried Shrimp and Scallops
    with Spinach, 212
  Fettucini with Scallops, 195
  Fried Scallops, 196
  Salmon with Scallops Filling and
    Lettuce Sauce, 153
  Sautéed Scallops, 196
  Scallop and Artichoke Soup, 46
  Scallop Brochettes, 23
  Scallop Ceviche, 73
  Scallop Salad, 73
  Scallop Stew, 54

Scallops in Butter and Brandy Sauce,
    197
  Scallops with Orange Sauce, 197
  Seviche, 26
  Warm Scallop Salad, 74
Scrambled Oysters, 194
Seafood Mousse, 24
Seafood Pasta Salad, 75
Seafood Salad in Papaya, 74
Seafood Stew, 54
Sesame seeds: Broiled Trout with, 174
  Oyster Stew with, 53
Seviche, 26
Shad: Baked Stuffed Shad, 156
  Broiled Shad, 154
  Oriental Baked Shad, 159
  Planked Shad, 157
Shad roe: Fettucini with, 157
  Shad Roe with Mustard Sauce, 158
She-Crab Soup, 47
Shellfish and Grapefruit Salad, 75
Shellfish Soup, 46
Shrimp: Avocado Shrimp Boats, 65
  Baja Shrimp, 210
  Baked Shrimp Parmesan, 9
  Bass Stuffed with Shrimp and
    Chestnuts, 114
  Batter Shrimp, 211
  Broiled Marinated Shrimp, 212
  Broiled Shrimp in Garlic Sauce, 211
  Cold Shrimp Soup, 40
  Corn and Shrimp Chowder, 40
  Curried Shrimp and Scallops with
    Spinach, 212
  Flounder with Shrimp and Clam
    Sauce, 126
  Fried Shrimp Romano, 213
  Island Shrimp Balls, 17
  Louisiana Shrimp, 214
  Pickled Shrimp, 214
  Shrimp and Cauliflower Salad, 76
  Shrimp and Corn Soufflé, 59
  Shrimp and Egg Bake, 63
  Shrimp and Rice Soup, 47
  Shrimp and Three-Bean Salad, 77, 82
  Shrimp Cocktail, 25
  Shrimp Creole, 215
  Shrimp Croquettes, 25
  Shrimp Curry, 215
  Shrimp Fritters, 27
  Shrimp Gumbo, 55
  Shrimp Jalapeño, 216
  Shrimp Mexicano, 216
  Shrimp on Tap, 111, 217
  Shrimp Pasta with Mozzarella, 217
  Shrimp Salad with Melon Balls, 76
  Shrimp-stuffed Tomatoes, 26
  Shrimp with Blackeyed Peas, 218
  Shrimp with Sun-dried Tomatoes
    and Goat Cheese, 218
  Shrimp with Zucchini, 87, 219
  Stuffed Giant Shrimp, 29
  West Coast Shrimp, 219
Skillet-steamed Fish, 99
Smelts: Pan-fried Smelts, 158
  Sautéed Smelts, 159
Smoked salmon: Salmon Dill Butter, 36
  Smoked Salmon Canapés, 23
  Smoked Salmon Casserole, 58

Stuffed Cherry Tomatoes, 28
  see also Salmon
Smoked Whitefish Appetizer, 24
Snow peas, Tuna with Mushrooms
  and, 181
Soft-shell Crabs à la Creole, 203
Sole: Baked Filets of Sole, 165
  Escabèche with Lime, 13
  Poached Sole, 166
  Poached Sole with Tomatoes, 166
  Saucy Creole Fish, 93
  Sautéed Sole, 165
  Sole in Orange Sauce, 168
  Sole with Green Sauce, 168
  Stuffed Sole in Creole Sauce, 169
Soufflés: Crab, 13
  Shrimp and Corn, 59
Soups, 38–47
Southern-fried Catfish, 121
Southern-style Tartar Sauce, 37
Soy Sauce: Broiled Swordfish with Soy
  Sauce Butter, 170
Spiced Flounder, 126
Spicy Fish Appetizer, 27
Spinach: Curried Shellfish with, 60
  Curried Shrimp and Scallops with,
    212
  Tuna Spinach Pâté, 32
Spread, Crabmeat, 12
Squid: Marinated Squid with Ginger,
    79
  Squid Salad, 78
Stews and casseroles, 48–63
Stir-fried Fish Fillets, 100
Stock, Basic Fish, 38
Stuffed Fillets Baked in Lettuce Leaves,
    100
Summer Clambake, 188
Sweet and Sour Fish, 101

Sweet and Sour Salmon, 63
Swordfish: Baked Swordfish Parmesan,
    170
  Broiled Swordfish with Soy Sauce
    Butter, 170
  Coated Swordfish Steaks, 171
  Marinated Swordfish Steaks, 171
  Swordfish with Apples, 172
  Swordfish with Peas, 172
  Swordfish Salad, 80
  Swordfish Stew, 56

Tarama Salad, 89
Tartar Sauce, 37
  Southern-style, 37
Tile Fish: Broiled Tile Fish with Parsley
  Butter, 173
  Tile Fish in Mustard Cream Sauce,
    173
Tofu Tuna Salad, 91
Tomato: Cold Mussels in Spicy Sauce,
    190
  Fish Soup with Onions, Cucumbers
    and Tomatoes, 42
  Flounder with Garlic and, 124
  Monkfish Catalan, 134
  Poached Sole with, 166
  Shrimp with Sun-dried Tomatoes
    and Goat Cheese, 218
  Shrimp-stuffed Tomatoes, 26
  Stuffed Cherry Tomatoes, 28
Trout: Baked Trout, 174
  Broiled Trout with Sesame Sauce,
    174
  Butter-stuffed Trout, 175
  Pan-fried Trout, 176
  Parmesan Fried Trout, 177
  Poached Trout with Scallions, 176
  Seviche, 26

Stuffed Sea Trout, 155
Trout in Red Wine, 178
Trout with Almonds and Pine Nuts,
    178
Trout with Seafood Sauce, 179
Tuna: Baked Tuna Steaks, 180
  Bean and Tuna Salad, 65
  Fancy Tuna Salad, 89
  Fresh Tuna Salad, 90
  Oriental Tuna, 181
  Scalloped Tuna, 62
  Tofu Tuna Salad, 91
  Tuna Crèpes, 30
  Tuna in Lime Marinade, 180
  Tuna Spinach Pâté, 32
  Tuna with Snow Peas and
    Mushrooms, 181

Vermouth: Baked Bass with Vermouth
  Sauce, 102
Vinaigrette, 37

Walnuts: Bass with Goat Cheese and
  Walnut Topping, 113
  Whitefish with Walnut Sauce, 183
Weakfish: Broiled Weakfish with
  Drawn Butter Sauce, 182
West Coast Shrimp, 219
Whitefish: Smoked Whitefish
  Appetizer, 24
  Whitefish Salad, 91
  Whitefish with Lemon Butter Sauce,
    182
  Whitefish with Walnut Sauce, 183
Whiting with Mushrooms, 183
Wine: Trout in Red Wine, 178

Zucchini, Shrimp with, 87, 219